CW01219136

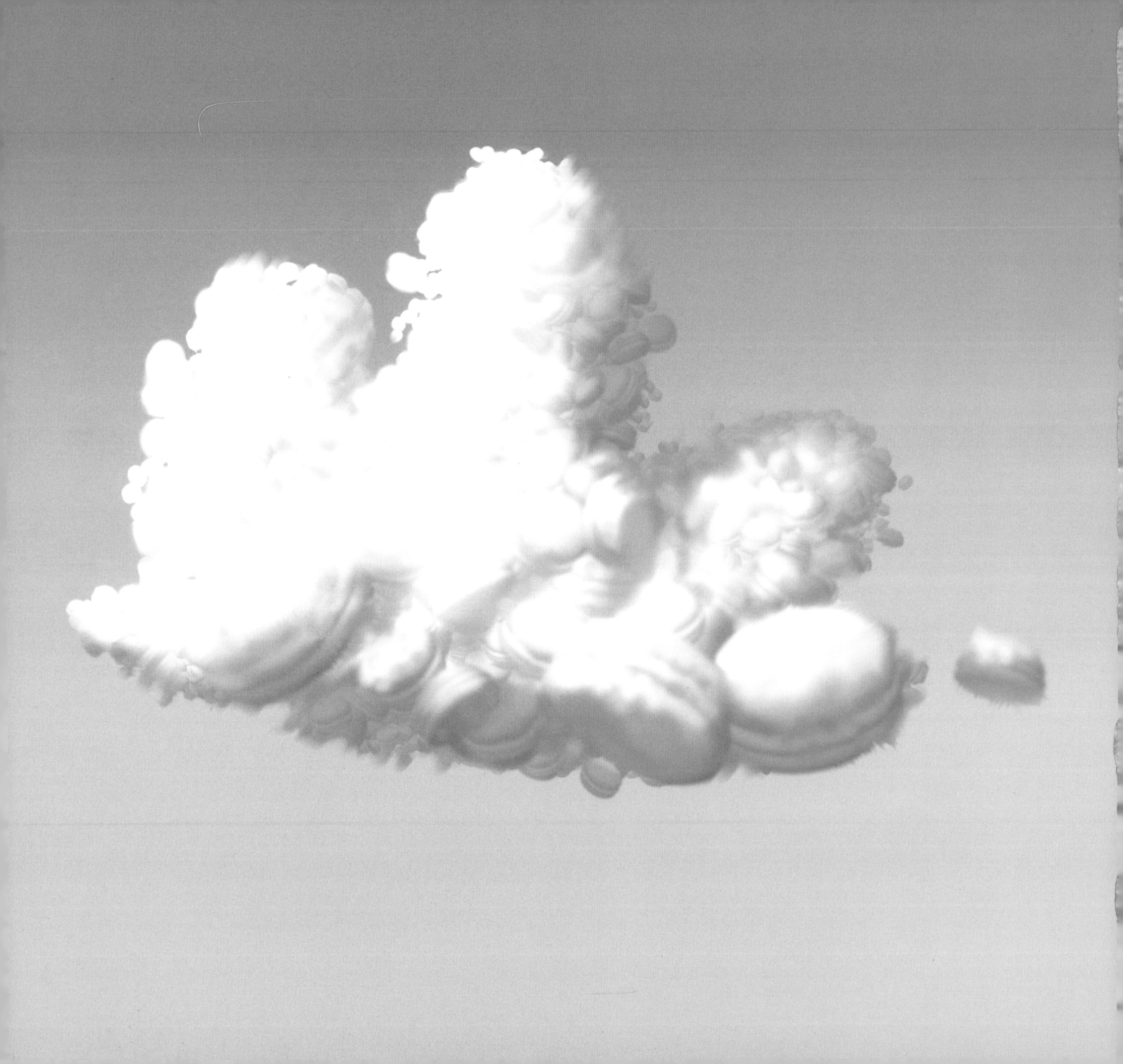

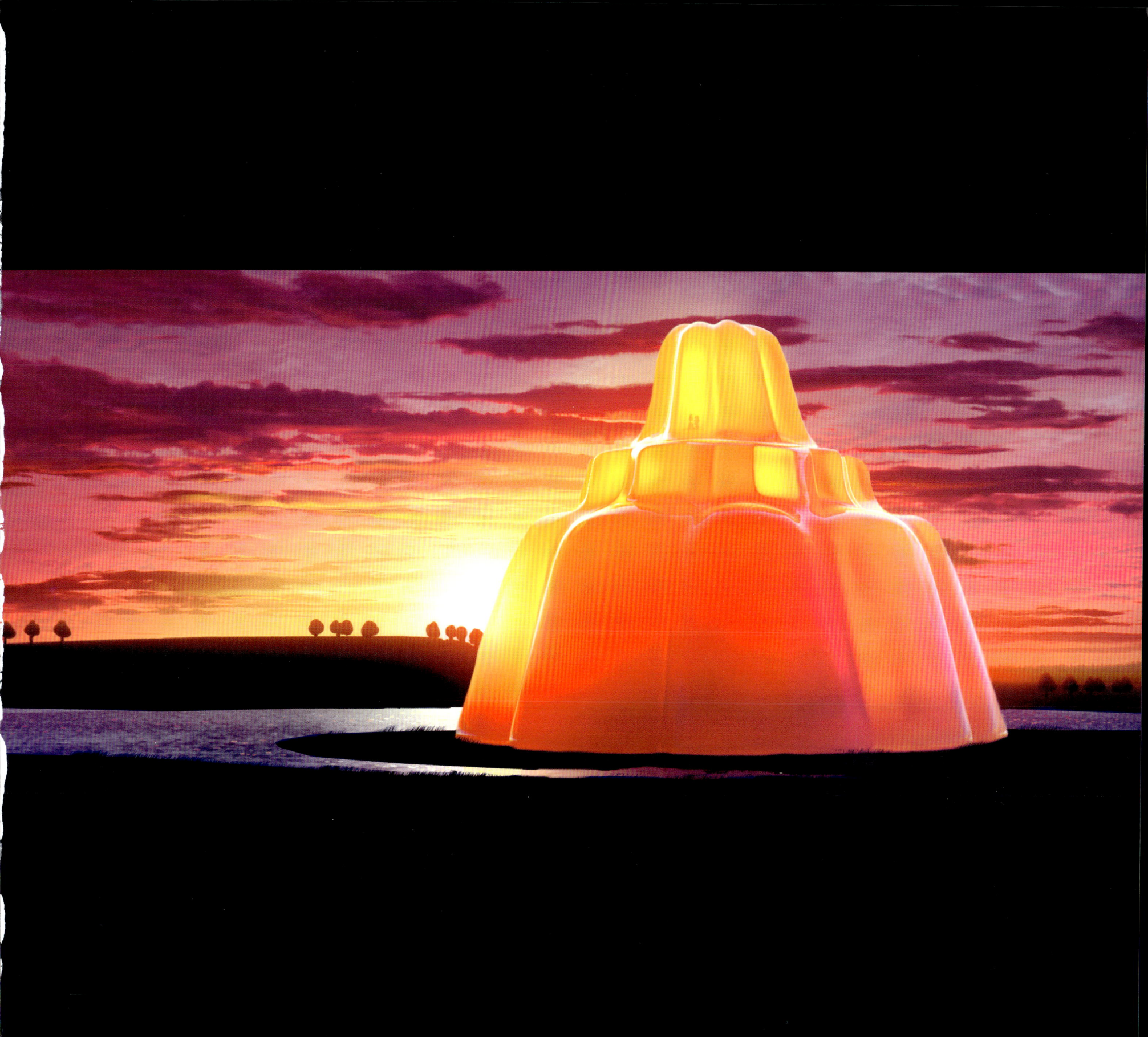

The Art and Making Of
SONY PICTURES ANIMATION'S

# Cloudy with a chance of MEATBALLS

Written by Tracey Miller-Zarneke
Foreword by Judi Barrett

TITAN BOOKS

# Contents

8 ★ Foreword by Judi Barrett

10 ★ Introduction

## Character Design

14 ★ A Bunch of Mixed Nuts

## Production Design

76 ★ Welcome to Swallow Falls

126 ★ The Many Flavors of Revitalization

176 ★ Afterword

179 ★ Acknowledgements

180 ★ Colophon

Page 1: Jell-O Mold at Sunset ★ *Dave Bleich*
Pages 2/3: Inside the Meatroid ★ *Chris Reccardi*
Pages 4/5: Weather News Network Studio ★ *Dean Gordon*
Pages 6/7: Flint's Lab ★ *Design: Justin K. Thompson, Paint: Michael Kurinsky*

WEATHER NEWS NETWORK

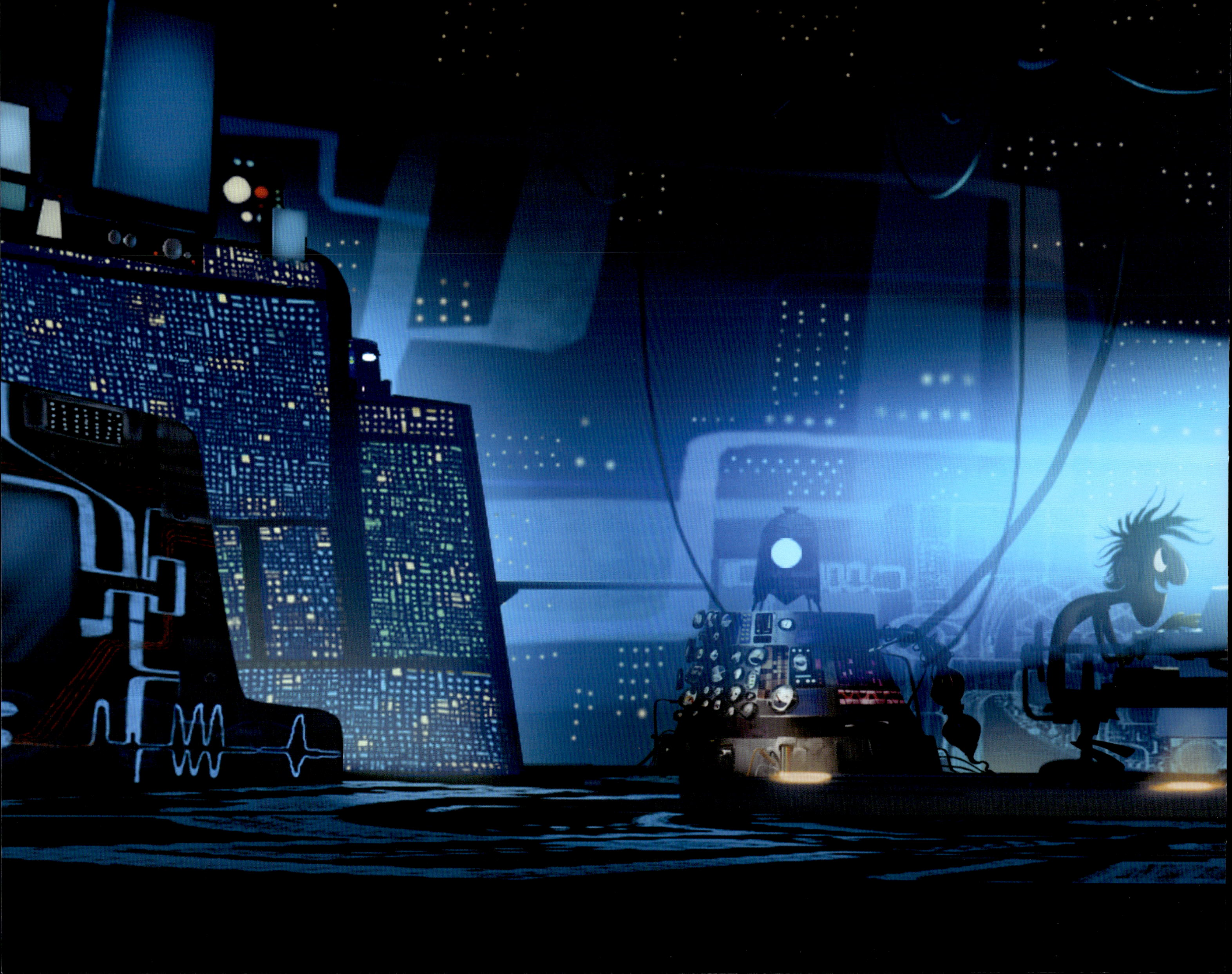

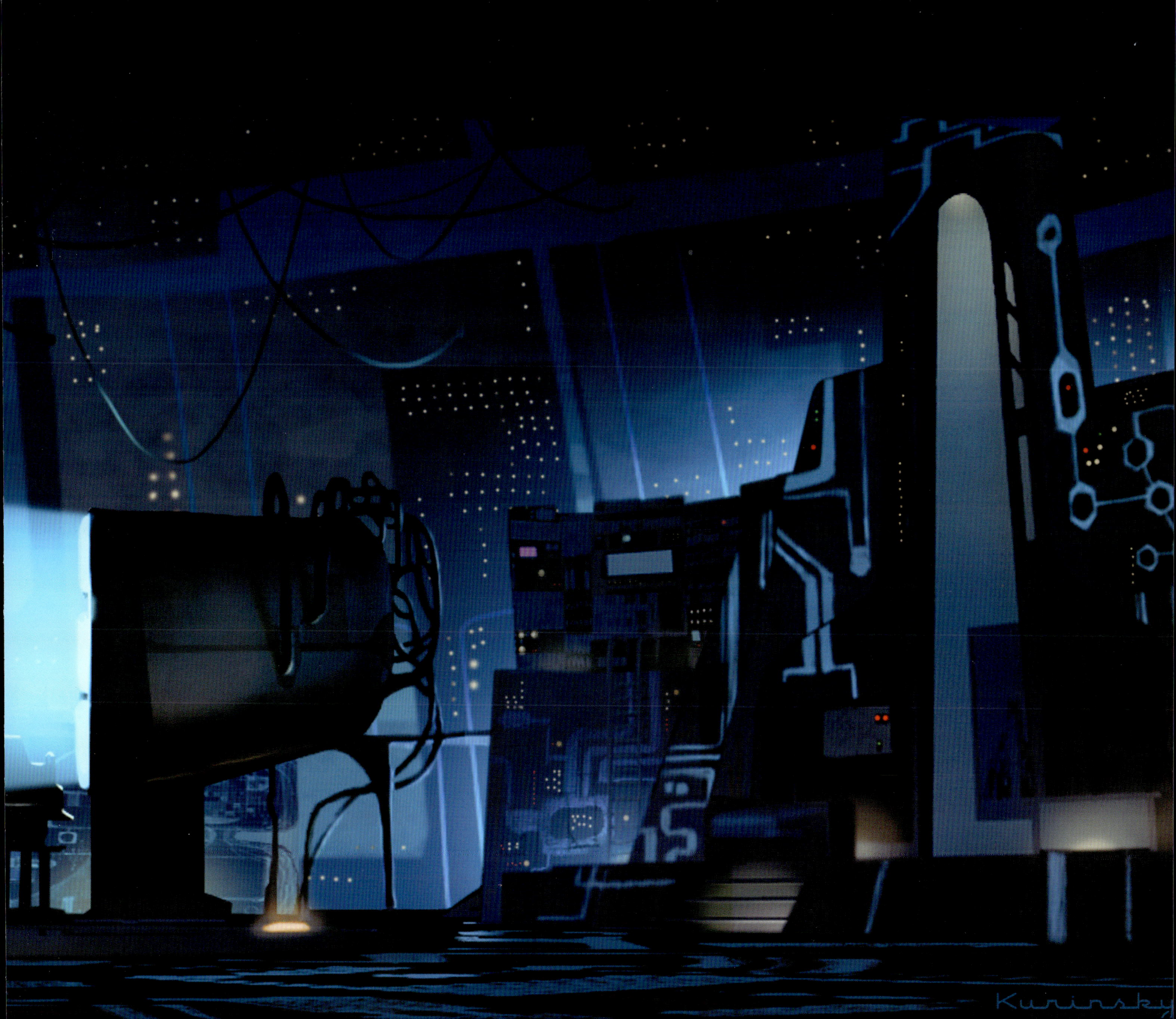
Kurinsky

# Foreword

**A**s a toddler, I wasn't the greatest eater according to my mother. So, she came up with a brilliant solution. She put a dollop of chocolate pudding, which I loved, on the spoon or fork in front of everything and anything she fed me. It worked! And so I ate my broccoli and string beans and all else that entered the portals of my mouth. Maybe it wasn't the healthiest of solutions, but it was successful and it certainly got me to eat all of my peas and carrots.

During that spoon-fed period, I also remember that my mom would repeat out loud, as she approached me with a food-laden utensil, "Chew and swallow, now chew and swallow." It was said in the hope that I wouldn't gulp down my food in record time, but would instead savor it, chewing it slowly and swallowing it prudently.

That cautionary expression stayed with me tucked away somewhere in my brain. It resurfaced one day many years later and appropriately became the name of the tiny town of Chewandswallow, which I created in my book, *Cloudy with a Chance of Meatballs*, but merged it into one word this time around. What a great name for that town, I thought.

Fortunately I broke with those youthful eating habits long ago, although I still dearly love chocolate pudding. What survived was a great love for food—reading about it, preparing it, cooking it, eating it, and most importantly, writing about it. It is one of the most enjoyable things in my life, both in my books and in my tummy.

One day, a few years after graduating college, for some reason that I can't account for, I thought of the provocative sentence, "Henry walked outside and got hit in the head with a meatball." And, as they say, the rest is history. I don't know where it came from or why. It was silly and it made me laugh. The image stuck with me and I thought that perhaps it might be the beginning of an idea for a children's book. Little did I know how right I was. From there, I began to play with words, creating food-related weather systems like a pea soup fog, a strawberry traffic jam, mustard clouds, a drizzle of soda, etc.

The idea grew and grew into what eventually became my book, *Cloudy with a Chance of Meatballs*, a story in which food rains down from the sky three times a day, for breakfast, lunch, and dinner. With the addition of Ron Barrett's brilliantly clever and glorious artwork, it eventually got published and has truly become a classic.

I always had the feeling that the original book would make a great animated movie, and it turned out that Sony Pictures Animation (SPA) did too. Although it needed stretching and development when it came to length, characters, and plot, SPA saw all its wonderful possibilities. The visual adaptation of the original book also had to be reinterpreted and redesigned so that the new images would fit into a 3D world using CGI technology.

The results are extraordinary and if you're a fan of the original book you'll certainly recognize some of your very favorite and most memorable moments in the movie. Sony Pictures Animation put together a phenomenal team of very special directors, producers, artists, and animators—a large family that made food coming down from the sky something you can believe in. The end results are mind-boggling. *Cloudy with a Chance of Meatballs* the film is a funny, wildly exciting, touching, amazing, and hunger-inducing movie for toddlers, adults, and everyone in between.

And to think that the seed of the strangely wonderful idea of food falling from the sky started to grow many years ago with a hungry little girl and a delicious lump of chocolate pudding.

—*Judi Barrett, 2009*

→ Cloudy With a Chance of Meatballs ★ Ron Barrett

There was a storm of pancakes one morning and a downpour of maple syrup that nearly flooded the town. A huge pancake covered the school. No one could get it off because of its weight, so they had to close the school.

*"This early image (below) helped us figure out where the directors wanted to go stylistically. Our discussion informed us that the schoolhouse was too quaint, the urban details like telephone poles/wires were good, the clouds were too whimsical, and the clean lines of the hills were good."*
—**MICHAEL KURINSKY** Art Director

↓ Beatboard ★ Michael Kurinsky

↑ Street Scene ★ Final Frame
→ Schoolhouse ★ Gaëtan & Paul Brizzi

# Introduction

An inventor must have a unique vision in order to create something no one has ever seen before. It's a vision that requires a fresh perspective fueled by endless energy. Flint Lockwood—diehard inventor and the main character in *Cloudy with a Chance of Meatballs*—certainly has this vision, and luckily directors Christopher Miller and Phil Lord have it as well.

Inspired by the 1978 best-selling children's book by Judi and Ron Barrett, *Cloudy with a Chance of Meatballs* has now evolved into a feature-length disaster movie, tempered with light-hearted humor and fun. "Chris and I had both grown up loving the book," recalls Lord. The directing duo was originally brought into Sony to talk about another film project, but upon discovering that the studio had the rights to this title, Lord and Miller were excited to pay tribute to one of their favorite childhood stories. "We actually think the book's whimsical absurdity helped develop our senses of humor, way back when we were kids," says Miller. The whole concept of the book is based on the absurd, with things that don't belong—namely food falling from the sky—existing on a scale that doesn't make sense, such as pancakes big enough to cover a school. To an adult who must question such anomalies, this lack of logic can be upsetting, but "when you're a kid, it's the greatest thing because you're engaged in figuring out how the world works all the time, and when things are off, it's stimulating," explains Lord.

While the film embraces a few key images, names, and story points from the original book, Lord and Miller introduce a whole new cast of characters in a much more action-packed adventure. "Their take on this story is crazy, irreverent, and fresh," says producer Pam Marsden. In the Lord/Miller version of *Cloudy with a Chance of Meatballs*, the central character is Flint Lockwood, whom Miller describes as "an outcast wannabe-inventor who tries to create a machine that will feed his hungry town. He accidentally launches it into the stratosphere, causing it to rain food. The town quickly becomes a tourist foodtopia where breakfast, lunch, and dinner shower down, making Flint a beloved hero. Wrapped up in his newfound adoration, Flint lets his invention get out of control, creating a delicious disaster of epic portions."

In preparation for bringing this story to the big screen, Lord and Miller spent many hours reviewing disaster films—everything from *The Swarm* to *Earthquake* to *Independence Day* to *Armageddon*. "We always wanted to do a cartoon version of a disaster movie," says Lord, because although they are meant to be dramatic action films, these stories play as "inherently funny because they have such a serious tone but really ridiculous things are happening. And we realized that we had exactly that situation with our film—a very silly thing that's happening that is actually perilous to the characters in that world," Miller explains.

To play to both the comedic and the action sides of the story, the directors looked to layout supervisor Dave Morehead to establish some rather surprising camera work, intermixing flat, locked-off, or slow-drifting camera shots with over-the-top, overly complicated deep-space camera moves that are inspired by the directorial style of Michael Bay, known for such action movies as *Armaggedon* and *The Rock*. As an added bonus, this camerawork naturally catches the audience off-guard, which the directors love to do. "You assert the story and certain realities, then you pull the rug out from

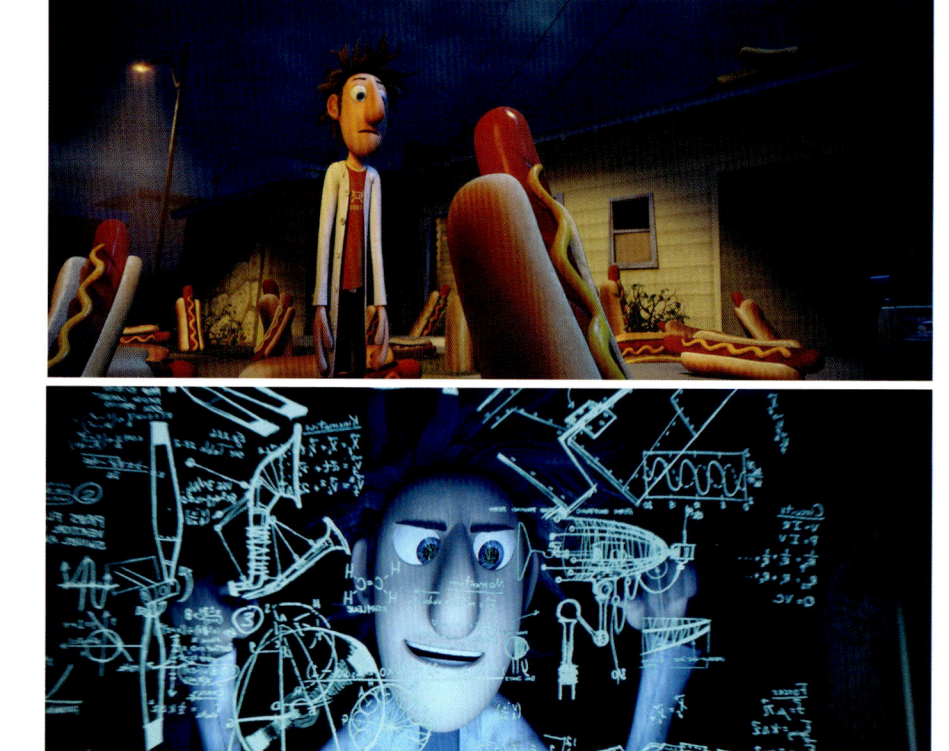

↑ Final Frames ★ *Digital*

"*The book has a sort of wish-fulfillment, fantastical side to it . . . kind of like how* **Jurassic Park** *is all about 'Wouldn't it be cool to see dinosaurs alive? That would be awesome. Oh wait, that wouldn't be awesome, that would be horrifying.'*"
—**CHRISTOPHER MILLER** Director, on the original *Cloudy* book

↓ Flint Expressions ★ *Carey Yost*

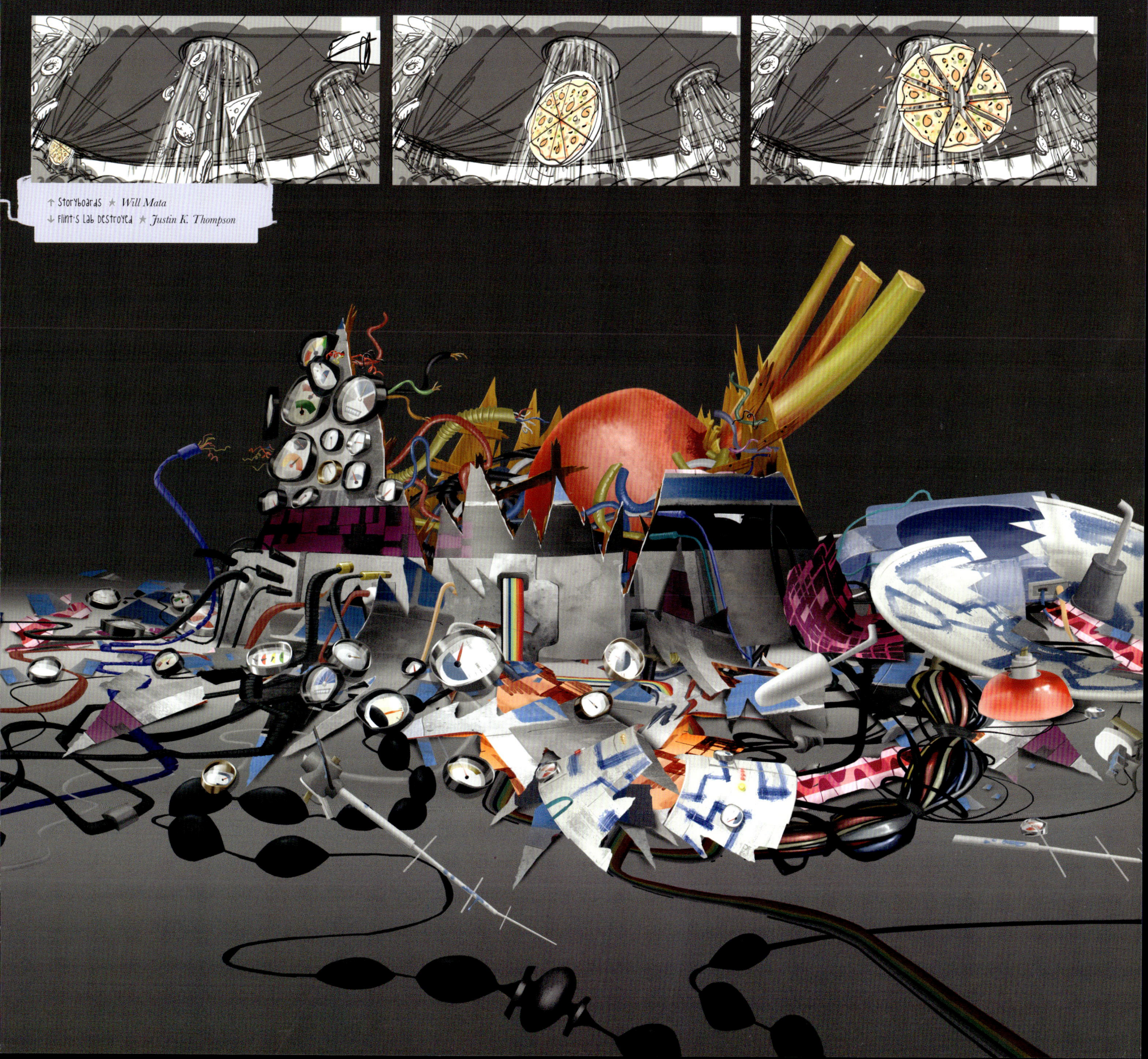

↑ Storyboards ★ Will Mata
↓ Flint's Lab Destroyed ★ Justin K. Thompson

under the audience, then put the rug back, then pull it out again," Lord says. "And the best thing about working in animation is that you can constantly and easily subvert reality," Miller adds.

For the look of the film, Lord and Miller drew upon the whimsical illustrations from the original book as well as from the imaginative perspective of Miroslav Sasek, an early–twentieth century children's book writer/artist from Czechoslovakia known for his travel pieces. "We have an affinity for superstylized yet simplified shape language," says Miller, and Sasek's style complied with their philosophy that "cartoons should look cartoony, and the whole point of animation is to exaggerate reality to convey truth," adds Lord. They brought in production designer Justin K. Thompson, along with Imageworks, to translate their vision into the CG (computer-generated) world, wanting to capture the playful use of pattern, the bold yet charming simplification of forms, and the cartoonlike sense of proportions to help convey the spirited energy of the film. Art director Michael Kurinsky then established a color theory that supports the use of texture while adding drama and intensity to reflect the twists and turns of the storyline.

In designing the characters for *Cloudy*, Lord and Miller envisioned the simplicity of Sasek's illustrations combined with the charm of the Muppets. "Animation is not about realism, it's about expressiveness," says Lord, "and the Muppets are so successful because they are simple, designed without a lot of fussy detail that would distract the eye and take away from their intended expressions." Plus, adds Miller, "the Muppets are appealing because they are the perfect translation of flat, graphic character design into 3D," which is exactly the vision that Lord/Miller had for their "cast."

"We often said to the directors, 'We have nothing if we don't have your vision,'" recalls Bob Osher, president of Sony Pictures Digital Production. To ensure that this vision made it to the final film, president of production Hannah Minghella credits Marsden's focus as "the perfect complement to Chris and Phil's boundless creativity. She has helped keep the entire team motivated and moving forward for the duration of a process that is incredibly long and involved." "Pam was the calm in the middle of the storm, especially when she had to work through several regime changes during the production," adds Osher.

The images shared in this book represent a small sampling of the tens of thousands of storyboards, character designs, and location concept pieces that were hand-drawn in pencil, colored by brush, or digitally painted and rendered during the development of *Cloudy with a Chance of Meatballs*. This exhibit is a tribute to the collective inventiveness at Sony Pictures Animation and the vision that it takes to produce a film as extraordinary as this.

*"Whether dealing with story, the jokes, the look, the animation, or whatever, Chris and Phil never rely on shortcuts or solutions that may be 'tried and true.' They always choose to find a new way."*
—**PAM MARSDEN** Producer

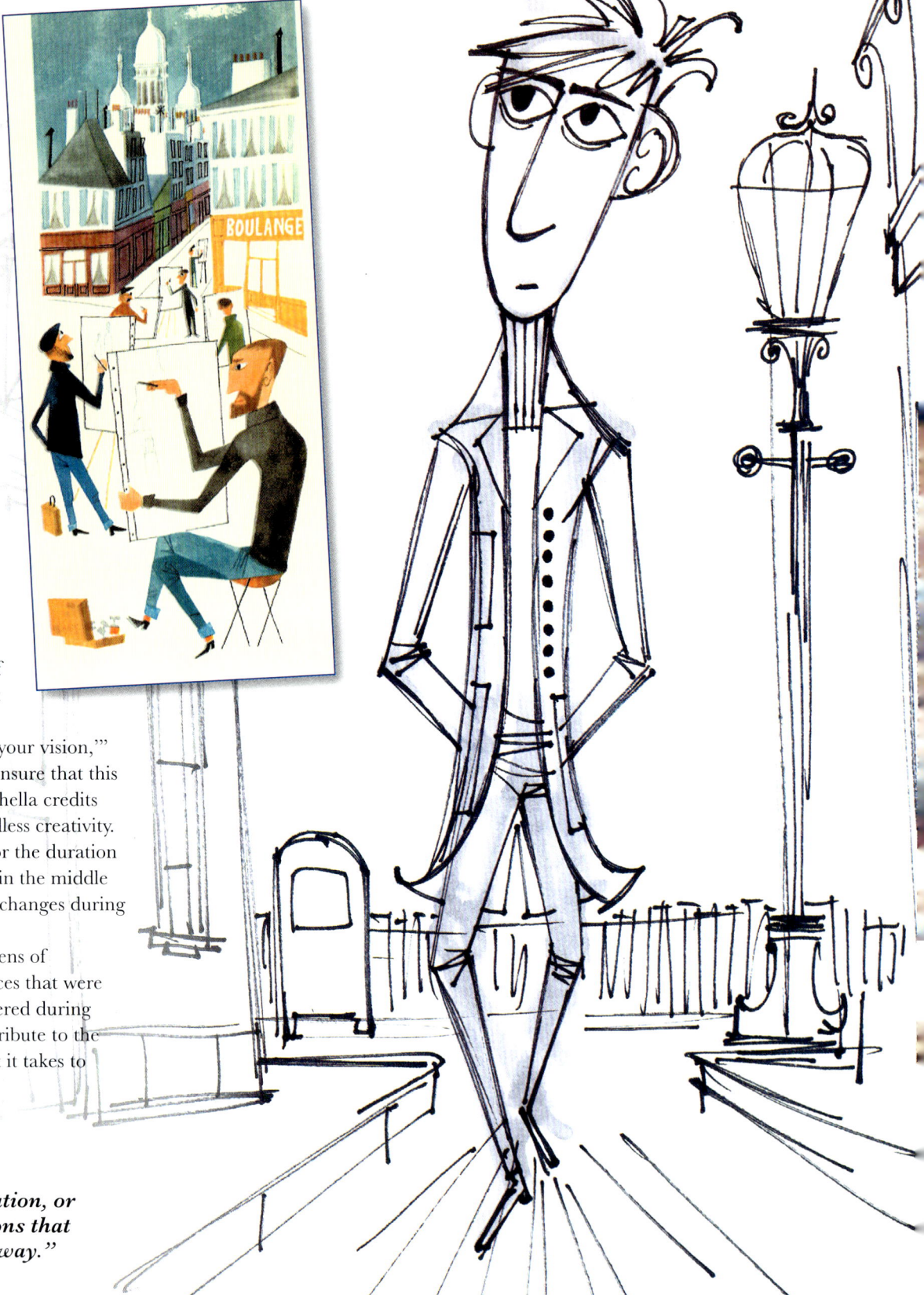

↑ The Painters of Montmartre ★ *Miroslav Sasek (from the book* This is Paris*)*
↗ Flint ★ *Chris Reccardi*
↗ Roofless Restaurant ★ *Will Mata*
→ Sascktown ★ *Michael Kurinsky*

PAY at CASHIER PAGUE EN LA CAJA

TACKLE
BAIT
WE HAVE WORMS!
COLD BEER
QUIK STOP
LIQUOR
insky

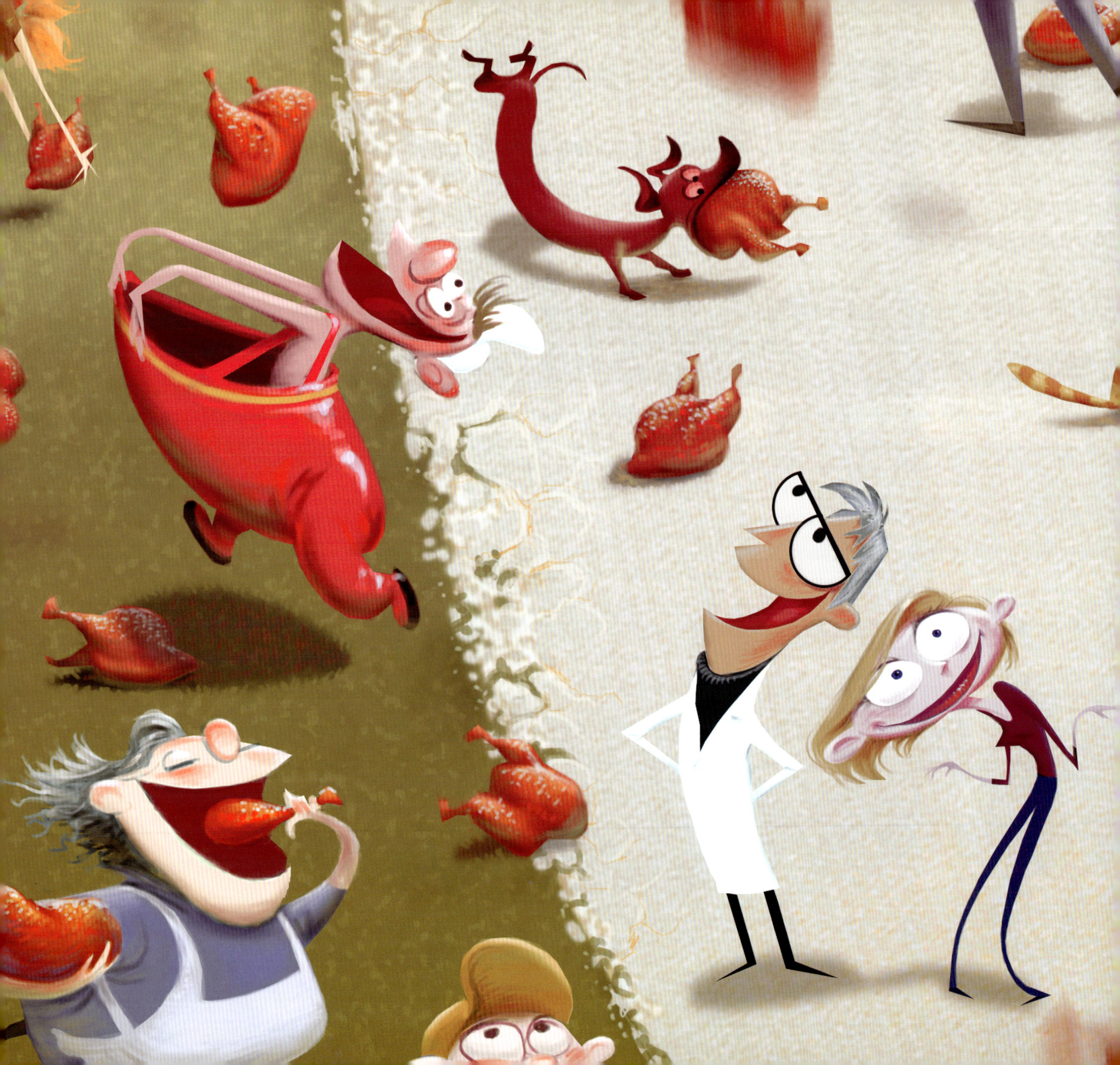

# Character Design
## A Bunch of Mixed Nuts

# Flint Lockwood

*"Flint has more than 1,000 facial controls, which gave our animators the ability to get pretty much any performance they wanted."*
—**STEPHEN CANDELL** Character Setup Lead

Flint Lockwood has always been a little different from his peers—his childhood bedroom was plastered with posters of famous scientists and inventors, and Flint was regularly mocked by his classmates, who thought his interests were nerdy. But one of his fondest memories of his mother is of her giving him his first real lab coat, inspiring him to keep on inventing because she knew he was "going to do big things someday." While most of his fellow Swallow Falls townsfolk simply wallowed in the depression that had hit their town once its livelihood had dried up, Flint persevered in his efforts to invent things to make life better, which is what led to the creation of his food machine, that plays such a prominent role in this disaster film.

Flint himself was reinvented time and again, both in design and personality. Early concept drawings of Flint show him with every imaginable hair color and style, standing at varying heights, weights, and manners of dress. Once the artistic decision was made to follow more cartoony influences, Flint's proportions were adjusted and tweaked from top to bottom: Flint was given a thinner body, long limbs, and an oversized head. A great deal of time was spent on his eyes, which were made sharper and more triangular, "but these proved less appealing and, therefore, not ideal for a main character," explains senior animation supervisor Pete Nash. "They wanted a Sasek 'feel,' but with more versatility," recalls character designer Carey Yost, who was told to keep pushing the proportions and shape language for Flint and the rest of the character lineup.

After Yost produced one particular concept drawing of Flint, the directors realized that this character should move in a very Muppet-like way. To support this more abstract than anatomical direction for animation, the modeling team built Flint with extra resolution in his limbs and hands to allow for humanly impossible flexibility. Modeling supervisor Marvin Kim explains that his team also gave Flint "more resolution in the face, particularly around the eyes, nose, and mouth to provide animators with the geometry to create expressions with wide eyes and mouths that opened to 180 degrees, like a hand puppet can do." The flexibility of the mouth shapes was a notable accomplishment, since being able "to go from a pin-sized hole to a gaping hippopotamus mouth with the same controls" required that new techniques be developed, according to CG supervisor Michael Ford. The look-development team also kept the skin surface simple,

↑ Voice of Flint Lockwood
★ *Bill Hader*

Previous pages Character Designs ★ *Andy Gaskill*
→ Flint ★ *Stephen Silver*

↘ Flint ★ *Carey Yost*

↑ Flint ★ *Pete Oswald*
← Flint ★ *Chris Reccardi*

FLINT IS WAY COOL

↑ Flint and Best Friend ★ *Phil Lord*

"This shows (above) where we started with trying to envision Sasek's influence to our world"
—**MICHAEL KURINSKY** Art Director

↑ ↗ Flint ★ *Stephen Silver*

↑ Flint ★ *Carey Yost*

← Young Flint ★ Carey Yost

making it "light on texture to support the desire to get graphic reads with clean lines," says visual effects supervisor Rob Bredow. In animation dailies sessions, the directors consistently gave notes to make Flint's motions less anatomical and more graphic, and regardless of how many times the animators had to redo shots, "they all had so much fun with this style of movement that I never saw a happier animation crew," recalls co-producer Lydia Bottegoni.

In character development, Flint had wavered back and forth between suave scientist and geeky guy who still lives with his parents, but the characterization that felt most right was basically "a subversion of the archetype of a very capable scientist—he *wants* to be that, but just isn't" explains director Phil Lord. Given a name that suggests an action hero, the original script positioned Flint as the most successful scientist in the world until his government-funded food machine got stuck in orbit over Swallow Falls, thus leaving him stranded in the small town while he attempted to fix his machine and redeem his reputation. But his initial arrogance kept the audience from connecting with him, and it was decided to make him a youthful resident of Swallow Falls, with more of an optimistic, genuine quality to his character.

This more innocent, dreamer personality proved the perfect fit for the simplified but joyfully expressive Flint who is able to easily connect with the audience. "His contraptions may be complicated, but he's a simple guy with simple dreams," says Miller, "and it's entertaining and inspiring to watch characters whose ambitions exceed their abilities."

Although he seems socially inept at first—Flint is much more comfortable in his lab than with a crowd of folks—"he learns to take responsibility for his actions as an inventor, both successes and failures, and by doing so he finds a way to fit into the human race," explains head of story Kris Pearn. Perhaps even more notable is Flint's example that a person should "embrace his weirdness" and be confident with who he is . . . a lesson he imparts to other characters and, ideally, the audience.

↑ ↓ Flint ★ Carey Yost

↑ Flint ★ Andy Gaskill

↑ Flint ★ *Michael Kurinsky*

← → Flint ★ *Carey Yost*

↑ Flint ★ *Carey Yost*   → Flint ★ *Final Frame*

↓ Flint ★ Chris Reccardi

↗ Flint ★ Andy Gaskill
→ Flint ★ Christopher Miller

20

↑ Flint Lineup ★ Stephen Silver

↑ Flint ★ Andy Gaskill
← ↓ Flint ★ Carey Yost

↖ ↘ Flint ★ Carey Yost

"Flint is a proponent of the 'let your freak flag fly' attitude."
—**PHIL LORD**
Director

↑ Handsome Flint ★ Design: Justin K. Thompson, Paint: Cristy Maltese

21

↑ ↑ Flint ★ *Sylvain Deboissy*

↓ Flint ★ Robin Joseph

"The animators love to play up Flint's social awkwardness by giving him nervous eye movement and odd choices of arm poses and adjustments to show that he doesn't know what to do with his hands."
—**PETE NASH** Senior Animation Supervisor

→ Flint ★ Andy Gaskill

# Tim Lockwood

Tim Lockwood is a man of few words and little expression, outside of the realm of fishing. Like most of his fellow townsfolk, he puts his nose to the grindstone and tries to keep his tackle shop afloat even though the sardine industry has long since expired in his community. The squareness of his shape echoes the small-town mindset of "not thinking outside of the box," and the rigidity of his movements is also symbolic of this sense of being locked into thinking "things are fine the way they are," says director Christopher Miller. He is a model citizen of Swallow Falls, representing the blue-collar worker who just doesn't understand someone like Flint, even if he is his own son. Tim's range of expression is quite small, with his mustache and unibrow further limiting his emotional readability, all of which reflect his rather stoic personality. This limited means of communication was a welcome challenge for the animation crew, who were "forced to be creative with other movements, such as posture and the speed of head turns," notes senior animation supervisor Pete Nash.

"Flint didn't always have a father in the story, but the relationship with Tim gives him more humanity and provides more of an emotional pull for the audience," explains head of story Kris Pearn. It is a relationship that everyone wants to see work, and when it finally does thanks to the assistance of yet another of Flint's inventions, the outpouring of emotion from Tim is a pleasant surprise—another unexpected, heartwarming moment that the directors are so fond of providing their audience.

↑ Voice of Tim Lockwood
★ *James Caan*

← Tim Lockwood ★
*Paint: Cristy Maltese*

*"Tim suffers no fools. He's like a lot of people that I admire, but am nothing like."*
—PHIL LORD Director

↓ ↑ Tim Lockwood  ★ *Carey Yost*

↓ ↑ Tim Lockwood  ★ *Carey Yost*

↑ Tim Lockwood  ★ *Paint: Noelle Triaureau*

← Tim Lockwood
★ *Mark Colangelo*

← ↓ ↑ Tim Lockwood  ★ *Carey Yost*

← ↑ Tim Lockwood  ★ *Carey Yost*

# Sam Sparks

"Samantha Sparks is the total opposite of Flint—she's outgoing, extroverted, talkative, and socially competent—but like him, she knows what it's like to feel alienated," says director Phil Lord. Whereas Flint has embraced his geekiness and let it lead his life's path, "Sam" Sparks has gone to great lengths to hide her true self: As a young, bespectacled girl fascinated with weather, she was mocked by her classmates for such interests. Sam then decided it would be easier to connect with others by dumbing herself down, getting rid of her eyeglasses, and playing up her cuteness—and this is her modus operandi when she meets Flint.

While Sam is enthusiastic about the prospect of moving up from intern to weatherperson, she is not entirely comfortable in her false persona, tripping up in her early broadcasts while trying to maintain the "cute" image. "Her comedy comes from her drive to be a successful weatherperson, but as she settles down and accepts her nerdy self in later broadcasts, she is more natural," notes director Christopher Miller. Her animation clearly alters when she switches back and forth between the true and false Sams: "Her eyebrows furrow, her eyes squint, and her mouth is asymmetrical when she is in geek mode, and her eyes get bigger and more blinky when she is playing dumb," explains senior animation supervisor Pete Nash.

Finding the right balance between geeky and cute in character design was a lengthy process, "especially when trying to make a comedic, graphic statement with her as well," recalls character designer Carey Yost. Carey and modeling supervisor Marvin Kim nearly cringe with repulsion when they recall a CG turnaround of an early Sam build that was simply "grotesque," in their independent opinions. Carey also realizes in hindsight that when they were trying to make every level of Sam funny, it got out of hand, even debating the question in an executive review session—"What is up with her hair, and what the hell is she wearing?" being the gist of the inquiry.

← Voice of Sam Sparks
★ *Anna Faris*

↑ Sam's Business Card ★ *Dean Gordon*
← Sam ★ *Final Frame*

Sam Sparks ★ Pete Oswald

To find the right look for Sam, her hairstyle was altered countless times, and each new "do" required a lot more work than just grabbing a curling iron or a pair of trimmers, "considering all the paint maps, procedural effects, and grooming that go into creating a hairstyle," explains hair and cloth supervisor Rodrigo Ibanez. Having the KAMI system in place really helped to economize this work—it's a proprietary hair-and-fur software package from Imageworks that can create multiple hair layers, add styling effects, and organize such information so that it renders more effectively than on previous Sony effects projects. Because KAMI provides simulations so quickly, it allows artists to spend more time creating and less time waiting to see their images, which makes it "one of the best tools in the industry, allowing artists to be artists," adds Ibanez.

After many iterations, the final Sam was discovered when visual development artist Pete Oswald did a take on Yost's earlier concept work. "At first glance, she is beautiful, with a subtle tribute to Farrah [Fawcett]'s 1970s hairstyle; but upon closer look, she's a little goofy, with big eyes and hands" explains Oswald. In Flint's eyes, she is most beautiful when she puts her glasses back on and pulls her hair back in a ponytail—a fun twist on the usual film makeover moment, when the geeky girl takes off her glasses, pulls her hair out of the ponytail, and lets it flow freely about her shoulders, blowing in the breeze. "Transformations are a big theme for the directors. Chris and Phil seem to love the redemptive quality of a nerd's story and the ridiculousness of the moment when simply removing one's glasses makes her suddenly beautiful," says Yost.

More importantly, Sam's psychological transformation serves both the story and the audience well. "She learns to accept herself for who she really is, and only by approaching herself and society with honesty and integrity can she see the dangers ahead and warn Flint—and the world—to head for cover. Also, by opening her mind to her true nature, she opens herself to falling in love with Flint," explains head of story Kris Pearn.

← ↑ *Young Sam*
★ Carey Yost

→ *Young Sam*
★ Paint: Noelle Triaureau

↙ Sam ★ Chris Reccardi

↑ Sam ★ Carey Yost
↓ Sam ★ Andy Gaskill

↑ Sam ★ Lynn Naylor

29

↑ Sam ★ Sylvain Deboissey   → Sam ★ Carey Yost
↓ Sam ★ Stephen Silver

30

→ Sam ★ Todd Pilger
↓ Sam ★ Takao Noguchi

"When Sam comes into Swallow Falls, right away you can tell she's an outsider: Her modern hairstyle incorporates highlights, lowlights, and layers, and her clothing has color and textures more sophisticated than any other character's in the film."
—**JUSTIN K. THOMPSON**
Production Designer

*"At one point we were asked to make her more foxy. Then we got feedback that said, 'Well, we know how she got where she is,' at which point we were asked to make her less foxy. So we redesigned her finally to be more cute and less 'vavoom.'"*
—**PHIL LORD** Director

↑ ↗ → Sam ★ *Carey Yost*

↖ ↑ Sam ★ Stephen Silver

↑ Sam ★ Deanna Marsigliese
↓ Sam ★ Final Frame

34 ↑ Flint and Sam ★ Chris Reccardi  → Beatboard ★ Gaëtan & Paul Brizzi

35

↓ → Flint and Sam ★ *Stephen Silver*

↑ Flint and Sam ★ *Jason Lethcoe*

↑ Anna Faris & Bill Hader

↓ ↑ Flint and Sam ★ *Carey Yost*

36

*"More important than the romantic component of Sam and Flint's relationship is their friendship and the story of Flint finally finding somebody who understands and admires him for who he is and who he, in turn, can allow to be who she really is."*
—**HANNAH MINGHELLA**
President of Production

↑ Flint and Sam ★ *Stephen Silver*
→ Flint and Sam ★ *Chris Reccardi*
↓ Flint and Sam ★ *Sylvain Deboissey*

# Steve the Monkey

Steve is more the average monkey than the average sidekick. Originally called Bonkers, Steve is intended to be a wild animal, not the anthropomorphized cartoon that most animated films present. "Since Steve doesn't talk, we wanted to make sure he could be expressive with his actions, posing his tail and limbs in both fluid and blocky shapes," says visual development artist Pete Oswald. "He never portrays emotions, just instincts" in true animal behavior, explains senior animation supervisor Pete Nash, and "he is very erratic and spontaneous in his animation, snapping into new poses quickly." To ensure that his movements were not like those of the other characters, "the character setup team even took away some functionality to keep his motions more limited and more animalistic," recalls character setup lead Todd Taylor. Steve is the bearer of one of Flint's earliest inventions, the thought-translator, with which Flint was hoping to show the world the deep inner workings of the animal brain. While Flint would like to interpret Steve's thoughts as much more intellectual than they actually are—for instance, mistaking Steve saying "can" as an affirmative answer to a question rather than the result of Steve actually looking at a sardine can—Steve serves a great purpose by being an ear for Flint's monologues, ushering the audience into Flint's thought process . . . which is much more robust than Steve's, apparently.

↑ Digital Character Poses

↑ Steve the Monkey ★ *Chris Reccardi*

↑ Steve the Monkey ★ *Phil Lord*

"*We really wanted to give him red eyes, because we liked that it said 'wild' and 'cute' at the same time. But we lost that battle.*"
—**PHIL LORD** Director

↓ ↘ Steve the Monkey ★ *Lynn Naylor*

↑ Steve the Monkey ★ *Lynn Naylor*

→ Steve the Monkey ★ *Carey Yost*

↑ Steve the Monkey ★ *Deanna Marsigliese*

39

← Steve the Monkey ★ Stephen Silver

↑ Steve the Monkey ★ Phil Lord

↑ Steve the Monkey ★ Stephen Silver

↑ Steve the Monkey ★ Eric Goldberg

↙ ↓ Steve the Monkey ★ Pete Oswald

# H2O MOLECULES ENTER

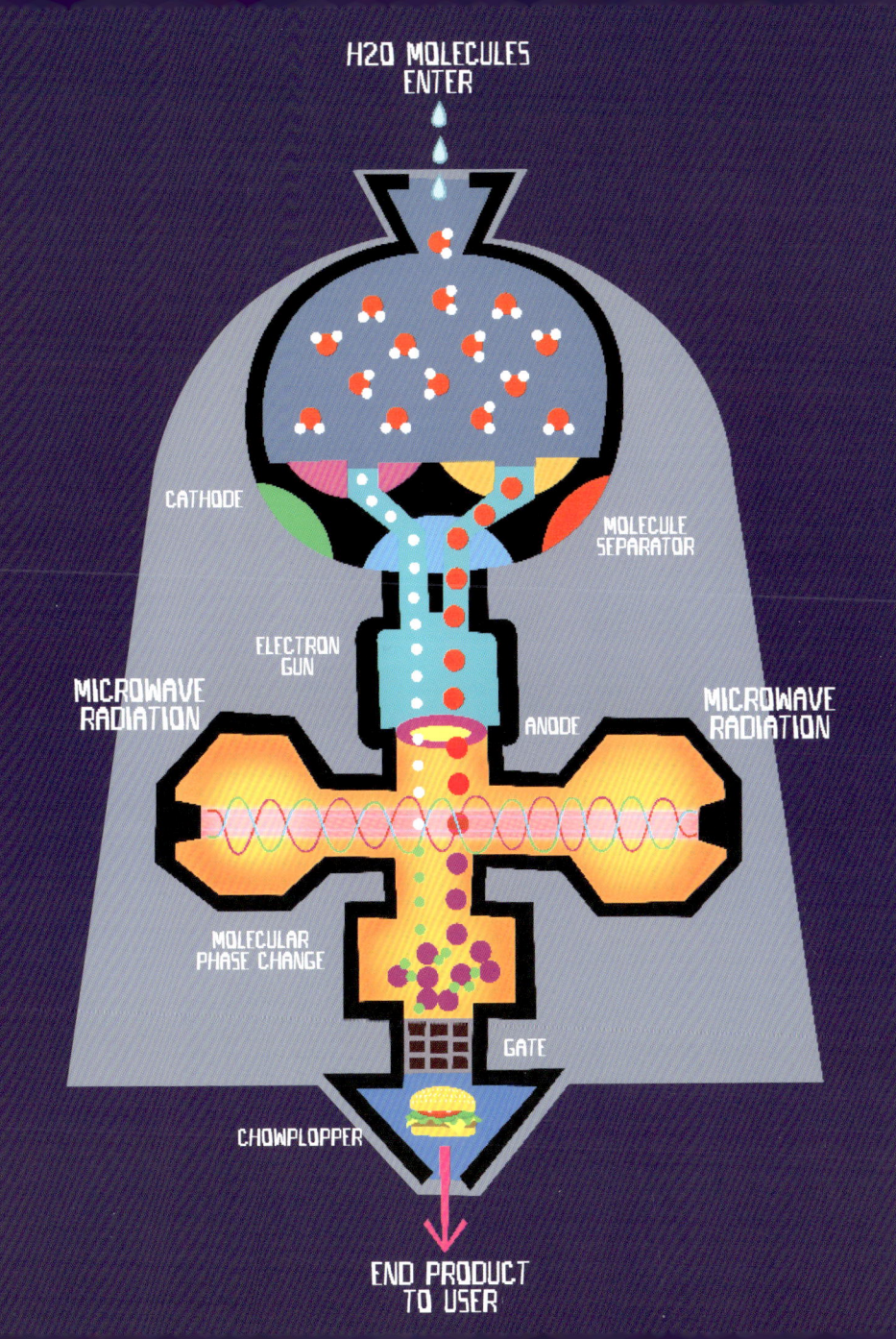

**CATHODE**

**MOLECULE SEPARATOR**

**ELECTRON GUN**

**MICROWAVE RADIATION**

**ANODE**

**MICROWAVE RADIATION**

**MOLECULAR PHASE CHANGE**

**GATE**

**CHOWPLOPPER**

# END PRODUCT TO USER

# Flint's Inventions

**M**ore often than not, Flint has been misunderstood in his need to create. "His ambition is to make things that are awesome first and functional second," says director Phil Lord. "In that sense, he's an artist more than a scientist." Since this is a town of little artistry, it's easy to see how Flint can be misunderstood, as Flint is clearly not cut from the same blue-collar cloth as are the rest of the townsfolk. Furthermore, many of Flint's inventions have backfired, making the town apprehensive of what other upsets he might cause with his prototypes. After all, his track record includes a remote-controlled television that was meant to walk to its owner so that he might change the channel, but instead it ran out the door and then ran amuck; a flying car that simply doesn't fly; a "hair unbalder" solution that made hair grow wildly out of control; and although it never made it to the final film, Flint also created an invisible coffee table that really "opens up the space" but caused more shin bruises than were worth the aesthetic benefit. "Flint has unlimited potential and amazing creative drive, but he just doesn't think everything through to the end," reflects production designer Justin K. Thompson.

Over Food Machine cutaway ★ *Design: Justin K. Thompson, Paint: Michael Kurinsky*

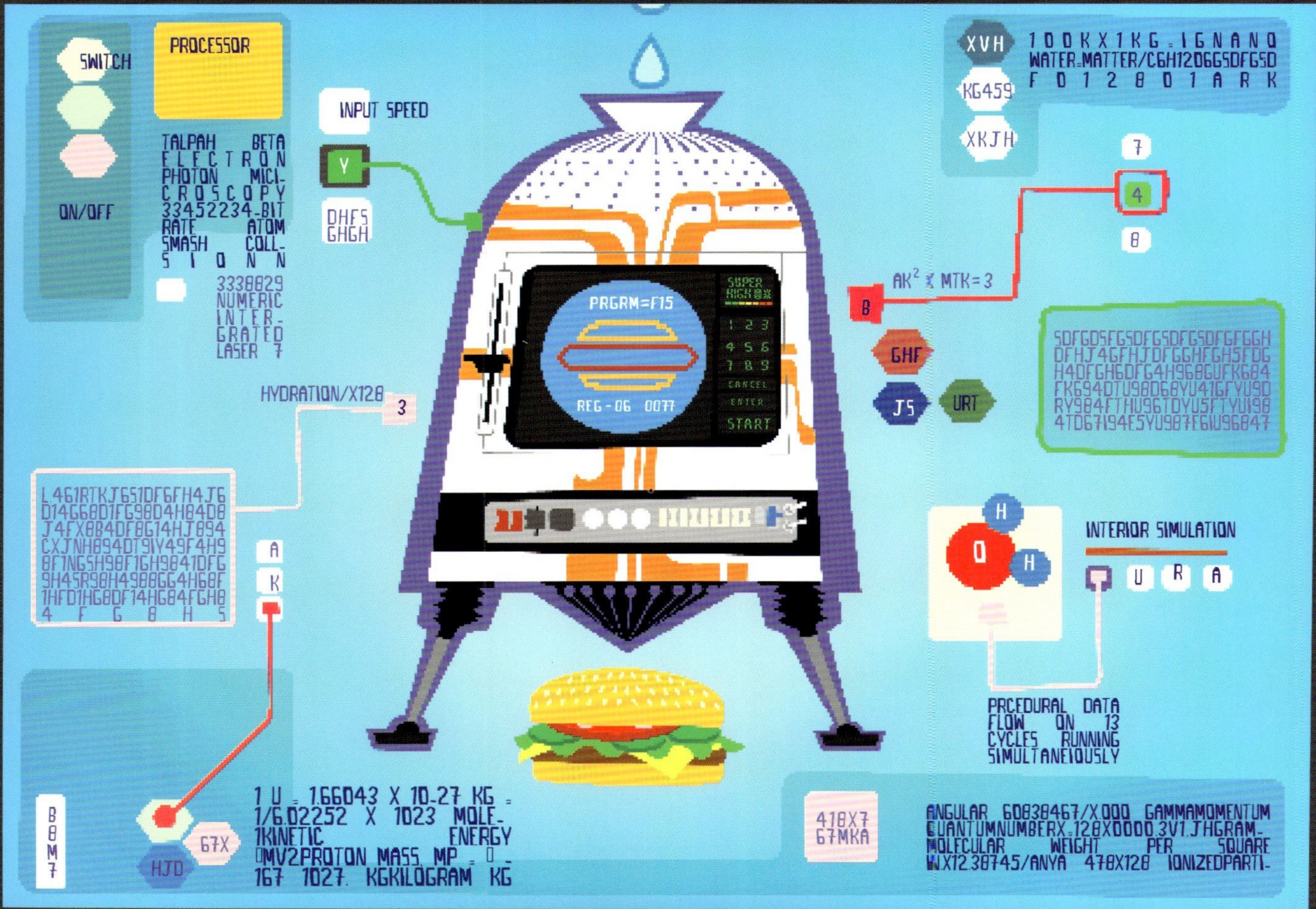
SWITCH
ON/OFF
PROCESSOR
TALPAH BETA ELECTRON PHOTON MICI-CROSCOPY 33452234-BIT RATE ATOM SMASH COLL-SIONN
3338829 NUMERIC INTER-GRATED LASER 7
INPUT SPEED
Y
DHFS GHGH
HYDRATION/X128
3
L461RTKJ651DF6FH4J6 D14G68D1FG98D4H84D8 J4FX884DF8G14HJ894 CXJNH894DT9IY49F4H9 8F1NGSH98F1GH9841DFG 9H45R98H4988GG4H68F 1HFD1HG8DF14HG84FGH8 4 F G 8 H S
A
K
B 8 M 7
HJD
67X
PRGRM=F15
REG-06 0077
SUPER HIGH
1 2 3
4 5 6
7 8 9
CANCEL
ENTER
START
XVH
KG459
XKJH
100KX1KG.IGNANO WATER.MATTER/C6H12O6G5DFG5D F012801ARK
7
4
8
AK² X MTK=3
B
GHF
JS
URT
SDFGDSFGSDFGSDFGSDFGFGGH DFHJ4GFHJDFGGHFGHSFDG H4DFGH6DFG4H968GUFK684 FK694DTU98D68YU41GFYU9D RY984FTHU96TDYU5FTYUI98 4TD67I94ESYU987E6U96847
H
O
H
INTERIOR SIMULATION
U R A
PRCEDURAL DATA FLOW ON 13 CYCLES RUNNING SIMULTANEIOUSLY
1 U = 1.66043 X 10-27 KG = 1/6.02252 X 1023 MOLE-1KINETIC ENERGY □MV2PROTON MASS MP = □ -167 1027 KGKILOGRAM KG
418X7 67MKA
ANGULAR 60838467/X.000 GAMMAMOMENTUM QUANTUMNUMBERX.128X0000.3V1.JHGRAM-MOLECULAR WEIGHT PER SQUARE WX12.38745/ANYA 478X128 IONIZEDPARTI-

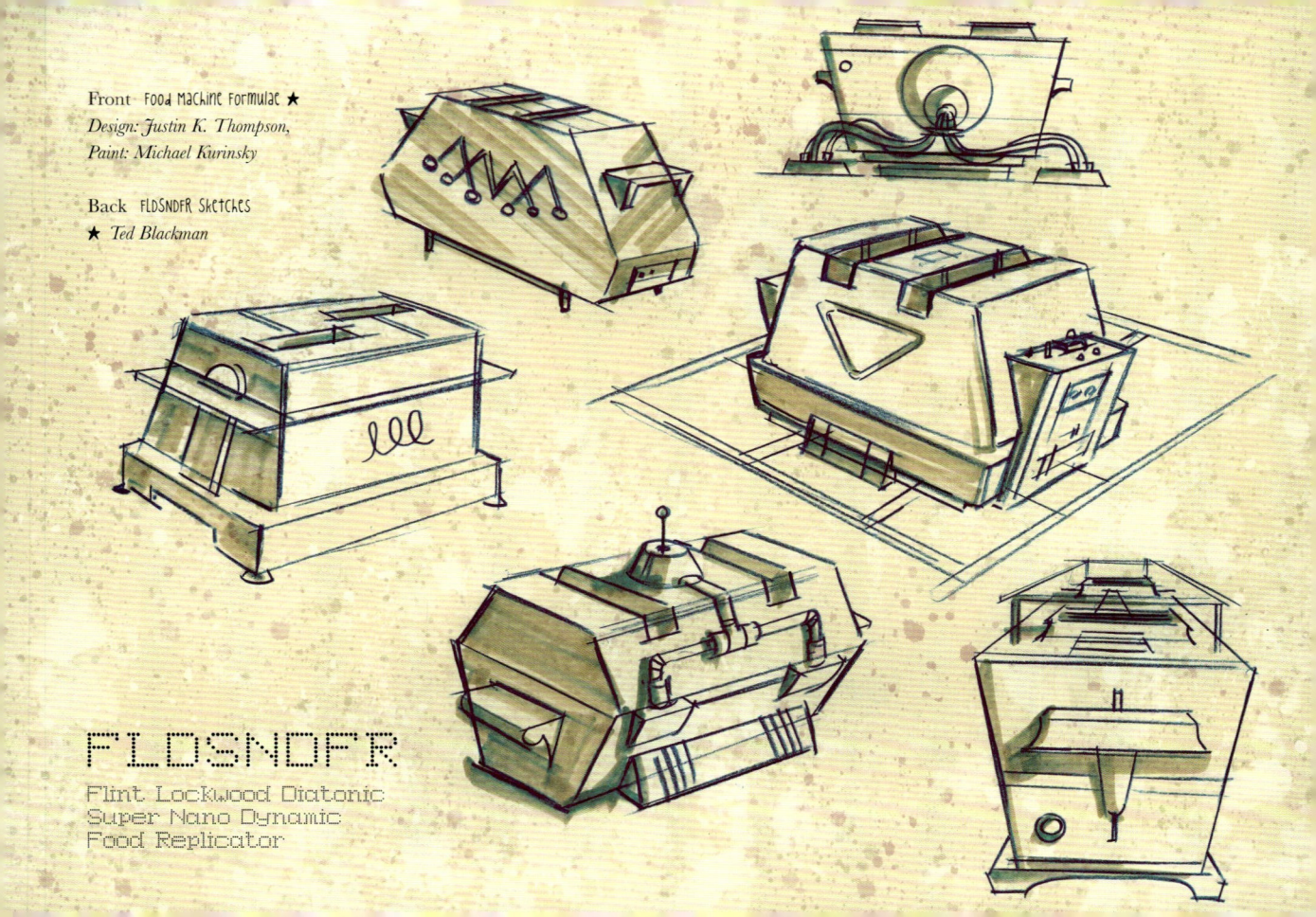

Front- Food Machine Formulae ★
Design: Justin K. Thompson,
Paint: Michael Kurinsky

Back- FLDSNDFR sketches
★ Ted Blackman

# FLDSNDFR
Flint Lockwood Diatonic
Super Nano Dynamic
Food Replicator

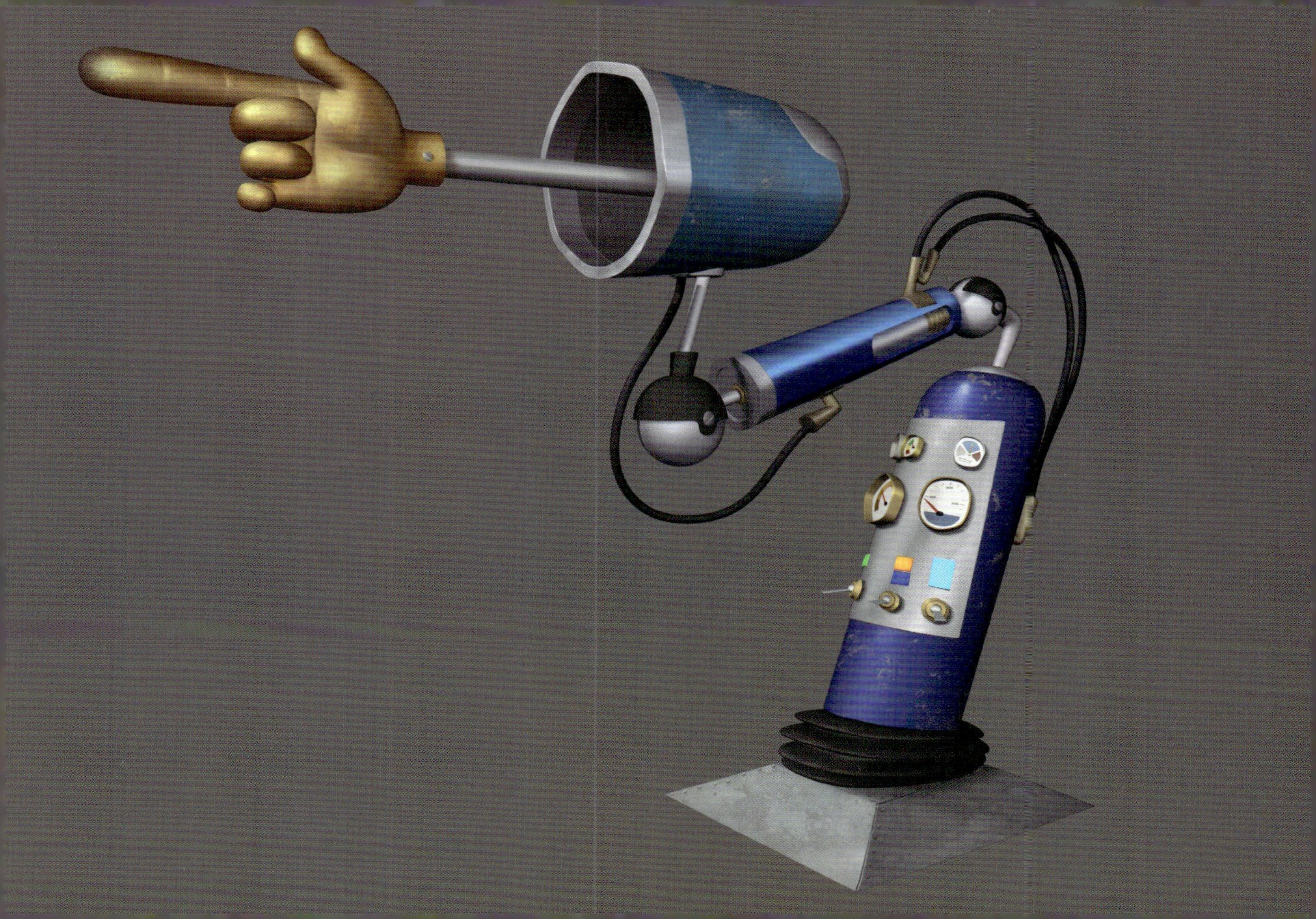

# ROBOT ARM: HAND CLOSE UP

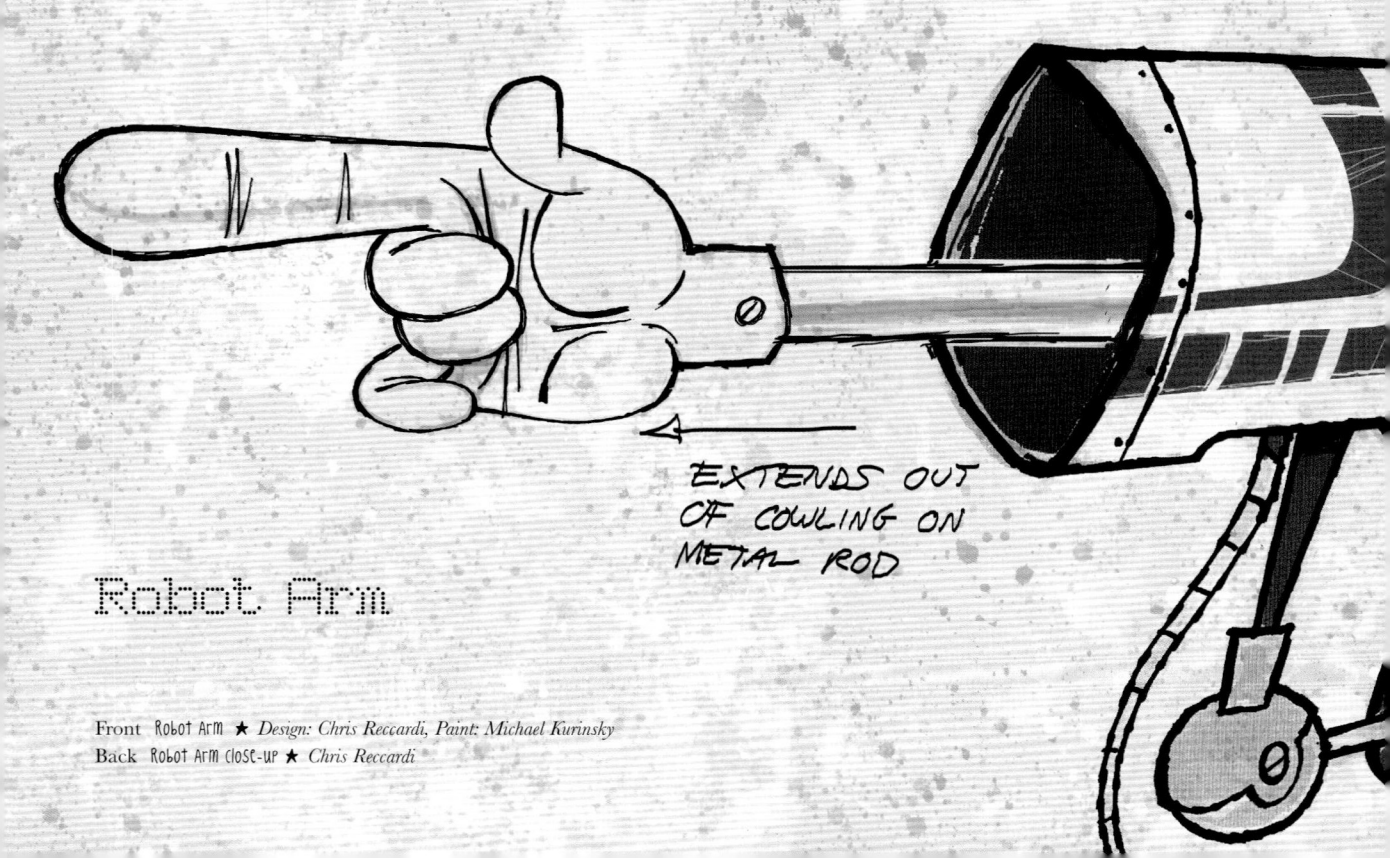

EXTENDS OUT OF COWLING ON METAL ROD

## Robot Arm

Front  Robot Arm  ★  *Design: Chris Reccardi, Paint: Michael Kurinsky*
Back   Robot Arm Close-up  ★  *Chris Reccardi*

Walking TV

# Rocket

Front Walking TV
★ Design: Justin K. Thompson,
Paint: Noelle Triaureau

Back Rocket
★ Chris Reccardi

↑ Flint at Home ★ *Michael Kurinsky*

↑ Flint and Steve ★ *Takao Noguchi*

↓ Flint and Steve ★ Design: *Stephen Silver*, Paint: *Michael Kurinsky*

↓ Flint and Steve ★ *John Norton*

42

← Steve the Monkey ★ Christopher Miller
↙ ↘ Steve the Monkey ★ Carey Yost

↑ Steve the Monkey ★ Stephen Silver

↑ Steve the Monkey ★ Sylvain Deboissey

41

"When we needed to make the label for eight-year-old Flint's invention of spray-on shoes, we adult artists just couldn't get it right. So we asked my seven-year-old son, Jack, to give it a try, and he readily took on the task, admitting earnestly, 'I'm not so good at shoes, but I'm really good at spray.'"
—Dean Gordon, *Visual Development Artist*

↑ Spray-on Shoes ★ *Noelle Triaureau*

↑ Hair Unbalder Bottle ★ *Dean Gordon*
← Flint's Phone ★ *Dean Gordon*

↑ Flint and Steve ★ *Sylvain Deboissey*

"Flint's inventions reflect a type of forward thinking that the town doesn't seem to have," notes art director Michael Kurinsky. Even from a young age, Flint has been compelled to invent things, generally to make the world a better place: His "spray-on shoes" were meant to help a problem that plagued his elementary school peers; his "thought translator" was meant to help facilitate communication efforts; and the ratbird—well, there's no real explanation for that other than the fact that "Phil and I wanted to think of the most messed-up combo animal he could create," explains director Christopher Miller.

"It was a challenge to make the ratbirds just the right amount of disgusting. We had to find the perfect combination of wetness, baldness, and diseased-looking detail that would get the point across without totally grossing out anyone."
—Dean Gordon, *Visual Development Artist*

"Ultimately, the ratbirds did work to represent a very important element of Flint's journey, namely his lack of ability to think through the consequences of his actions as an inventor."
—Kris Pearn, *Head of Story*

↓ Food Cannon ★ *Bruce McCall*

← Spray-on Shoes Can ★ *Dean Gordon*,
Label Design: *Jack Gordon*

↑ Ratbird ★
*Ted Blackman*

↘ Ratbird ★ *Ted Blackman*

→ Ratbird
★ *Carey Yost*

43

# Manny

**M**anny is the most efficient and effective character in the film—a bold statement for a supporting character, but essentially true. He is a man of few words and great talent: An immigrant from Guatemala, Manny has apparently gathered skills as a doctor, a pilot, and a comedian in his career prior to becoming a cameraman. His design and walk are both strongly influenced by the animation style of UPA Pictures from the 1940s and 1950s (think Mr. Magoo or Gerald McBoing Boing), and his shape is reminiscent of the Inspector from the *Pink Panther* cartoons. Manny's movements are "never wasted and are smooth as silk," says senior animation supervisor Pete Nash. "He is not designed to have a great deal of movement, considering his short limbs," adds visual development artist Pete Oswald. It's a physical limitation that naturally complements his personality of being efficient, all part of Manny's "more than the average eye can see" charm.

← Manny ★ Omar Smith
↘ Weather News Network Logo ★
Design: Justin K. Thompson,
Paint: Michael Kurinsky

↑ Manny ★ Pete Oswald

↑ Manny ★ Pete Oswald

*"The UPA held-cel style of animation is much more suited to Manny's character than the energetic movements of the Muppets."*
—**PETE NASH** Senior Animation Supervisor

← ↑ MANNY ★ *Pete Oswald*

↑ MANNY ★ *Carey Yost*
→ MANNY ★ *Pete Oswald*

→ MANNY ★ *Robin Joseph*

# Mayor Shelbourne

Like Flint, Mayor Shelbourne went through many design iterations before his true look was discovered. But whether he appeared older or younger, balding or bouffant, with moustache or without, his personality has been consistently that of a shyster, someone not to be trusted. In his final form, "he has this stereotypical 'used car salesman' expression, baring his teeth instead of having his whole face smile," explains senior animation supervisor Pete Nash. In fact, the 1970s "used-car salesman" vibe resonates all the way down "from his perfect hair to his white patent leather shoes," adds visual development artist Pete Oswald. His political presence lies somewhere between "the mayor from *Jaws* and the ineffectual government of Flint, Michigan, from *Roger and Me*," notes director Phil Lord.

The Mayor serves a very important role in the story, testing Flint's ethics when he forces him to make a choice about continuing to run the food machine or not. Perhaps more importantly, the Mayor plays out the politics-of-food theme, "but we were careful not to let his character suggest an association between evil and fat, instead turning it on its end to show how greed can lead to obesity," explains head of story Kris Pearn. Mayor Shelbourne's greed literally turns him into a glutton who is then trapped within his own body—he is immobilized to the point of needing a motorized cart to get around, and he can't even reach its handlebars due to his girth. The prominence of the Mayor's mouth also adds to this symbolism: He has broad, Muppet-like mouth shapes that show he is a big talker, then a big eater—actions which all come back to haunt him, like the worst heartburn imaginable.

↑ Mayor Shelbourne ★ Pete Oswald

↑ Mayor Shelbourne ★ Carey Yost

"For a long time we resisted making him so sleazy. But it turned out that the sleazier he got, the more people liked him. What does that say?"
—**PHIL LORD** Director

"We treat his body like a bean, a silly bean that bends in place when he walks. We do this to offset his diabolical, serious nature. It's as though his body is betraying the way he wants to be portrayed."
—**PETE NASH** Senior Animation Supervisor

↖ Mayor Shelbourne ★ Pete Oswald

"The Mayor (and Brent and Flint) all have very puppet-like facial capabilities, where the corner of the mouth can go all the way up under the ear to unhinge the head. To achieve this we needed to disobey anatomy, so we gave the animators a 'skull control' to lift the top of the head."
—**STEPHEN CANDELL** Character Setup Lead

↓ Storyboards ★ Jeff Ranjo

↑ Mayor Shelbourne ★ Robin Joseph

MAYOR: A PIZZA STUFFED INSIDE A TURKEY AND THE WHOLE THING IS DEEP FRIED AND THEN DIPPED IN CHOCOLATE

MAYOR: IT'S ME, THE MAYOR.

MAYOR: THANKS FOR NOTICING!!!

↖ The Mayor ★ *Stephen Silver*
↙ The Mayor ★ *Deanna Marsigliese*

"He is a bitter pill, in both shape and attitude."
—**JUSTIN K. THOMPSON**
Production Designer

48    ↑ The Mayor ★ *Lynn Naylor*    ↑ The Mayor ★ *Pete Oswald*

↑ The Mayor ★ Pete Oswald

↑ The Mayor ★ Phil Lord

↑ ↓ The Mayor ★ Stephen Silver

↑ The Mayor ★ Dean Gordon

49

# Earl Devereaux & Family

↑ Voice of Earl Devereaux ★ *Mr. T*

**E**arl Devereaux is way more cop than the quiet town of Swallow Falls really needs, except when Flint's inventions get out of control, as is often the case. Earl is all about playing by the rules, and he will enforce those rules with great energy: He will pull ten backflips while pursuing a suspect, and he has no hesitation in literally tackling a jaywalker. "His dynamic shape supports this athleticism and suggests an action-hero type," explains production designer Justin K. Thompson. A hero is precisely what the directors wanted to see in him because they felt that his voice talent, the one and only Mr. T, greatly defined him. As director Phil Lord explains, "Mr. T is a real hero, who always tries to teach everyone to do the right thing, and we love him for that." In a former version of the story, Earl was the P.E. teacher at school while also serving as the volunteer police chief, equally capable of making citizen's arrests or of asking people to drop and give him twenty.

The only loophole in Earl's hard-line rulebook involves his son, Cal, for whom he has a soft spot bigger than his own stature. Earl is overtly expressive in his love for Cal, and this affectionate relationship stands in dramatic contrast to that of Flint and Tim. While the Devereaux family seems complete with both parents present and a whole lot of love to go around, there is still a lesson to learn from their situation: Because Earl really can't say no to his son, Cal ends up overeating to a point of endangering his own life, and this serves as a subtle reminder to all parents that sometimes love means saying no, and that kids need some discipline and limitations in order to flourish. Eventually, Earl "learns how to love his son with more boundaries and expectations, and how to see the rest of the world with less," adds head of story Kris Pearn.

Cal had a much bigger role in earlier versions of the film, but he has always been a kid who wants to be older than he really is, which explains the voice casting of Tracy Morgan, a deep-talking, full-fledged adult. His proportions are so pushed that in order to properly model his head shape, character designer Carey Yost sculpted a head to give the modeling department for exact reference. "Cal's head is square with a roundness to it, and because his features are so large on such a small face, we had to build the flow of motion to go from eyes to ears in order to make it work," explains modeling supervisor Marvin Kim. And why all the hard work to make this character so diminutive? "Chris and I were both short growing up," director Phil Lord explains, "so I guess we have an affinity for small kids who want to be treated like big kids."

↙ ↓ Earl Devereaux ★ *Lynn Naylor*
↘ ↓ Earl Devereaux ★ *Stephen Silver*

*"He is actually a very smart character, and he defines the big message of the film about collective responsibility for one's own actions."*
—**KRIS PEARN**
Head of Story

↑ Earl ★ Carey Yost

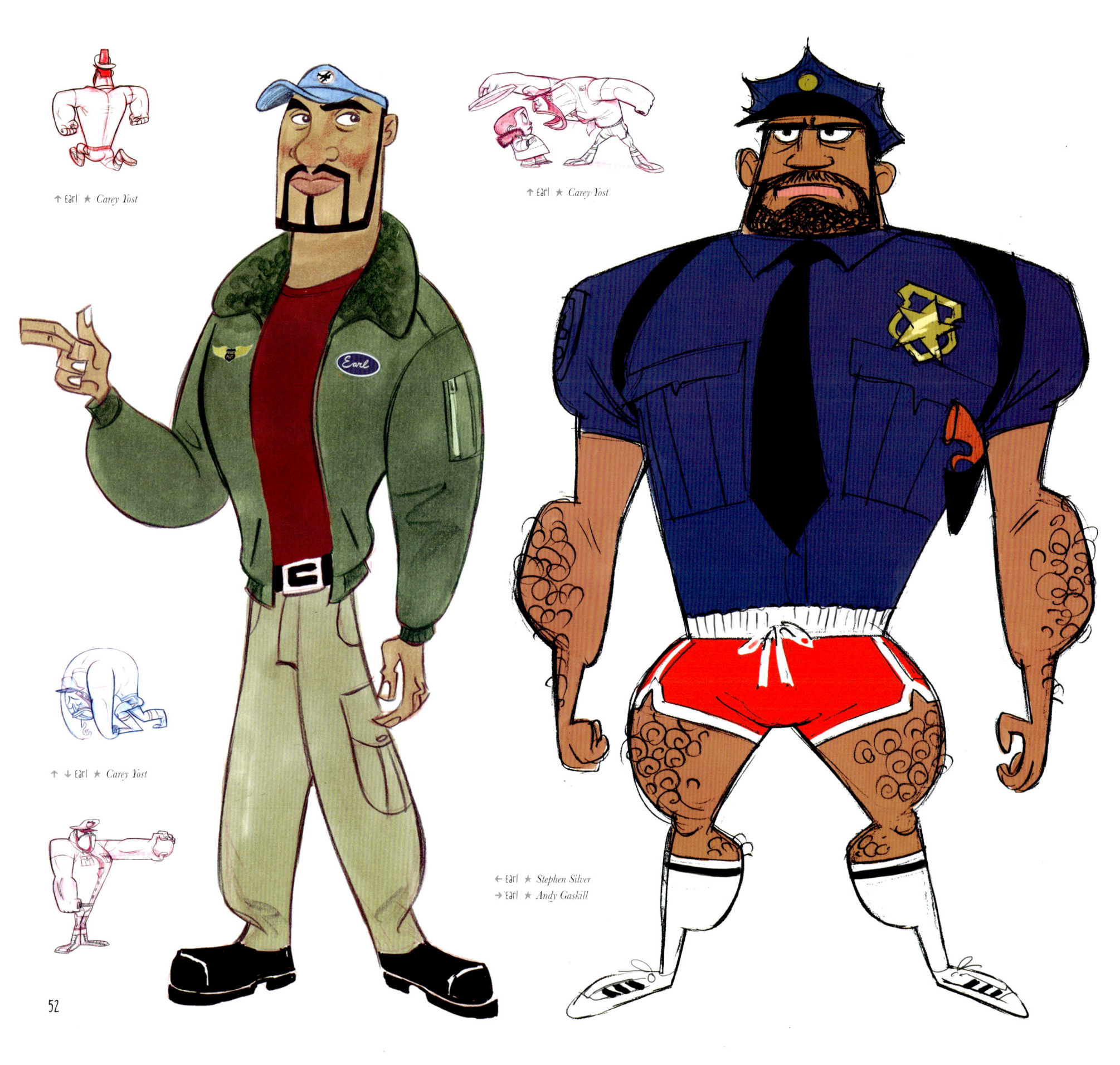

↑ Earl ★ Carey Yost

↑ ↓ Earl ★ Carey Yost

← Earl ★ Stephen Silver
→ Earl ★ Andy Gaskill

52

↖ Earl ★ Carey Yost

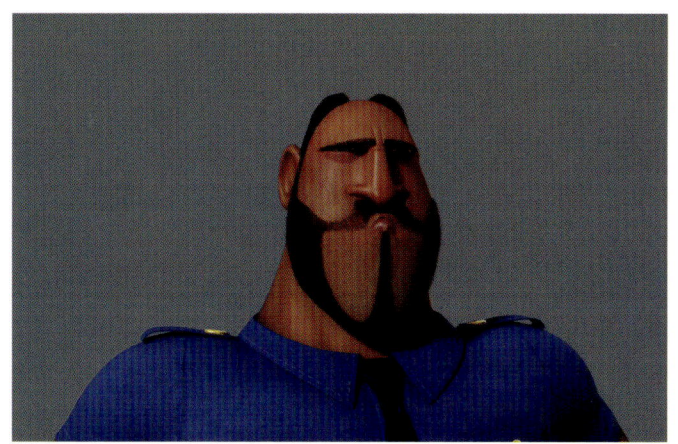

↑ Earl ★ Noelle Triaureau
↑ Earl ★ Stephen Silver
→ Earl facial expressions ★ Digital
↙ Earl ★ Carey Yost

↑ Cal ★ Carey Yost

↑ Cal ★ Deanna Marsigliese
↓ Cal ★ Carey Yost

↓ Cal ★ Carey Yost

↑ Cal ★ Carey Yost

54

↑ ↗ Regina Devereaux ★ Carey Yost

↙ Earl confronts Flint (with Cal watching in disguise)
★ Carey Yost

55

# Baby Brent

Brent McHale (a.k.a. Baby Brent) is a small-town celebrity, riding on the fame he gained when he was a baby chosen to be the namesake and spokesmodel for the town's main business—much like the Coppertone Baby, but hawking sardines instead. Just as the town of Swallow Falls can't let go of its past and its ties to the long-defunct cannery, Brent is "locked into that moment in time, down to still wearing the diaper," notes director Phil Lord. Brent has grown accustomed to being treated like he's royalty, and his walk cycle shows he is "very loose in his movement, like he's never had a moment of stress in his life" says senior animation supervisor Pete Nash. He's also not the smartest fish in the school, as characterized by his stock facial expression that is "half-lidded and dopey, featuring angled eyes with bisecting pupils."

Brent was actually the first character built, and he was a fun task for the modeling department "due to his girth, especially trying to pack that into a diaper," recalls modeling supervisor Marvin Kim. Brent also happens to be the only character besides Flint who is built in detail all the way down to his toes, since he wears sandals during most of the film. Along the lines of Brent baring it all, the look-development team had to spend an inordinate amount of time "trying to make him look less creepy with all that skin, body hair, and nipple showing," explains CG supervisor Stirling Duguid. Brent's body hair alone was the focus of a lot of character designer Carey Yost's energy as well, exploring everything from squiggles to jagged stubble to corkscrew curls.

The cloth department also had its work cut out for it when trying to put a warm-up suit over Brent's belly, especially when charged with having the fabric follow the shape and silhouette of the character like bound cloth. "We needed to provide high resolution in certain patches for the fabric to support specific textures and wrinkles, and we were thankful to have the TANGO system online to make that work," says hair and cloth supervisor Rodrigo Ibanez. TANGO is Imageworks' in-house cloth simulator that gives the artists more flexibility in managing cloth issues than commercially available systems do, and it is this unique ability to rework just a portion of the fabric (as opposed to redoing the simulation for an entire cloth object) that makes it so efficient and user-friendly—kind of like just replacing a button instead of reknitting the whole sweater.

Brent carries himself with a blissful confidence for most of the film, then is stripped of his self-esteem and "forced to rebuild himself, which he achieves while encased in an oversized chicken body, no less," explains director Christopher Miller. It's a thoughtful turnabout on the former bully, having to face his own truth while looking so ridiculous. "He learns what it means to work for something and to throw your heart (or giblets) into a cause greater than one's own self," says head of story Kris Pearn.

↓ Young Brent McHale ★ Carey Yost

"*I am very curious about bullies. I have always wanted to know how they work. Brent is an attempt to understand them.*"
—**PHIL LORD** Director

↑ Brent McHale ★ *Carey Yost*
↗ Brent McHale ★ *Chris Reccardi*
↓ Baby Brent Sardine Can Prop ★ Design: *Carey Yost*, Paint: *Michael Kurinsky*

↗ Brent and Sam ★ *Andy Gaskill*

↖ ↙ ↓ Brent McHale ★ Chris Reccardi

"Brent is very deluded about the value of his accomplishments. He almost always has a half-lidded expression, to show a high level of confidence that has been fueled by years of effortless adoration."
—**PETE NASH** Senior Animation Supervisor

↙ Brent McHale ★ Ted Blackman

"I think hairy backs are appealing."
—**CAREY YOST**
Character Designer

58

↘ Brent McHale ★ Chris Reccardi

↑ Brent McHale ★ Mark Colangelo
↓ Brent McHale ★ Chris Reccardi

↗ → Brent McHale ★ Noelle Triaureau
↓ Brent McHale ★ Stephen Silver

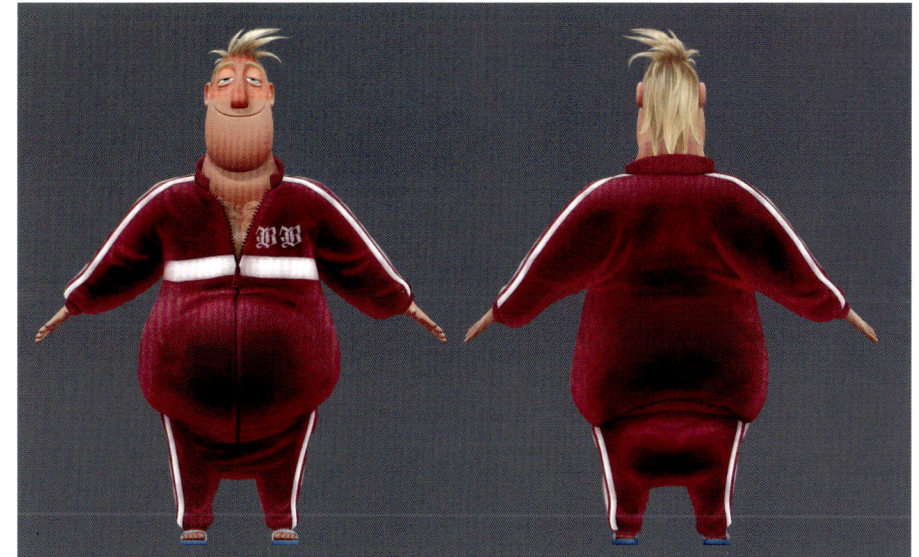

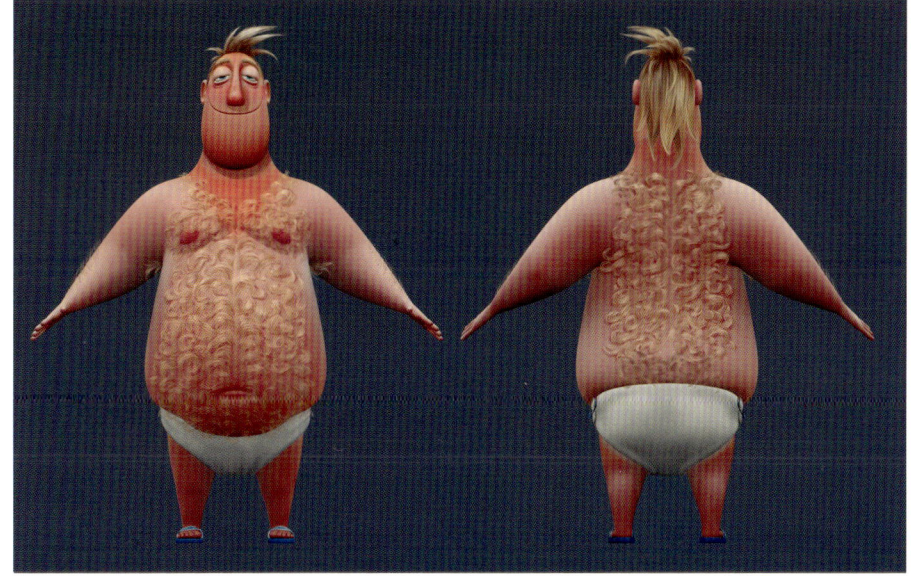

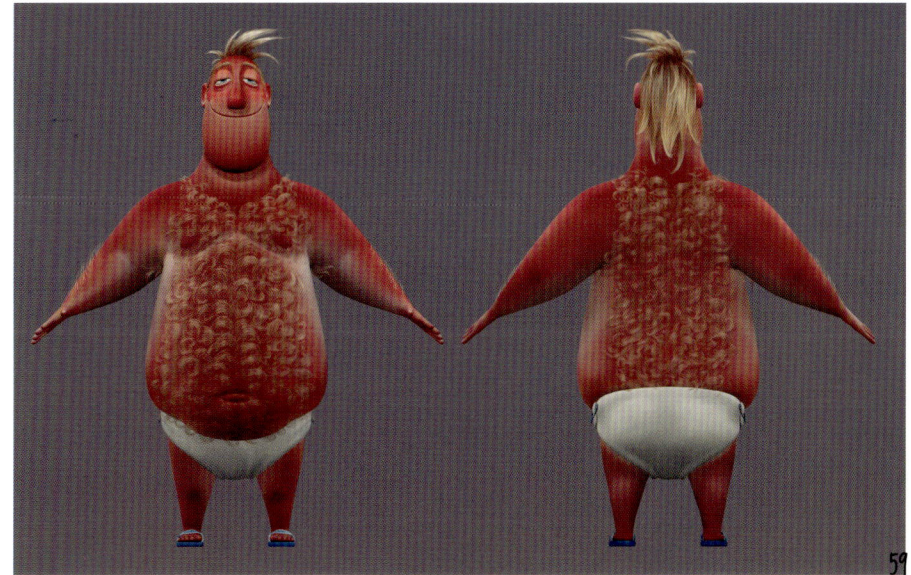

59

# Fran Lockwood

Although Flint's mother, Fran Lockwood, had a much bigger role in earlier versions of the story, she still provides a valuable piece to the puzzle that is Flint. "In the great disaster film tradition, our main character has lost a parent early in his life, which creates a void in him that propels him to do what he does," explains director Phil Lord. This loss drives Flint to continue to invent in the hopes of making this world a better place, since it was Fran who put the idea into his head that he would someday "do great things." Her absence also makes the relationship between Flint and Tim that much more tenable, giving the audience a much stronger investment in hoping that this father-son relationship really comes together.

↗ Fran Lockwood ★ *Mark Colangelo*
→ Fran Lockwood ★ *Paint: Cristy Maltese*
↙ Fran Lockwood's Grave ★ *Simon Rogers*

↓ Fran Lockwood  ★ Carey Yost

*"Fran's absence creates a rooting interest for Flint: If his Mom loves him, then there must be something there to love, but if she's the only one who really gets him, and we take her away, then he is truly in an underdog scenario."*
—**KRIS PEARN** Head of Story

# Townsfolk

What would a disaster film be without crowds of people running and screaming in the climactic scenes? The crowds in *Cloudy* utilize the same technology originally developed during work on *The Polar Express*, but the models were newly constructed in order to bring them into the design realm for this film. "They all have a 1970s influence to them, representing a town that is stuck in the past," says visual development artist Pete Oswald. "The generic adult and kid crowd models were scalable to account for their weight gains once the food started falling, but this scalability also allowed us to create quite a diverse range of 'supergenerics' with great efficiency," recalls character setup lead Todd Taylor. "We started with simple blank slates that were easily customized with generous rigging capabilities," explains production designer Justin K. Thompson, and with that, dissimilar nose shapes and costumes were added to make individuals in the crowd different enough to not look like clones but similar enough to not distract from the main characters.

To animate the crowd's movements, a software package called SWARM was vital. "Without Dave Davies' SWARM system, there was no way we could have done those big action scenes where so many characters are running and climbing and hiding," recalls co-producer Lydia Bottegoni.

↓ → Townspeople Super variations ★ *Pete Nash*

↓ Generic Kids ★ *Carey Yost*
→ Youth ★ *Lynn Naylor*

← Digital Kid ★ *Paint: Michael Kurinsky*

↑ Generic Baby ★ *Carey Yost*
↖ ← Townspeople ★ *Digital*

→ Townsfolk ★ *Stephen Silver*

↙ TOWNSPEOPLE ★ *Deanna Marsigliese*

← ↖ character lineups ★ *Pete Oswald*
↘ Generic Youth ★ *Robin Joseph*

↖ ↑ Townfolk ★ *Pete Oswald*

Generic Townfolk ★ Robin Joseph

# Dearly Departed Folks

A few beloved townsfolk moved away before filming began . . . or perhaps they were simply cut due to story changes and time limitations.

Rufus is the local, not-so-attractive newsperson who gets pushed aside by the Mayor when he wants to unveil to the world the new Swallow Falls bearing the face of a much cuter television personality, Sam Sparks. After that, "Rufus became understandably indignant," recalls director Phil Lord, and Rufus voices his dismay rather clearly in telling Sam, "I hope you fail." "The thing that really made Rufus funny was that in spite of his outward bitterness, underneath it all he still clung to his dream of the 'big time.' This egotism made him a bit of a bastard, and the combination of flaccid ambition colliding with a fortress of bitterness made him almost likable," explains head of story Kris Pearn.

Salty Peppers is a rather creepy-looking old man who had a recipe for a sardine-based salad dressing that could eat through anything. "At one point it was revealed that his full name was Salvatore Pepperoncini Cardini, the twin brother of Caesar Cardini, whose more popular Caesar salad caused the rise of the anchovy industry and the subsequent fall of sardines," explains director Christopher Miller. "We thought he was hilarious for a year or so, and then all of a sudden he wasn't," says director Phil Lord. "I guess we matured and moved on to more sophisticated monkey-poop humor."

Many of the crewmembers were singing the blues at the departure of the Jukebox Repairman, who first appeared in the tackle shop in a version of the story that had Flint shopping for invention supplies in the store that his father didn't own. Reminiscent of a scene in a Western film that would take place in a saloon, "the town freak walks in, and all the locals hanging out immediately stop talking," explains director Christopher Miller. "As a twist on the classic 'record scratch' moment from movies and TV shows, there was a record scratch, and then we cut over to a jukebox, and the Jukebox Repairman sticks his head out and says 'Sorry, my fault.'" It then became a running gag throughout the movie, whenever a dramatic statement was made: "You'd hear a record scratch, and there Jukebox Repairman would be, having bumped the jukebox, even if the scene was outside," recalls Miller.

German Basketball Kid isn't really a character so much as a decoy that Cal set up so that he could sneak out to play at one point. Director Christopher Miller explains that "Cal had placed a basketball wearing a Kaiser helmet atop a metal bucket in his room to fool his dad," and when Earl discovered the body double, he yelled at the inanimate object, "German basketball-faced kid, you've fooled me for the last time!" "Not everyone got this bit—I think it made our bosses' heads explode," recalls director Phil Lord.

↑ ↗ Rufus ★ *Carey Yost*

*"Rufus was a fantastic character we were using to add flavor to Sam's story. He shone a denuded light on the shallowness of the media, where intelligence will always fall to beauty—at least this is the windmill that Sam ultimately must battle in order to grow as a character."*
—**PHIL LORD** Director

↓ Jukebox Repairman ★ *Phil Lord*

*"We cut him [Jukebox Repairman] after we realized the movie was three hours long."*
—**PHIL LORD** Director

↑ German Basketball Kid ★ *Phil Lord*

→ Salty Peppers ★ Michael Kurinsky
↓ Salty Peppers ★ Stephen Silver

# vance LaFleur & Cathy

**V**ance LaFleur is the coolest scientist in the world, modeled after the "super-scientist hero from 1950s B-movies and dressed in a full-length lab coat with extra-long tails that were tended by his 'science babes,'" recalls director Phil Lord. The suave Vance is considered a hero for creating a reverse nuclear bomb as well as saving the world from giant ants.

Cathy is the sassy recepionist who works with LaFleur, and she is never hesitant to share her opinion.

↑ vance LaFleur ★ *Deanna Marsigliese*

↑ ↗ vance LaFleur ★ *Carey Yost*

↖ ↗ Cathy ★ Carey Yost

→ Cathy ★ Omar Smith

↑ ↗ Cathy ★ Carey Yost

# The Science League

**B**esides being incredible in his own right, Vance LaFleur is also the charismatic leader of the Science League, an elite club headquartered in Iceland, where he and other great minds mostly hang out drinking martinis and smoking bubble pipes while reveling in their past successes. Flint dreams of being invited to join this prestigious group based on his food machine but falls short—as he is informed by Cathy, his invention needs more "snapadoo" to make it stand out.

The Science League travels to Swallow Falls to see Flint's invention for themselves and arrive in the most awesome mode of transport imaginable, a pod that has "concentric rings which spin at high speed to teleport the pod to its location of choice," explains the aircraft's designer, visual development artist Chris Reccardi. When Vance finally asks Flint to join the League, Flint decides he really belongs at home and that maybe the League isn't all he had imagined it could be. After all, says head of story Kris Pearn, "he learns that Vance was the creator of those giant ants in the first place and has the blasé attitude of 'Who hasn't almost destroyed the world?'"

Although the story line involving Vance and the Science League was cut from the film, a poster of Vance remains hanging in Flint's bedroom.

↑ League HQ ★ *Ted Blackman*
← Poster ★ *Pete Oswald*
→ ↗ Copters ★ *Chris Reccardi*
Opposite Page Science League HQ
★ *Ted Blackman*

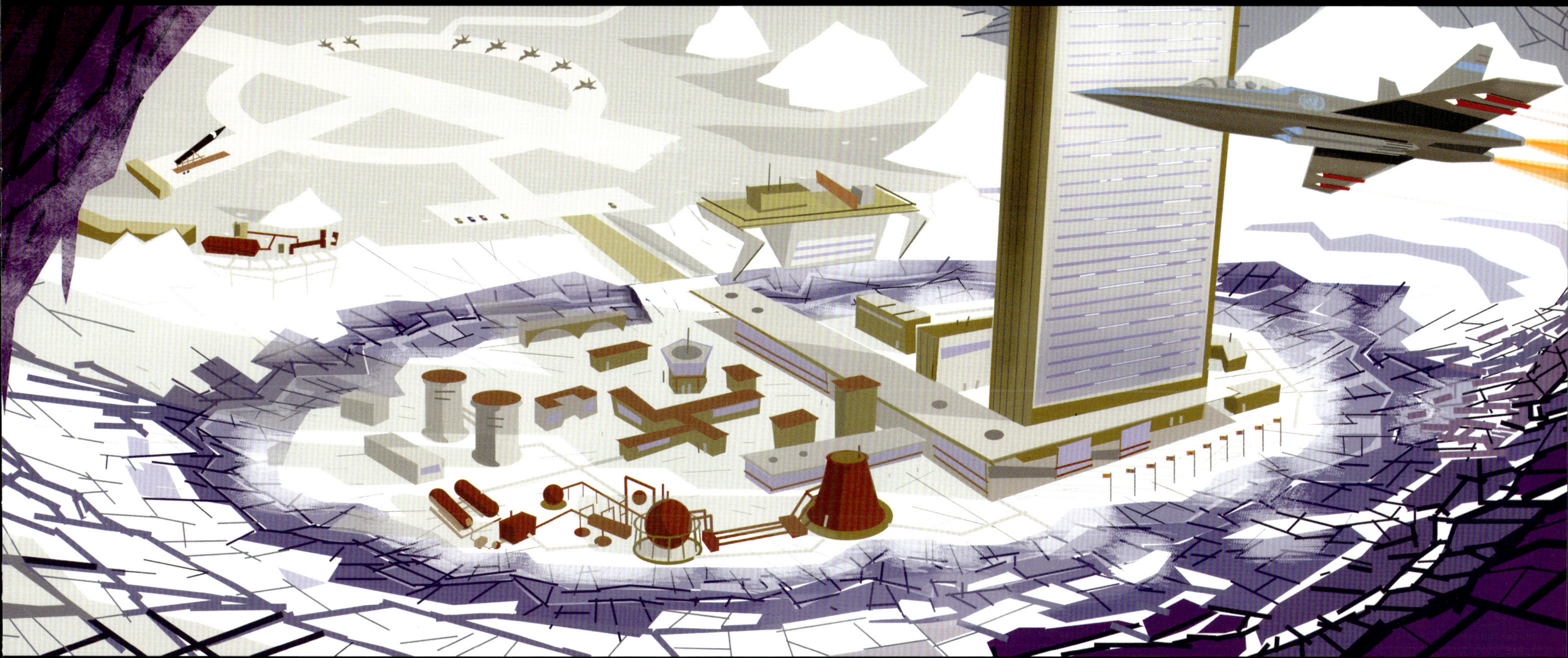

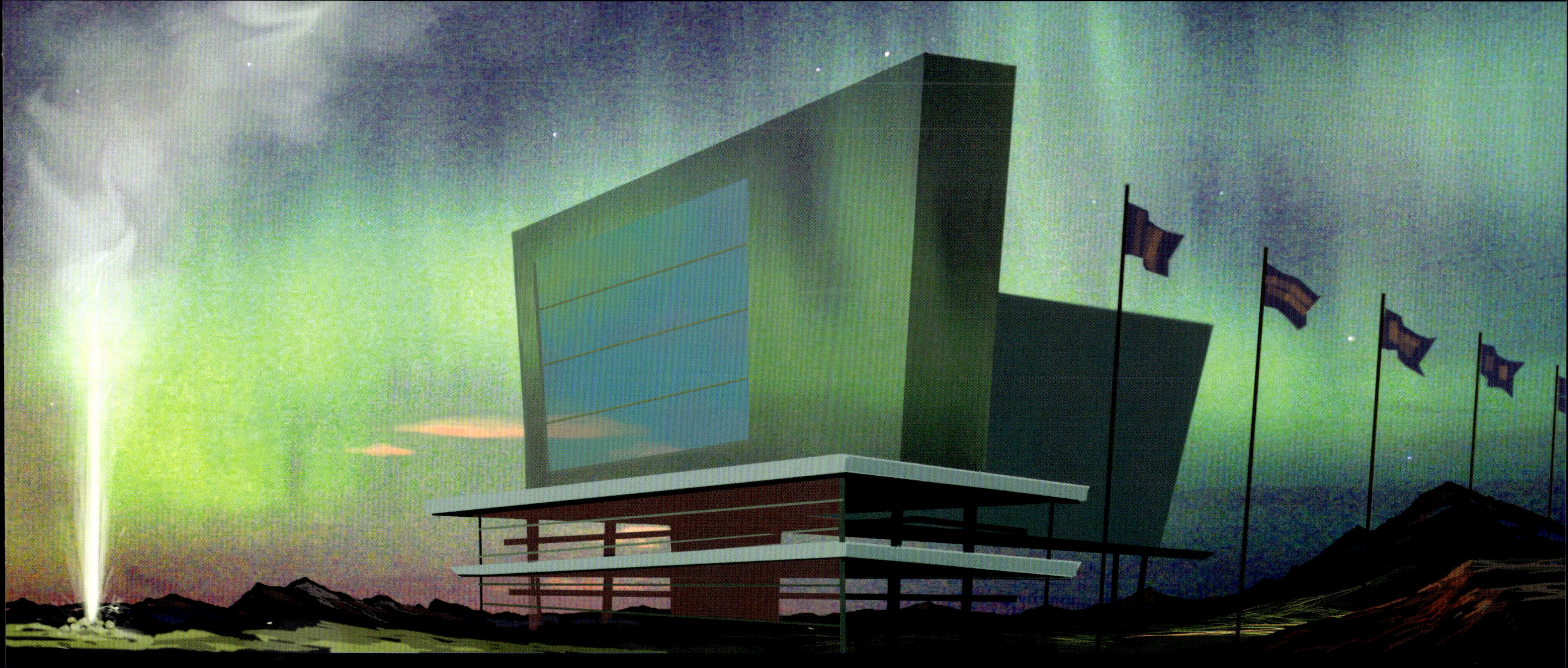

# The Food Monster

Instead of having to travel through the stratosphere to defeat the out-of-control food machine, an early version of the story had Flint and Sam confronting a giant food monster off the coast of the island. "The Mayor had the food machine shot out of the sky and it fell into the ocean, and since the machine runs on water, a huge monster emerged," explains director Phil Lord. The monster was eventually cut because it was too similar to that of another Sony film.

↑ ↓ Food Monster ★ *Todd Wilderman*   ↑ Food Monster ★ *Kris Pearn*

↑ Food Monster ★ *Gaëtan & Paul Brizzi*

← ↑ → Food Monster ★ Todd Wilderman

↑ Food Monster ★ Ted Blackman

→ Food Monster ★ *Design: Ted Blackman, Paint: Michael Kurinsky*
↘ Food Monster ★ *Bruce McCall*

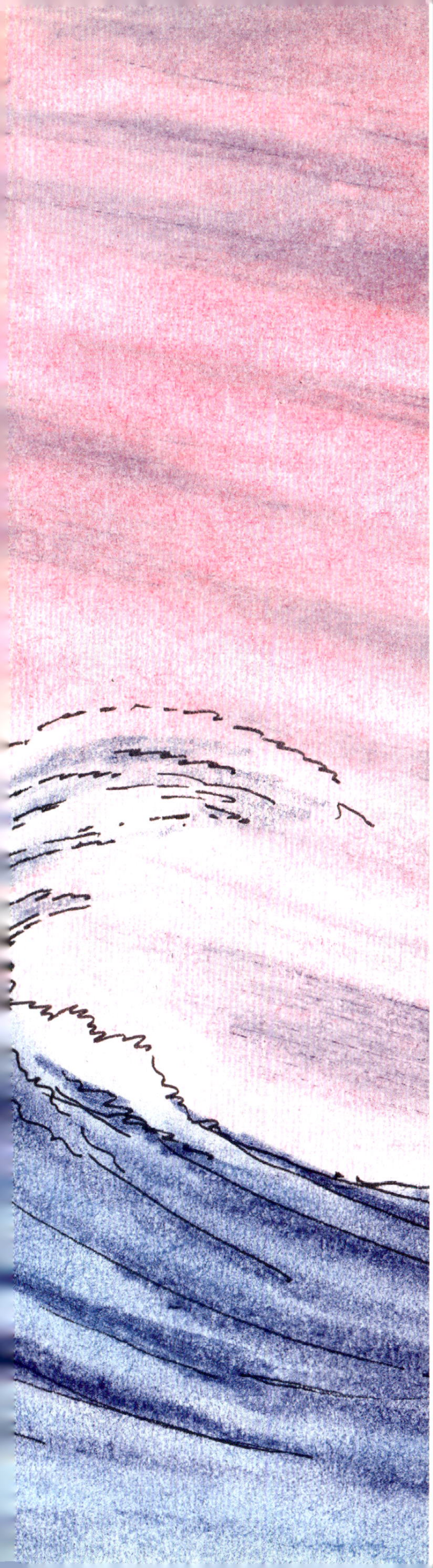

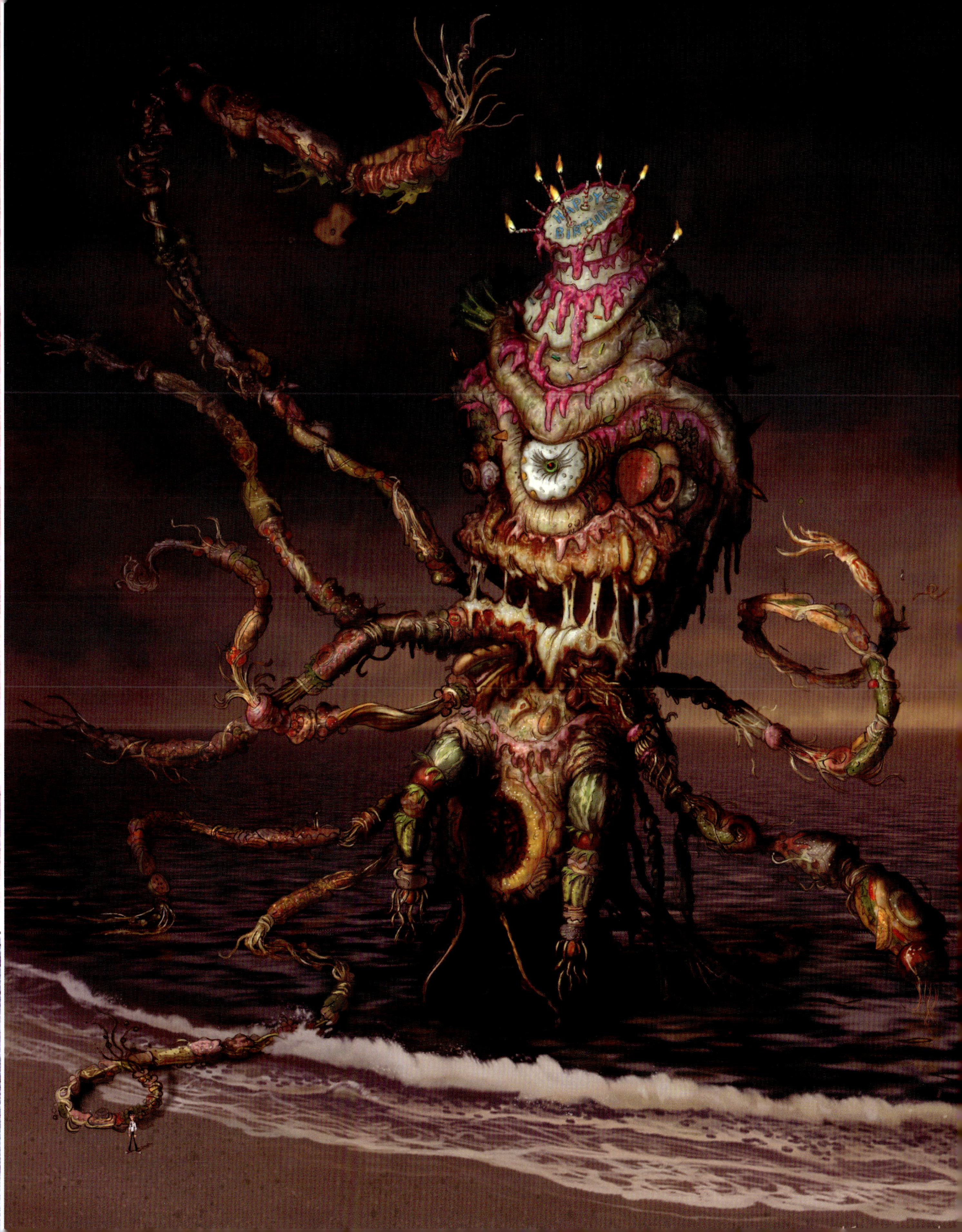

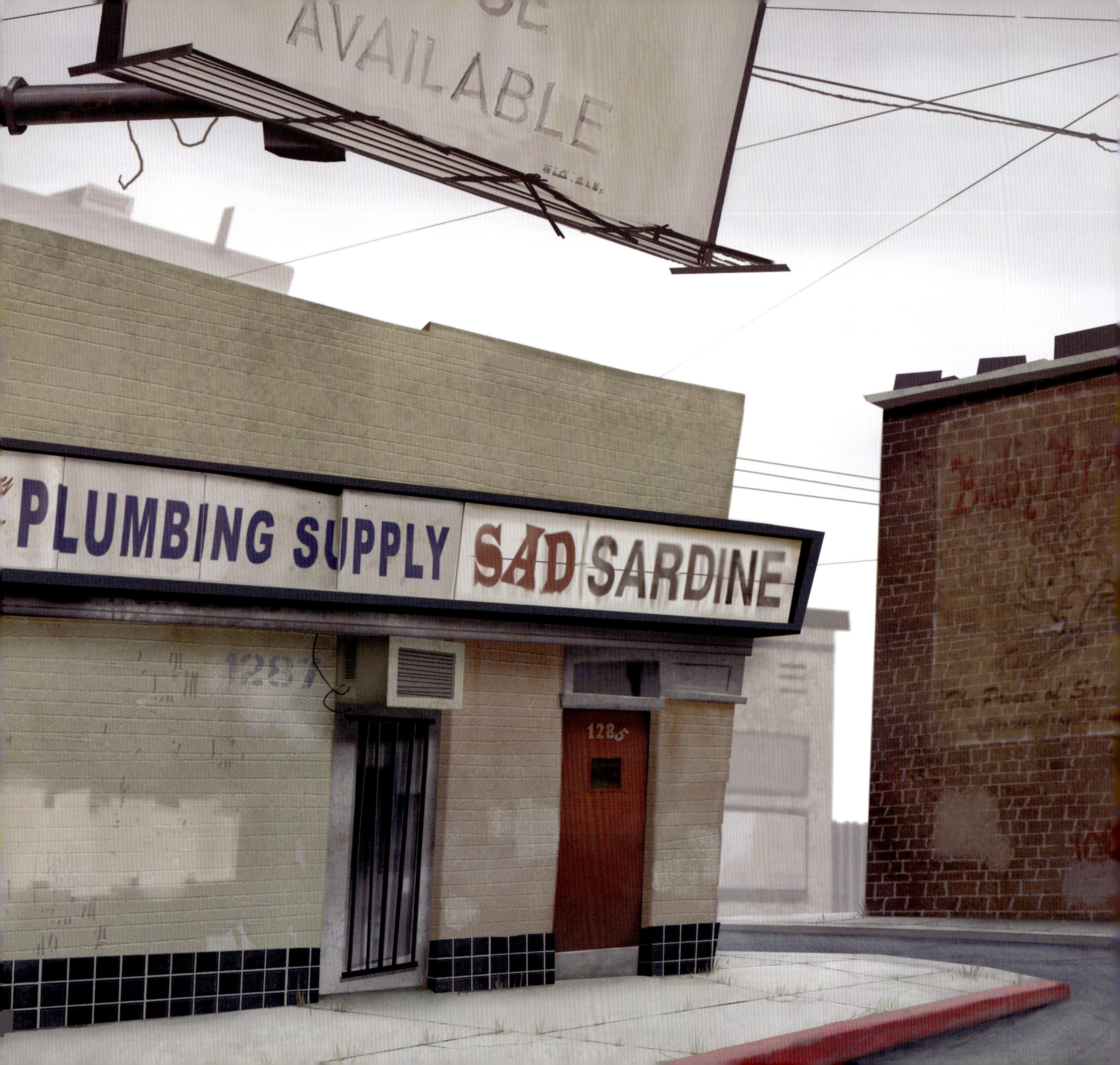
AVAILABLE
PLUMBING SUPPLY
SAD SARDINE
1287
1285

# Production Design
## Welcome to Swallow Falls

Previous Spread **Swallow Falls** ★ *Design: Dan Quarnstrom, Paint: Michael Kurinsky*

# Swallow Falls' Dull Palate

Flint's hometown of Swallow Falls has seen better days. Ever since the world realized that sardines were "super gross," the famous Baby Brent Sardine Cannery was forced to close its doors, and thus the island town lost its main source of revenue. Almost every business in the downtown district known as Sardine Circle had hung its economic hat on the sardine theme—from the Sardonuts Shop to the Sardiner—which shows how heavily the community relied on one particular source of income and hope . . . both of which have long since dried up. To that end, the town looks like it is in a state of disrepair and has the sad melancholy of a place that has ceased trying to move forward.

→ **Sardine Truck** ★ *Justin K. Thompson*
↓ **Welcome to Swallow Falls** ★ *Design: Andy Gaskill, Paint: Michael Kurinsky*
→ **Swallow Falls Docks** ★ *Final Frame*

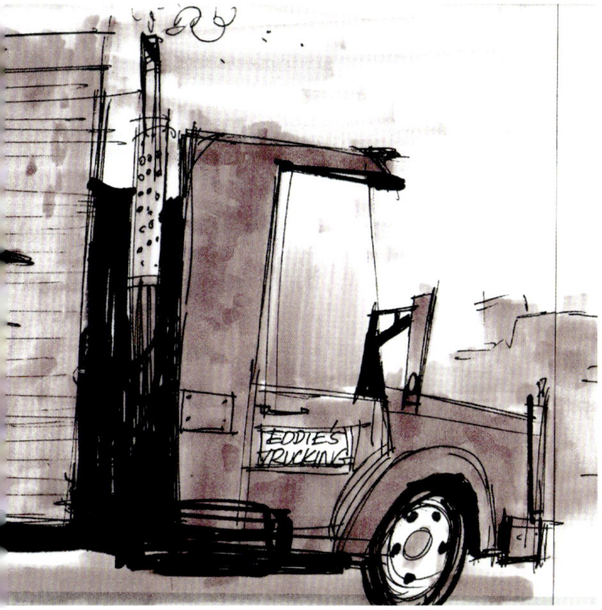
EDDIE'S
TRUCKING

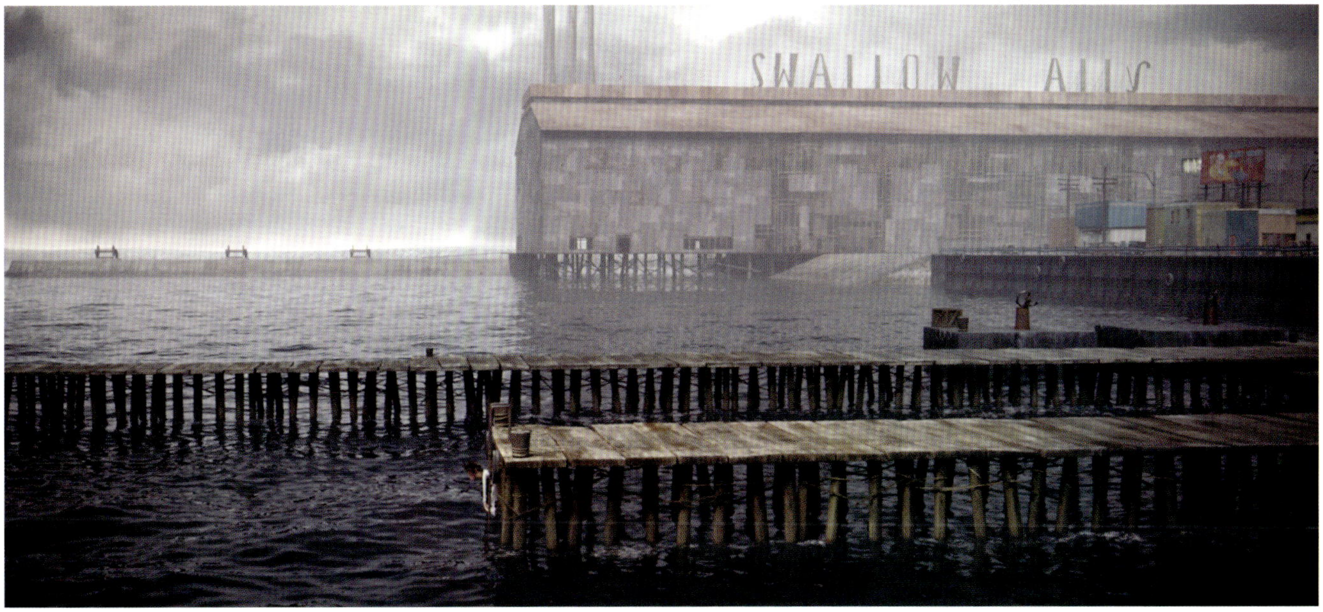
SWALLOW

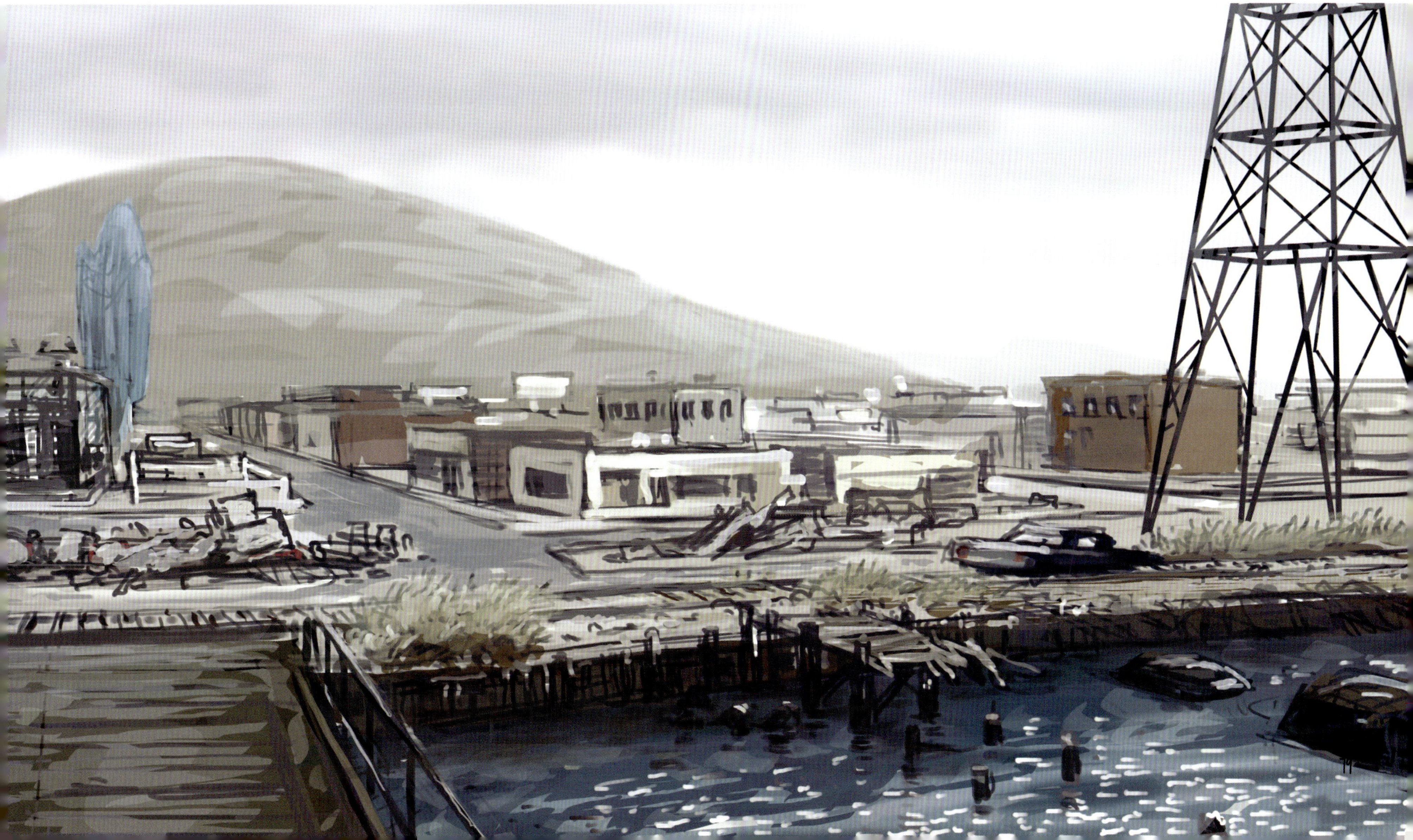

Thoughtful production design and art direction clearly convey the state of depression of Swallow Falls. "Our assignment was to create a city based on a stern look, with architecture that reflects a demoralized economy with little diversity and low culture," says visual development artist Antonio Canobbio. The structural shape language is all squares and rectangles to signify the "stuck in a box" mindset of the community. "We looked to the industrial buildings near our studio for inspiration when we were working on architectural layouts," recalls visual development artist Armand Serrano, who designed a series of six L-shaped building blocks that are efficiently reused throughout the town but differentiated by smart look changes. When viewed from above, it is easy to see that Swallow Falls is a pattern of rectangles and squares. "Pattern is one of the biggest design elements we used to create depth, space, and texture in the film," explains production designer Justin K. Thompson. "We were inspired by Sasek's use of pattern, created by repeating shapes, and Justin was great at visualizing it for a CG world," recalls director Christopher Miller.

"We worked consciously to oversimplify things, making none of it slapstick or playful," says visual development artist Marcelo Vignali, whose work in the park delivers a prime example of intentional simplicity: The trees are pruned rather harshly, and while such a "chop job" adds some interesting visuals with the lines of the tree branches, it also suggests that Swallow Falls has a general lack of care for the aesthetic and is more about basic functionality. "There is also a note of irony in the town's details, such as in the store banner that announces 'We make banners,'" Vignali continues, pointing out a rather unsophisticated attempt to put the best face on a service: While the intended purpose of a banner itself is to make things look appealing, this banner clearly is not. The blank bulletin board at the nondescript structure that is city hall is a comment on the lack of vitality and energy in the community as well.

To further bring down the vibe, the skies over Swallow Falls are gray and overcast, and the environment is comprised of subdued hues. "The town has color, but it is fairly desaturated when we first see it," notes art director Michael Kurinsky. It appears that layers of grime have put a damper on any color that once graced the town, and that no one has painted his business for years, with one excepted practice: In a subtle yet visually effective way, the element of pattern is applied to the look of buildings by suggesting walls that may have been defaced, then painted over haphazardly with a roller.

The thoughtful use of texture also adds to the sense of a timeworn community. To achieve this look, Kurinsky actually hand painted, salted, wrinkled, and then scanned watercolor paper and instructed his team of artists to apply and layer these textures in everything they painted digitally. As Michael explains, "the resulting indentations, brush strokes, and extrusions on walls make Swallow Falls a much more tactile world, avoiding the cold and synthetic feel that is often the case in CG sets," therefore allowing the audience to better settle into the environment. This effect, in turn, permits the audience to better connect with the characters: After all, "the purpose of art direction is to create backdrops for the characters and nothing more," says Thompson.

↑ Swallow Falls ★ Ted Blackman

↑ ↓ Swallow Falls Street Frontage ★ Antonio Canobbio

↓ Swallow Falls Street Frontage ★ Justin K. Thompson

↑ Swallow Falls ★ *Ted Blackman*  → Welcome to Swallow Falls ★ *Digital*

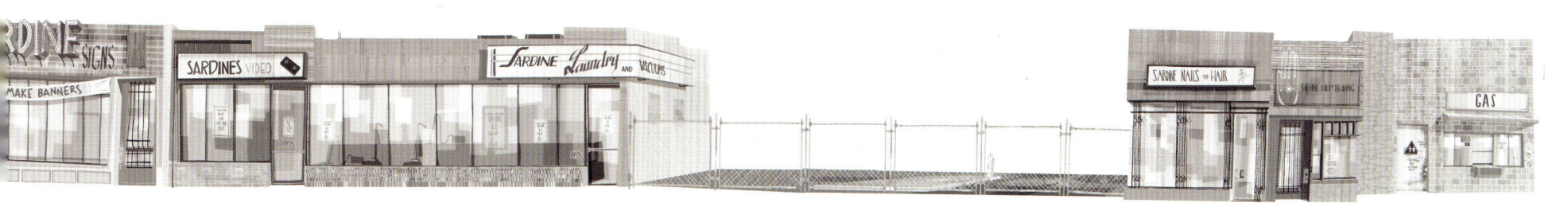

"I love designing ugly. It's a challenge to find beauty and interest in it."
—**ANTONIO CANOBBIO** Visual Development Artist

"When you enter the town, without anyone saying a word, the colors and designs give you so much information that it sets you in a mood, telling you that you are entering into depressing times."
—**BOB OSHER** President of Sony Pictures Digital Productions

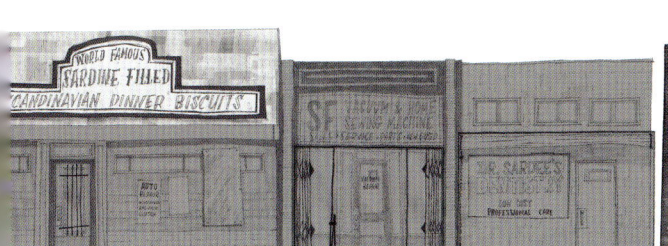

*"The task of asset management on this film is huge: There are more characters, more effects, and more environments than in any other animated film Sony has done so far."*
—**PAM MARSDEN** Producer

Early visual development of Swallow Falls made it look like too wonderful a place to live, in production designer Justin K. Thompson's opinion. "When the town gets destroyed, I didn't want it to be such a nice place that viewers would feel the loss so strongly . . . think of *Titanic*. When the boat sinks, the viewer (necessarily) kind of feels sorry for it, practically empathizing with it", he explains.

↑ → Swallow Falls ★ Andy Gaskill
← Sardine Tower ★ Design: Ted Blackman, Paint: Michael Kurinsky
↘ Swallow Falls map ★ Chris Reccardi

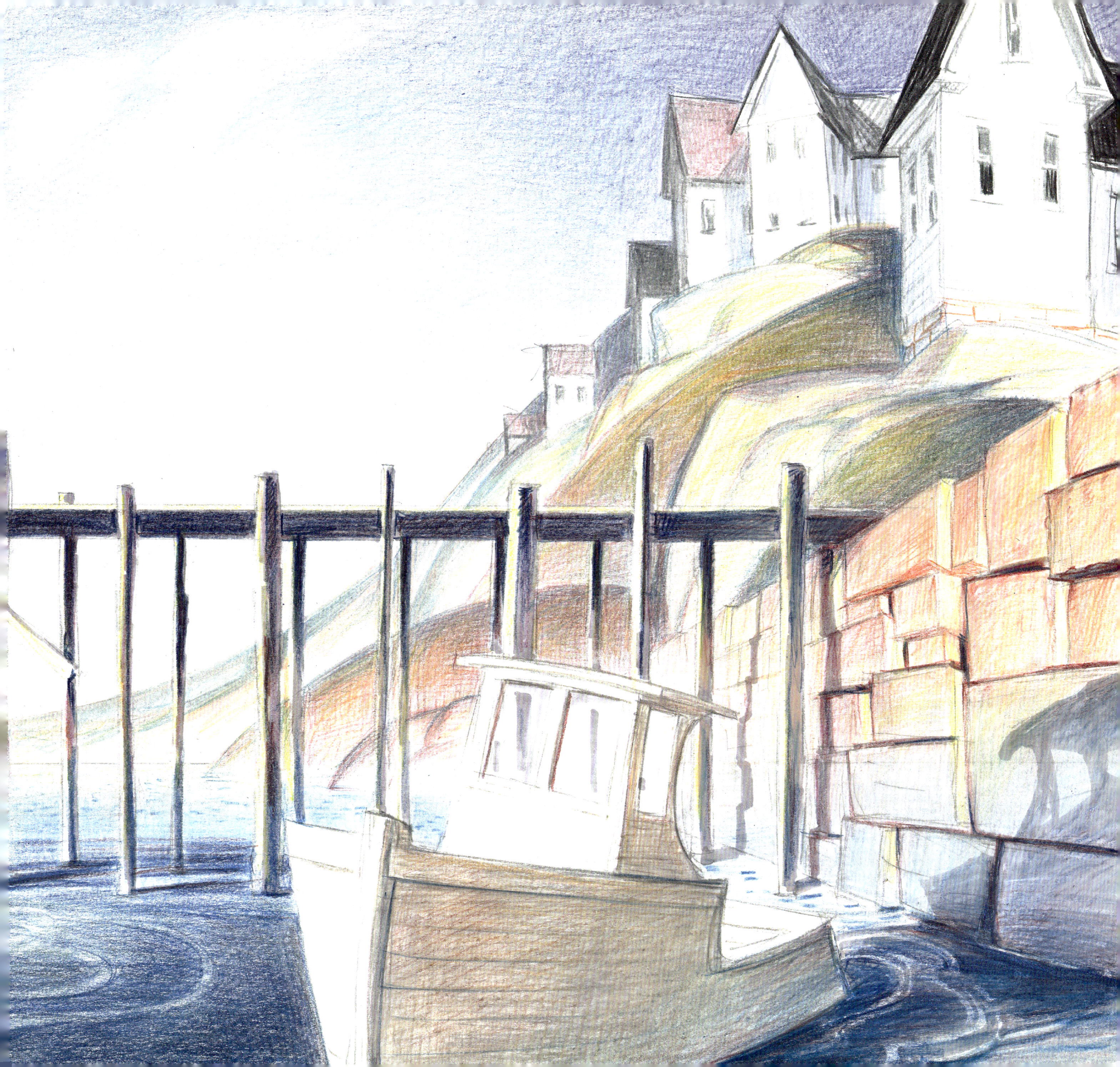

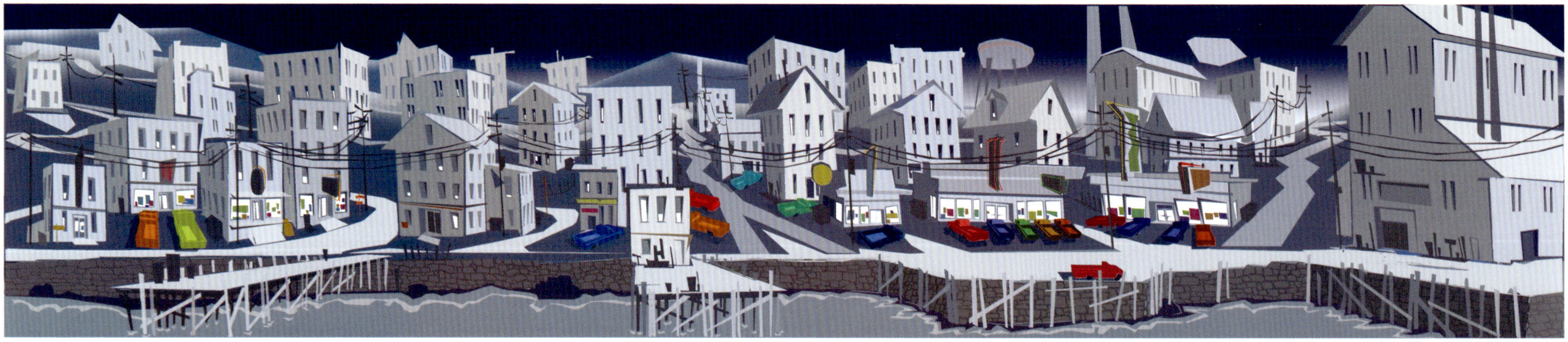

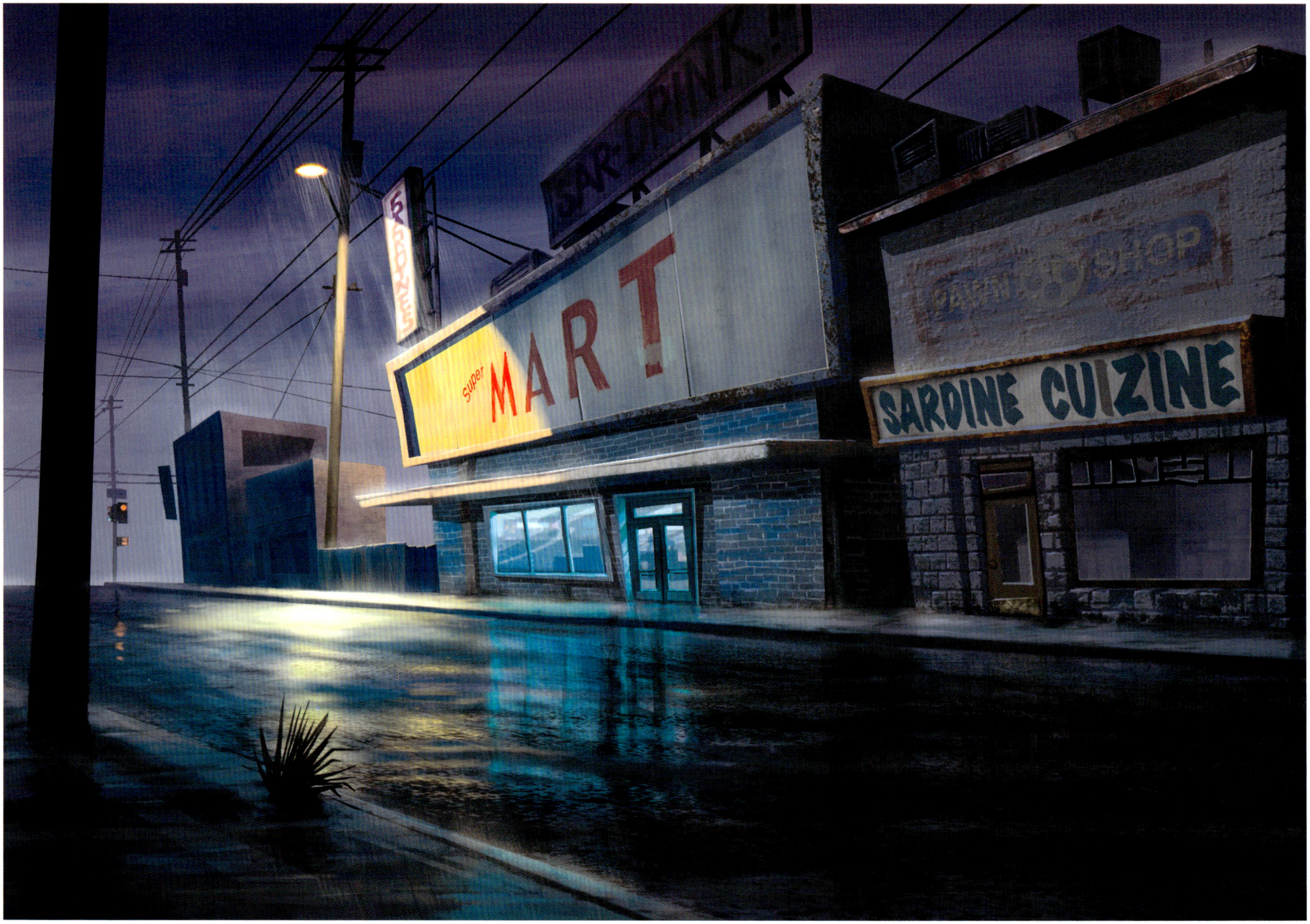
SAR-DRINK!
super MART
PAWN SHOP
SARDINE CUIZINE

↑ Swallow Falls ★ *Ted Blackman* → Swallow Falls ★ *Andy Gaskill*

*"The simplicity of the town was like having a fresh canvas for each act, allowing me to easily create new lighting and color scenarios."*
— **MICHAEL KURINSKY**
Art Director

↖ Swallow Falls ★ *Dan Quarnstrom*
← Swallow Falls Street ★ *Jerry Loveland*
→ Swallow Falls Lighting Studies ★ *Michael Kurinsky*
↓ Swallow Falls ★ *Design: Dan Quarnstrom, Paint: Michael Kurinsky*

# Local Merchants

The used-rugs store was the first building on which production designer Justin K. Thompson and art director Michael Kurinsky combined their efforts, and it proved they were in the same mindset with regard to the look of the film. "It was amazing how little verbal communication we needed on this, but we both had our eyes on the same goal, so it just worked," recalls Kurinsky. This structure also exhibits a good showing of what the production calls "roof furniture," namely items such as billboards, television antennas, and vent pipes. It's the kind of thing that most shows want to eliminate from their sets, since it's rather distracting detail, but it is exactly the right motif for a town such as Swallow Falls—more about function than aesthetic. In fact, Thompson and Kurinsky seem to enjoy incorporating the lines of telephone wires into shots for added visual interest.

At one point in development, the Mayor also commissioned the construction of an upscale food-themed supermall, complete with Tuscan village–style façades much like those appearing on shopping centers all over Los Angeles in recent years. "I have a term for this style: Megaterranean," says director Phil Lord, who agrees with production designer Justin K. Thompson's assessment of these structures as being "new and appealing, but rather soulless, homogenized architecture." Upon further discussion, it didn't seem to be the kind of establishment that Swallow Falls could afford or would have the vision to create, considering its much more "design on a dime" approach to revitalization.

While the saying goes that "beauty is in the eye of the beholder," one would have to be quite beholden to find it in the structure that visual development artist Ted Blackman designed when asked to "come up with some buildings for the worst, most depressing place in the world," as director Phil Lord recalls. Although the beauty supply store called Beauty World seems simply ironic at first look, the pattern created by the faded wood siding and the iron fencing perfectly captures the totally functional, never fanciful way that Swallow Falls "portrays beauty in the mundane," as production designer Justin K. Thompson says. "It cracked us up so much that we designed the whole town to feel like that," notes Lord, even if this particular location never made it into the final film.

↑ Swallow Falls Street Scenes ★ Dan Quarnstrom

↑ The Supermall ★ Justin K. Thompson ↓ Beauty World ★ Ted Blackman

← The Supermall ★ Chris Reccardi

↑ Sardy Nan's Used Rugs  ★ Design: Justin K. Thompson, Paint: Michael Kurinsky

# waterfront Street

**W**aterfront Street, the address for Tim's Tackle Shop, has as much charm as you would imagine a block that includes a bail bondsman's shop would have. Visual interest comes from more creative rectangular patterning in both layout and design, with brickwork, paint, and patches of asphalt displaying such detail. This location also has a generous amount of "street furniture," namely parking meters, streetlights, phone booths, and mailboxes and includes detail "even down to the staples in the telephone poles to give a sense of history and longevity in not worrying about pretty things," notes visual development artist Antonio Canobbio.

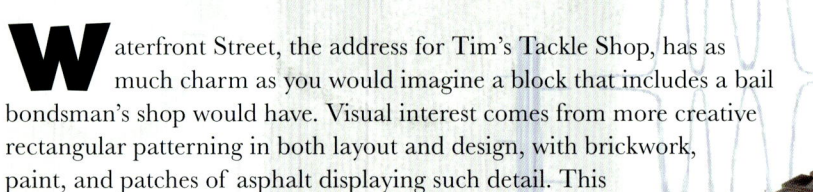

*"The ability to blend whimsical and photorealistic styles so successfully is a tribute to the collaboration between Justin and Michael."*
—**HANNAH MINGHELLA** President of Production

↖ ↑ Telegraph Wire Studies ★ Phil Lord 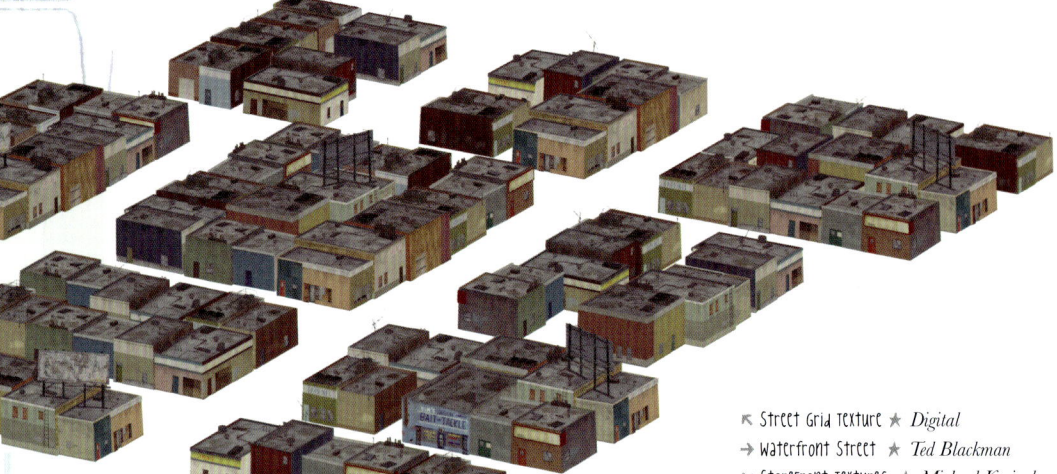
↖ Street Grid Texture ★ Digital
→ Waterfront Street ★ Ted Blackman
↘ Storefront Textures ★ Michael Kurinsky
↓ Waterfront Street ★ Antonio Canobbio

SAD SARDINE

SIR DEEN'S

BLACKMAN

A

OFFICE

B

C

D

# Sardiner

While the Sardiner appears to be nothing more than the local greasy spoon, it is actually quite well stocked in terms of meaningful design detail. Propagating the Swallow Falls lackadaisical attitude towards appearance, it looks as if the restaurant had started as a small diner that bought up additional square footage as needed, but simply couldn't be bothered with remodeling the whole façade—a mix of stucco, rock, and brick, with nothing aesthetically appealing about it. Awnings and windows don't match. "You can imagine customers at one particular table complaining about the bright sunlight which forced the owners to add the small awning on the left," explains visual development artist Antonio Canobbio. "It's a fun challenge to be limited to designing with simple shapes and to have to find ways to make them interesting." Canobbio clearly succeeded in this challenge by working the rectangular patterning into the paint-overs and water stains on the exterior, as well as into the wood paneling, flooring, and various reflections on the interior. In every imaginable way, the Sardiner is a smorgasbord of unrefined, simple construction, intentionally cooked up by a top-notch design crew.

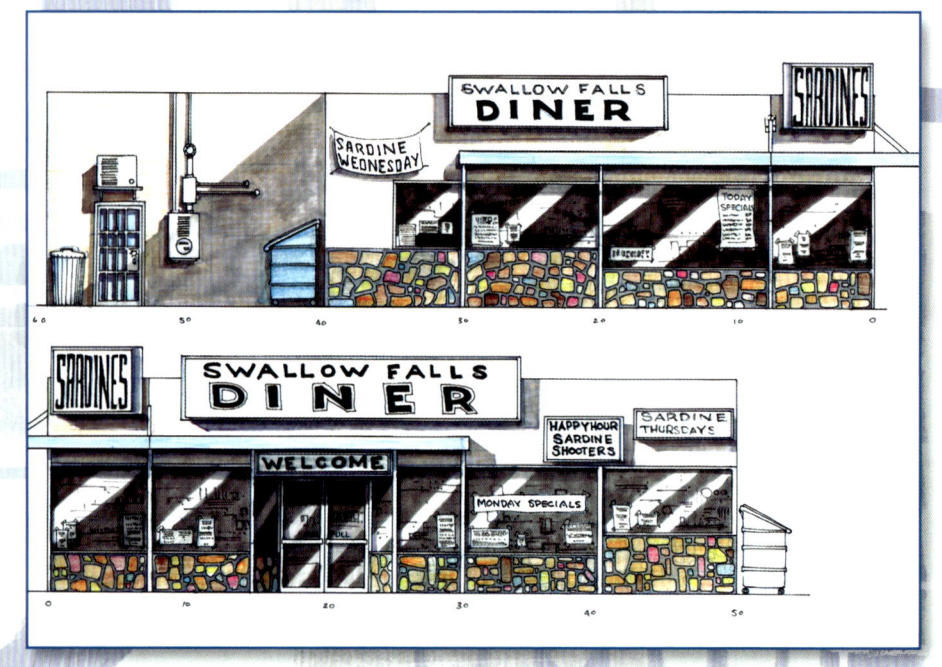

↑ Brent outside the Sardiner ★ *Digital*

↓ Sardiner Interior ★ *Antonio Canobbio*

↑ Swallow Falls Diner ★ *Dan Quarnstrom*
Overleaf Swallow Falls Street ★ *Design: Antonio Canobbio, Paint: Michael Kurinsky & Jerry Loveland*

↑ Sardiner Exterior ★ *Antonio Canobbio*

The inside of the diner also presents a glaring example of how unsophisticated the town is, by virtue of what the townsfolk consider "art"—in this case, a very simple, rather uncultured painting of a mermaid. "It's an homage to the mermaid mural that was inside a restaurant just down the street from our studio where we would go on Fridays for shrimp soup, beers, and good conversation. That mural was so bad it was good," recalls art director Michael Kurinsky.

↑ Mermaid Mural ★ *Antonio Canobbio*

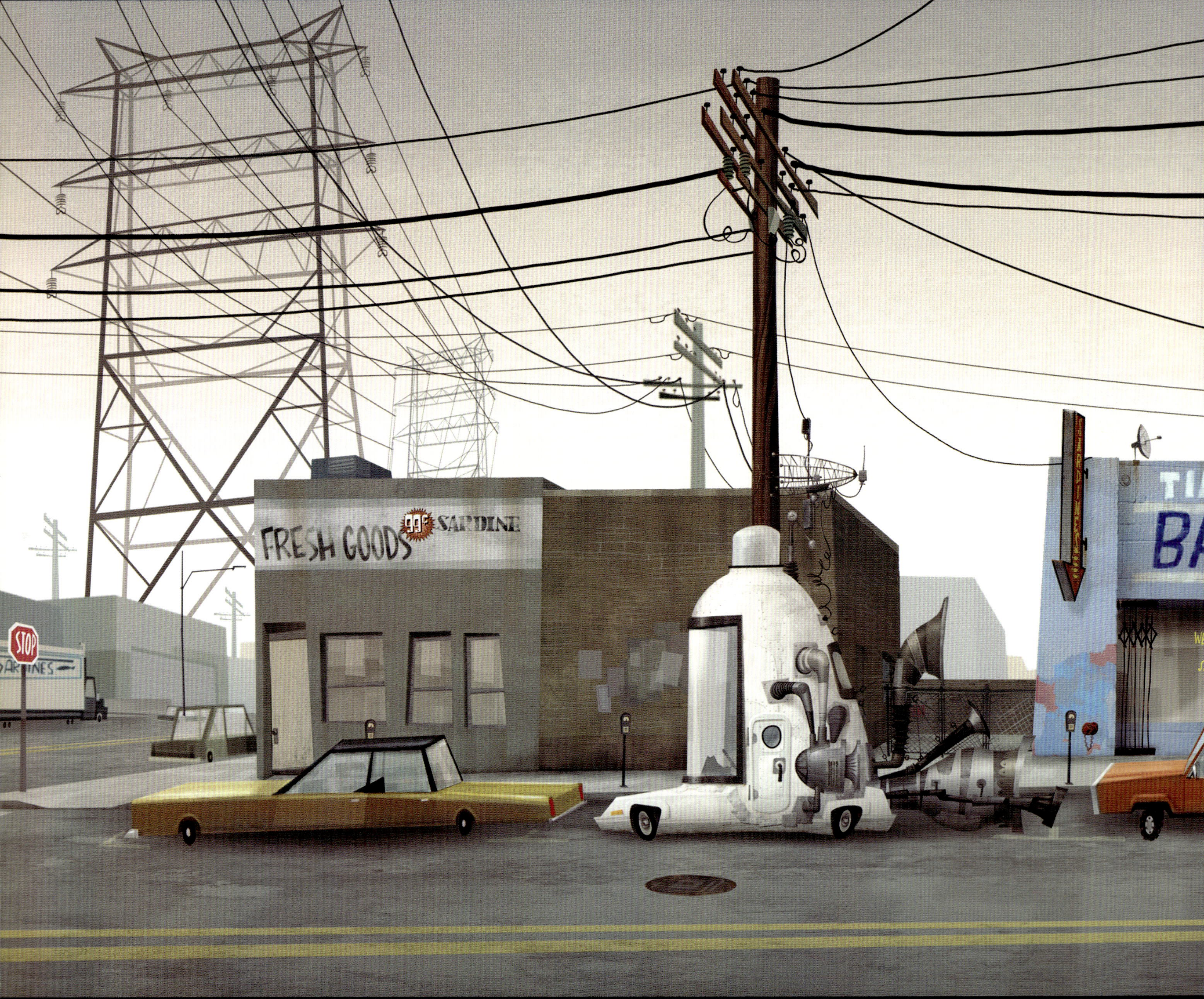
FRESH GOODS
99¢
SARDINE
STOP

SARDINE
T AND TACKLE
TIM'S SARDINE BAIT AND TACKLE
• LIVE SARDINE BAIT
BAIL
PHONE
PHONE
PHONE

# Tackle Shop

As mentioned previously, the entire town of Swallow Falls actually looks like a pattern of rectangles and squares when viewed from above. "As you get closer, it works like a fractal, continually breaking down into smaller and smaller squares and rectangles until you are in Tim's Tackle Shop, and the same pattern is repeated right down to the individual items for sale," notes production designer Justin K. Thompson. The palette in the shop is cool with warm accents, and it serves as a prime example of the desaturated color that characterizes Swallow Falls. Heavy texture usage also suggests that like all of the local businesses, the store is "worn and run-down, a sign of the times, as Tim hasn't been able to keep up the shop" since the sardine industry went bust, explains art director Michael Kurinsky. It is an environment that is very much stuck in the past, and this aura clearly makes the forward-thinking Flint uncomfortable, especially when the idea is presented that this could be his future.

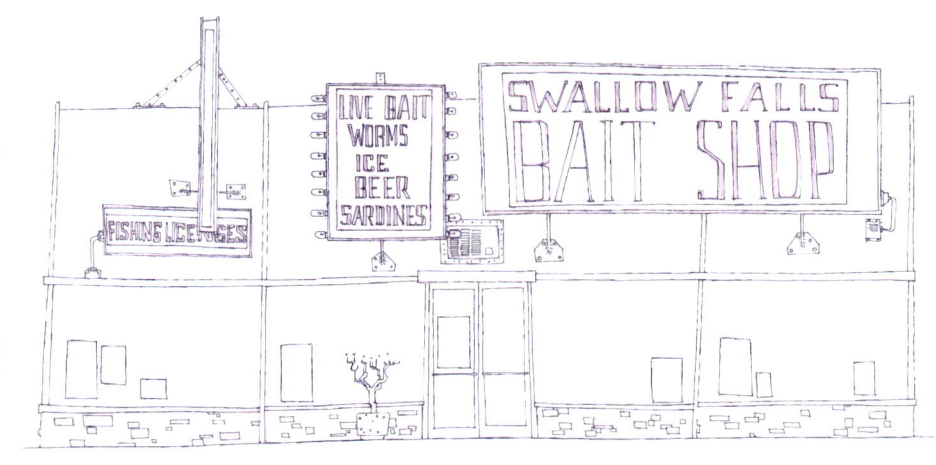

↓ Tackle Shop ★ *Digital*

↑ Tackle Shop ★ *Dan Quarnstrom*

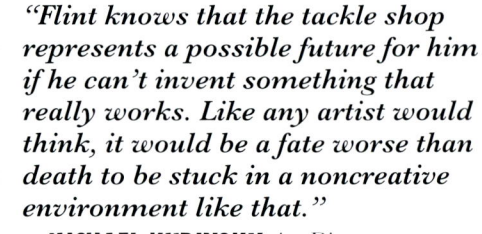

*"Flint knows that the tackle shop represents a possible future for him if he can't invent something that really works. Like any artist would think, it would be a fate worse than death to be stuck in a noncreative environment like that."*
—MICHAEL KURINSKY Art Director

↓ Tackle Shop ★ *Jerry Loveland*

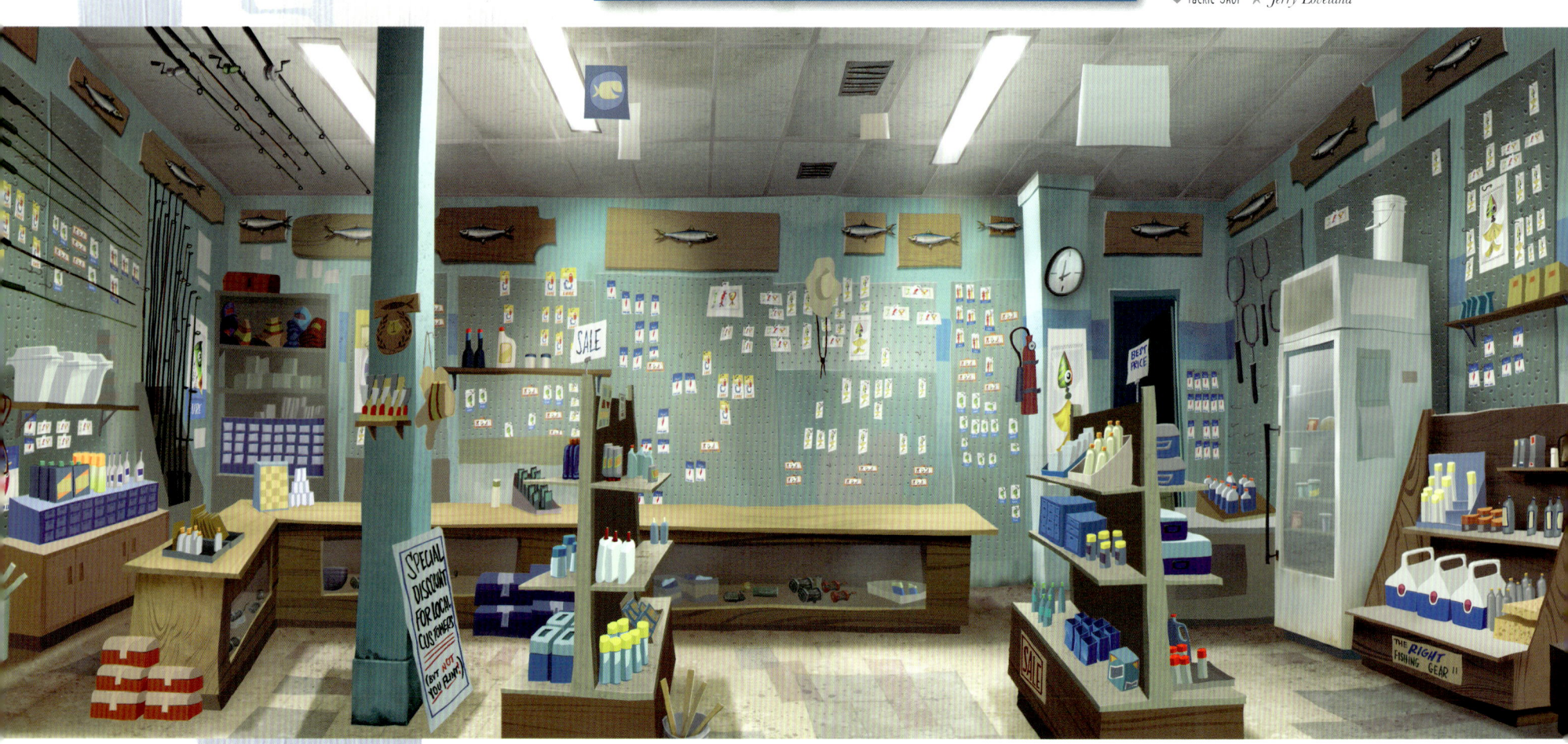

# MAKING THE PERFECT BURGER

# EAT-&-RUN

HOME OF THE 1000 POUNDER

"DO THE MUSTARD AND KETCHUP ON BURGERS SQUIRT OUT WHEN THEY CRASH DOWN? IMPORTANT DISCUSSIONS LIKE THIS HAPPENED REGULARLY." — DAN KRAMER, DIGITAL EFFECTS SUPERVISOR

**TOP BUN**

MUSTARD AND KETCHUP

PICKLE SLICES

TOMATO SLICES

LETTUCE LEAF

**CHEESE**

meat

**BOTTOM BUN**

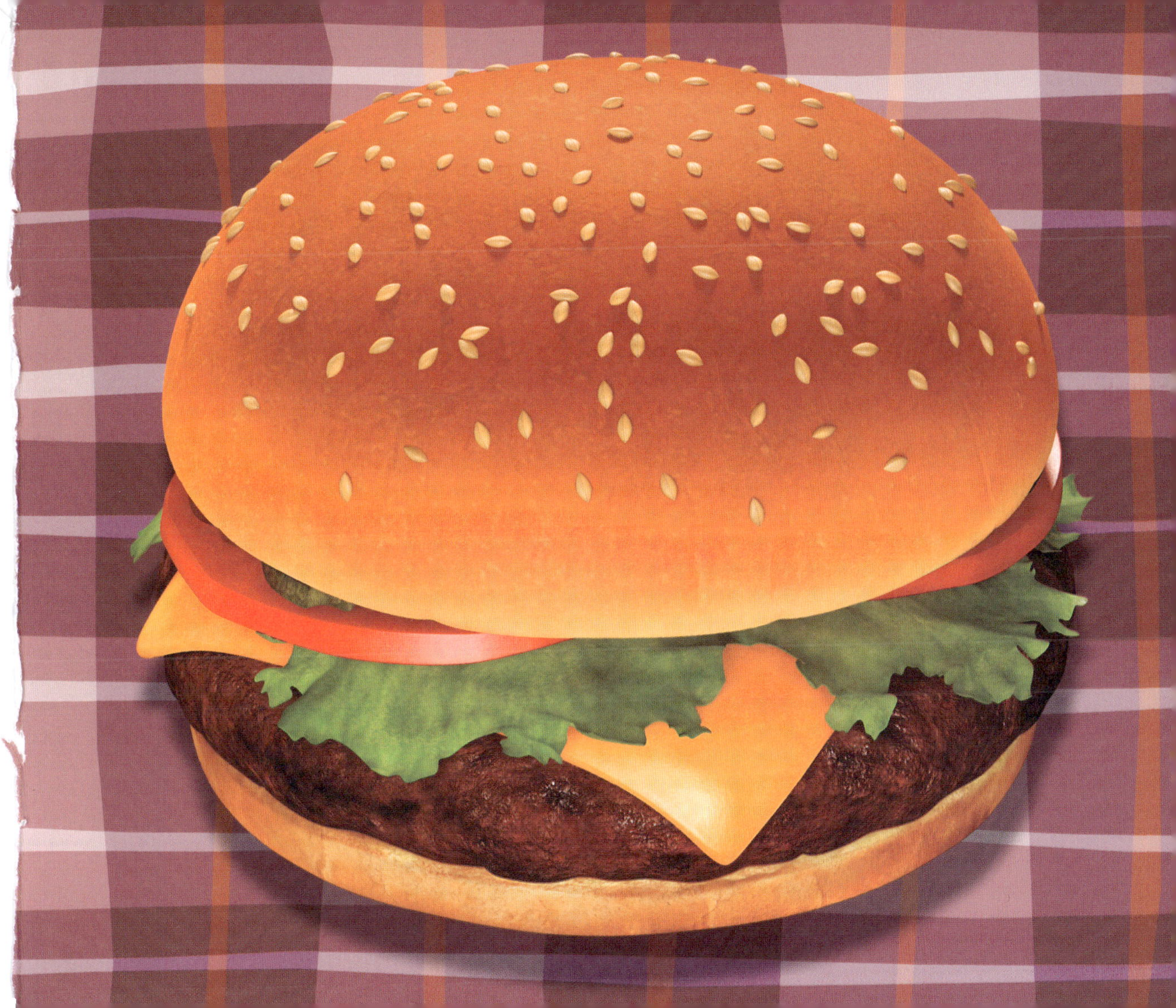

$H_2O$  $H_2O$  $H_2O$

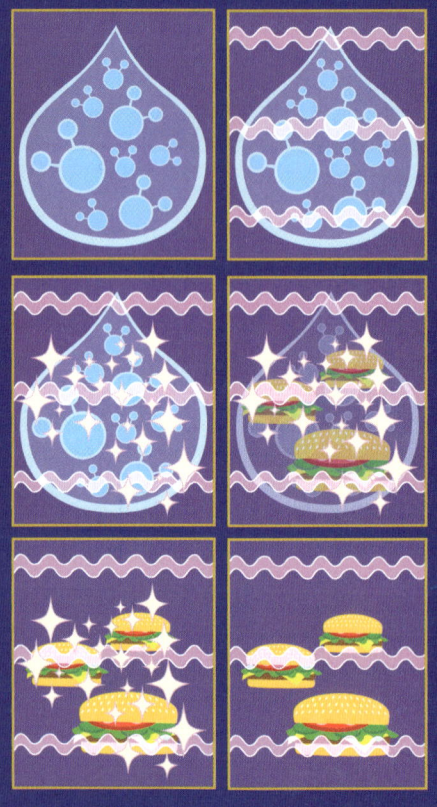

Free Radicals

# KETCHUP
# MUSTARD

Time. Pressure

$c(P \leq) \frac{SP}{ST} = \frac{2\pi r}{\sqrt{F_n}}$

$\frac{z^2 \cdot b^2}{m \sqrt[9]{+//}}$

ARCSIN ∠ 22

ARCSIN ∠ 22

ARCSIN ∠ 22
ARCSIN ∠ 22
ARCSIN ∠ 22

LETTU
PICK
TOMA
CHEE

HAMBURGE
PATTY

OUTPUT 30°  30°

↑ Motion Graphics ★ *Justin K. Thompson*
→ Blueprint ★ *Dean Gordon*
→ Cheeseburger & Elements ★ *Michael Kurinsky*

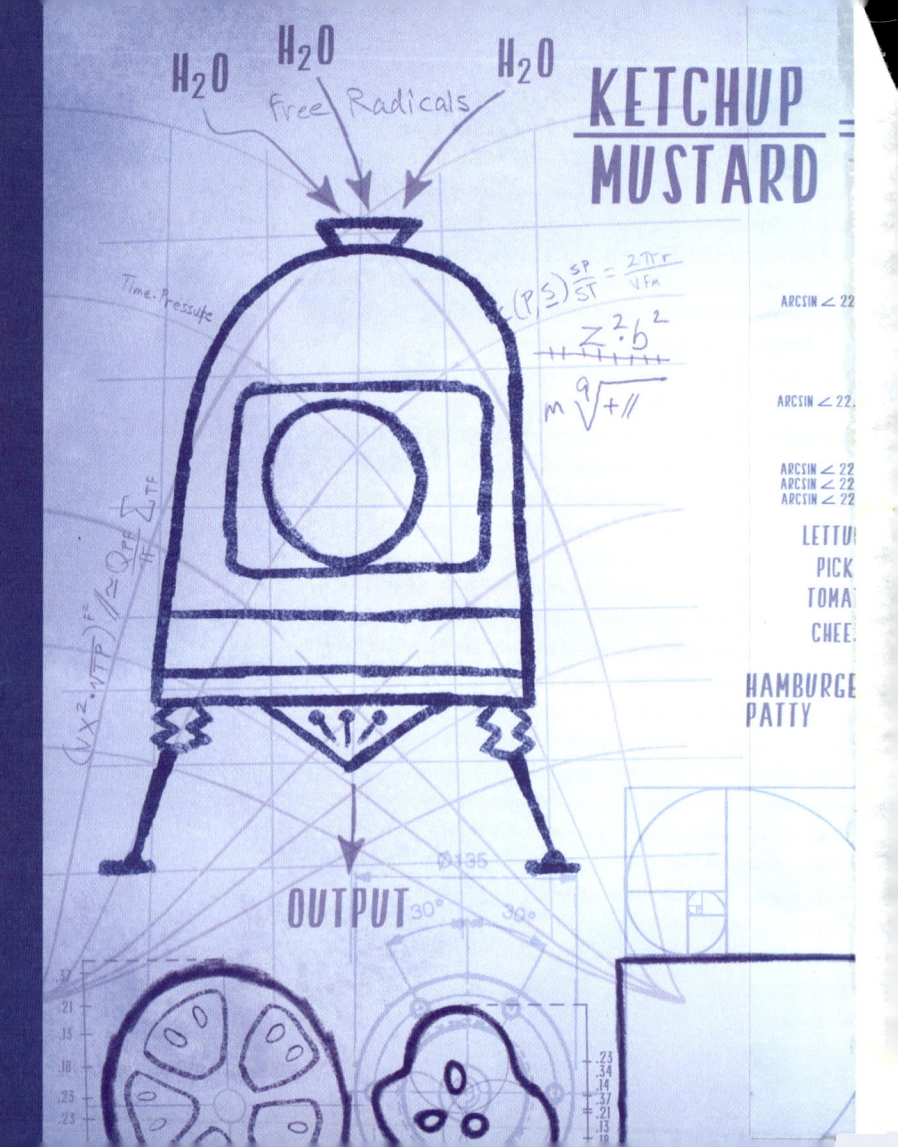

↗ Tackle Shop ★ Dan Quarnstrom
↘ Tackle Shop ★ Justin K. Thompson

# vehicles

**W**ith stretched chassis proportions, small wheels, and high windows, these vehicles could have appeared too toylike and distracting within this dreary town, "but the design gets more grounded when you add textures and lighting," explains art director Michael Kurinsky. There are four basic car models—station wagon, coupe, sedan, and pickup—and designing them was a fun assignment for visual development artist Chris Reccardi because he's "always asked to do 'cool stuff,' and it was a nice change to be told to picture what would be driving around Flint, Michigan, in the 1980s recession." To achieve this goal, Reccardi made sure the generic cars show signs of neglect, with primered fenders, mismatched replacement doors, peeling racing stripes, and bubbling window tint—all perfect details for the car unenthusiasts of Swallow Falls.

There are, however, two vehicles that don't look like they rolled off the same assembly line as the generic cars, and those are Sam's news van and Flint's car.

The Weather News Network's news van is clearly a lot more organic than the cars of Swallow Falls, unique in its sweeping curves and contours. Reccardi looked to the late 1980s and early 1990s Chevrolet models for inspiration on designing the news van since he "was going for a retro feel, but something not stuck as far in the past as the town is." The fact that it has a decent paint job in a vivid teal further differentiates it from the town's fleet of vehicles.

↑ ↗ Generic Truck & MidSize Car ★ *Chris Reccardi*

↑ Generic Truck ★ *Ted Blackman*

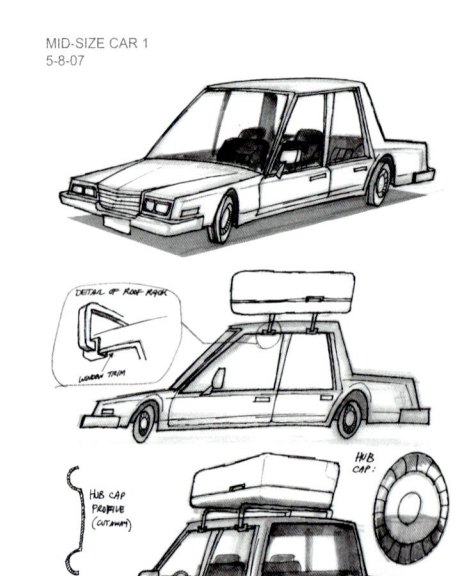

↑ News Van ★ *Dean Gordon*

↑ Flint's Car ★ *Digital*

→ Cruise Ship ★ *Design: Simon Rodgers, Paint: Dave Bleich*

**Flint's Car: Before & After!**

# FLINT'S CAR: GEAR - REAR VIEW

To design Flint's Car, director Christopher Miller did a sketch to start the wheels rolling, and visual development artist Chris Reccardi took what he considers a tame approach to building upon that image. "The directors encouraged me to do something completely ridiculous, so I decided to make a crazy Victorian machine to play up how Flint is more of a nerd than a scientist," recalls Reccardi. To build his automotive masterpiece, Flint apparently took a late 1970s Mustang–inspired body and enhanced it with a big dome of sheet metal to create a roomy cabin. Its interior is stocked with a conglomeration of old monitors and keyboards that hearken back to the days of Tandy computers—a mix of speakers, subwoofers, and synthesizers fresh out of the 1970s, plus a fascinating maze of cables, wires, and vacuum tubing, all fastened with the not-so-handyman's tool of duct tape. It's not the usual cool, science-fiction vehicle that one expects from inventors, but it's a magic combination of found objects that is more visually fun than logically useful, which Flint is so adept at creating.

Front Cover Flint's Car ★ *Chris Reccardi*
Back Cover License Plate ★ *Michael Kurinsky*
↑ Flint's Car: Gear-Rear View ★ *Chris Reccardi*

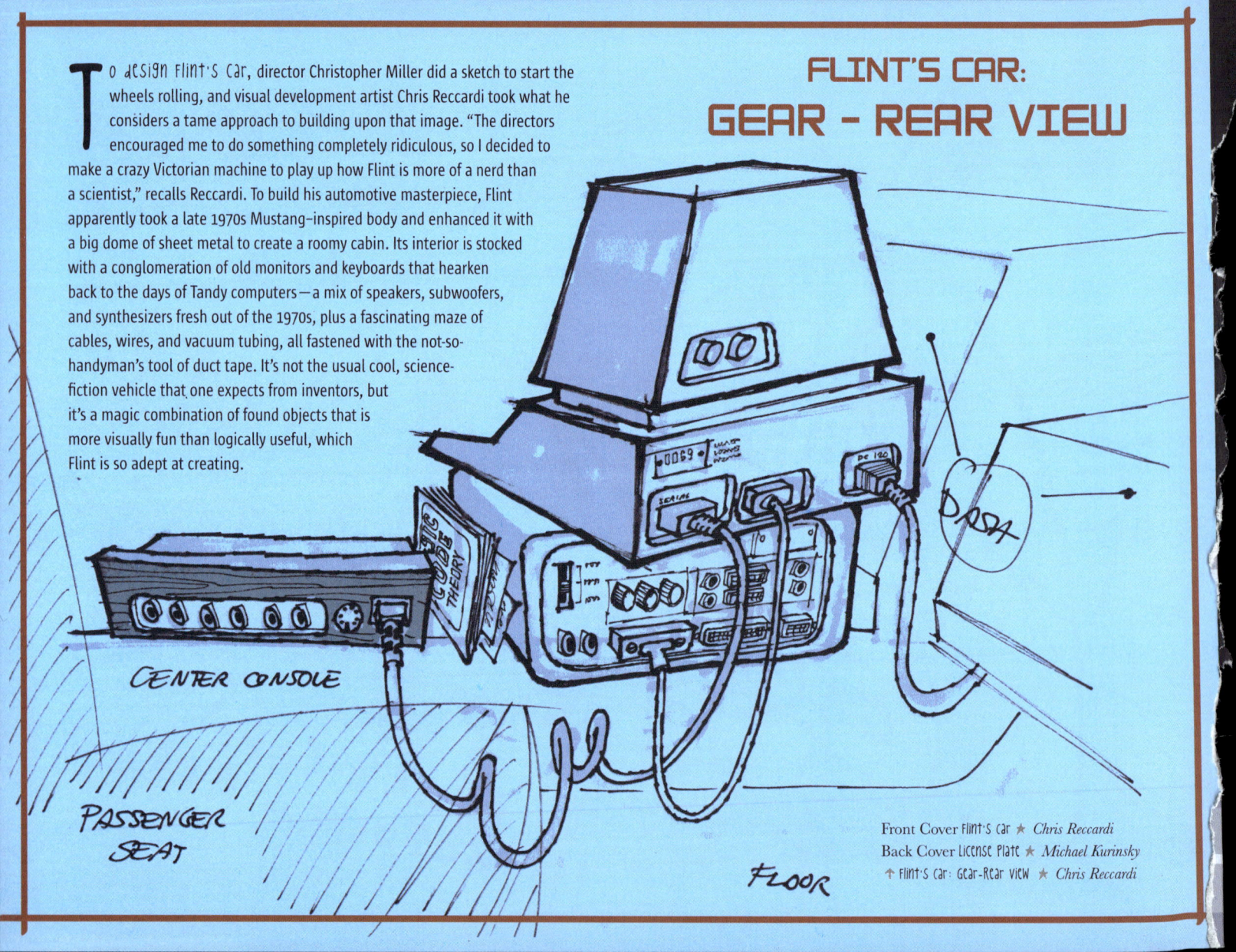

↑ Flint's Car ★ *Chris Reccardi*

↘ Flint's Car ★ *Chris Reccardi*
→ Flint's Car ★ *Michael Kurinsky*

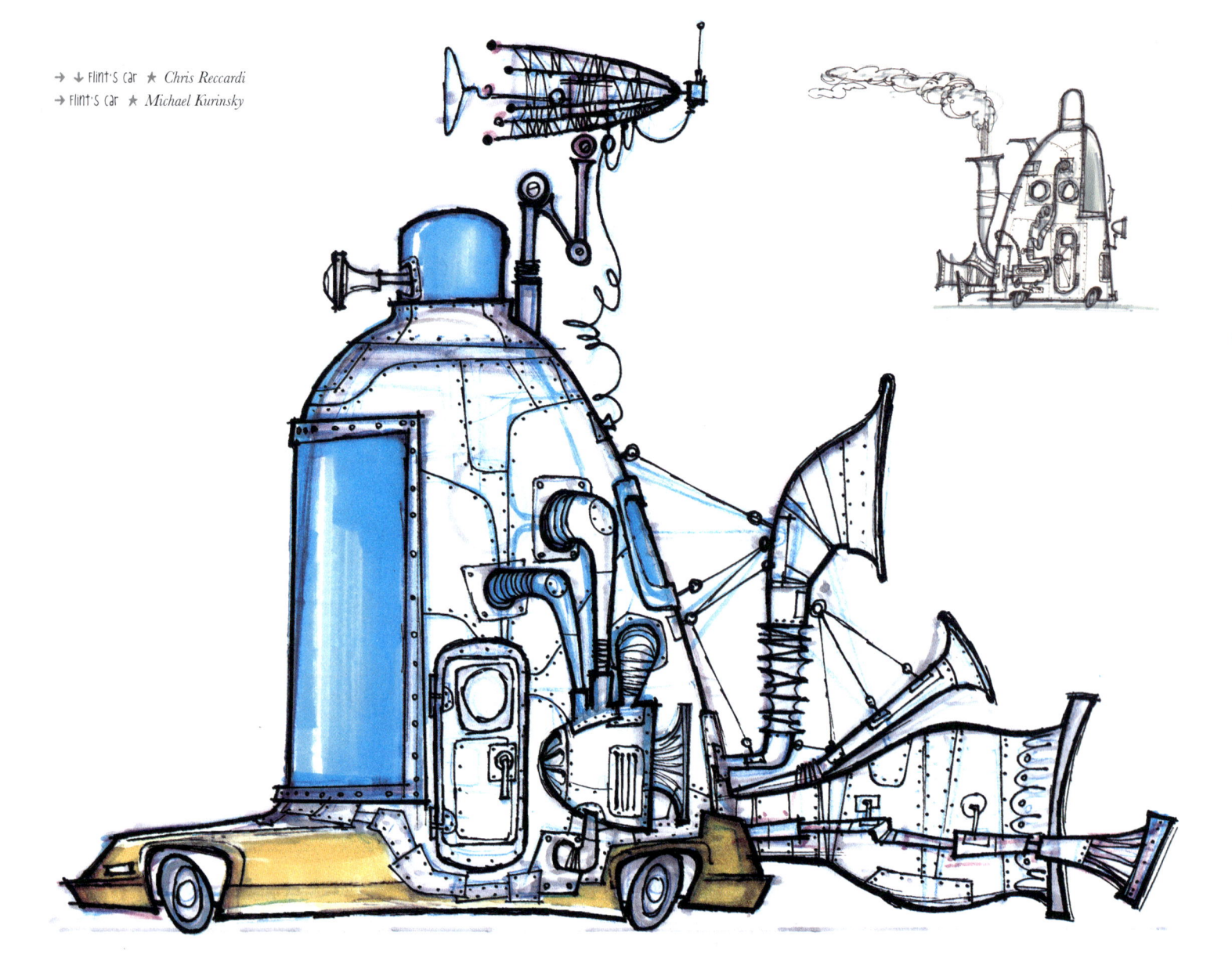

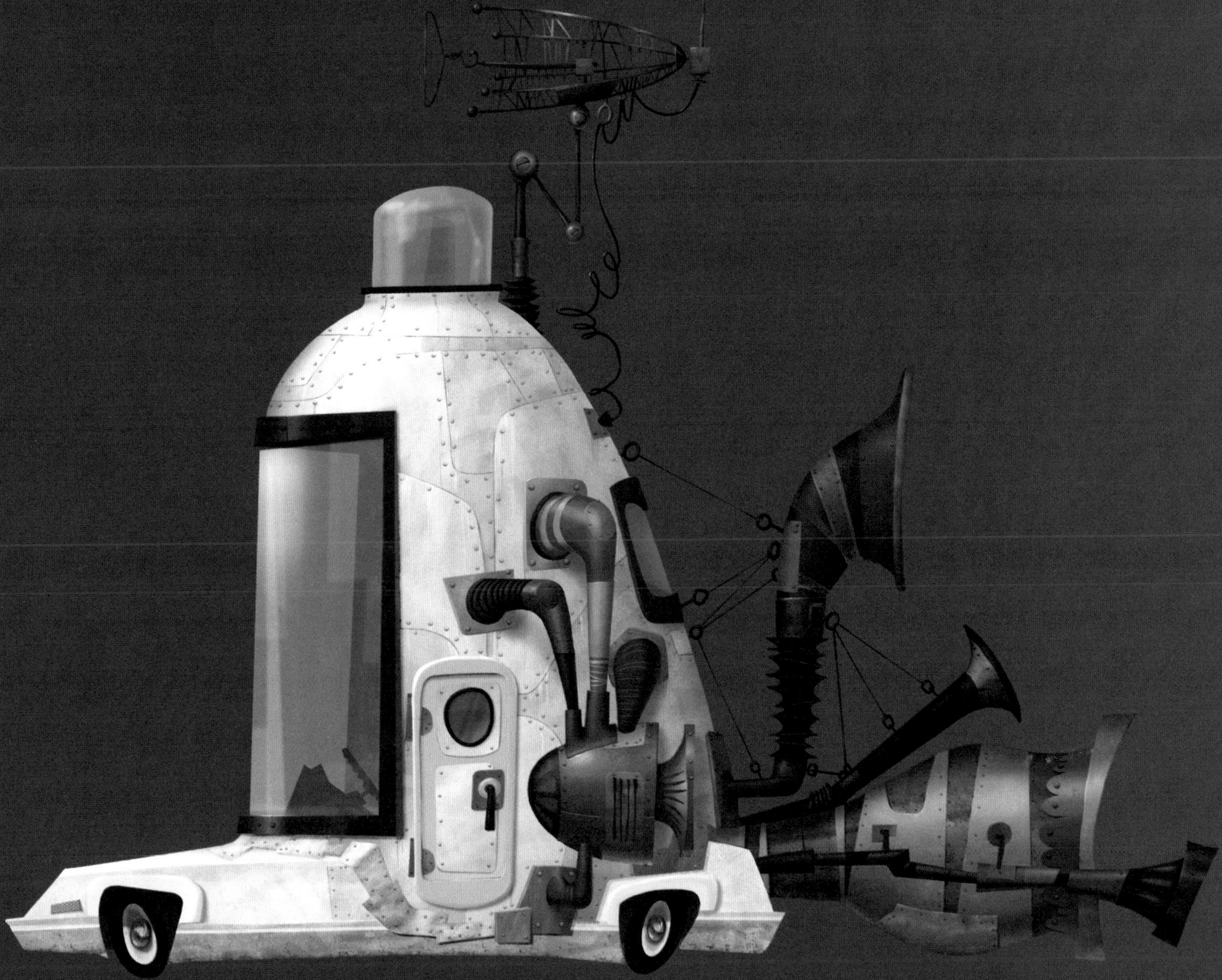

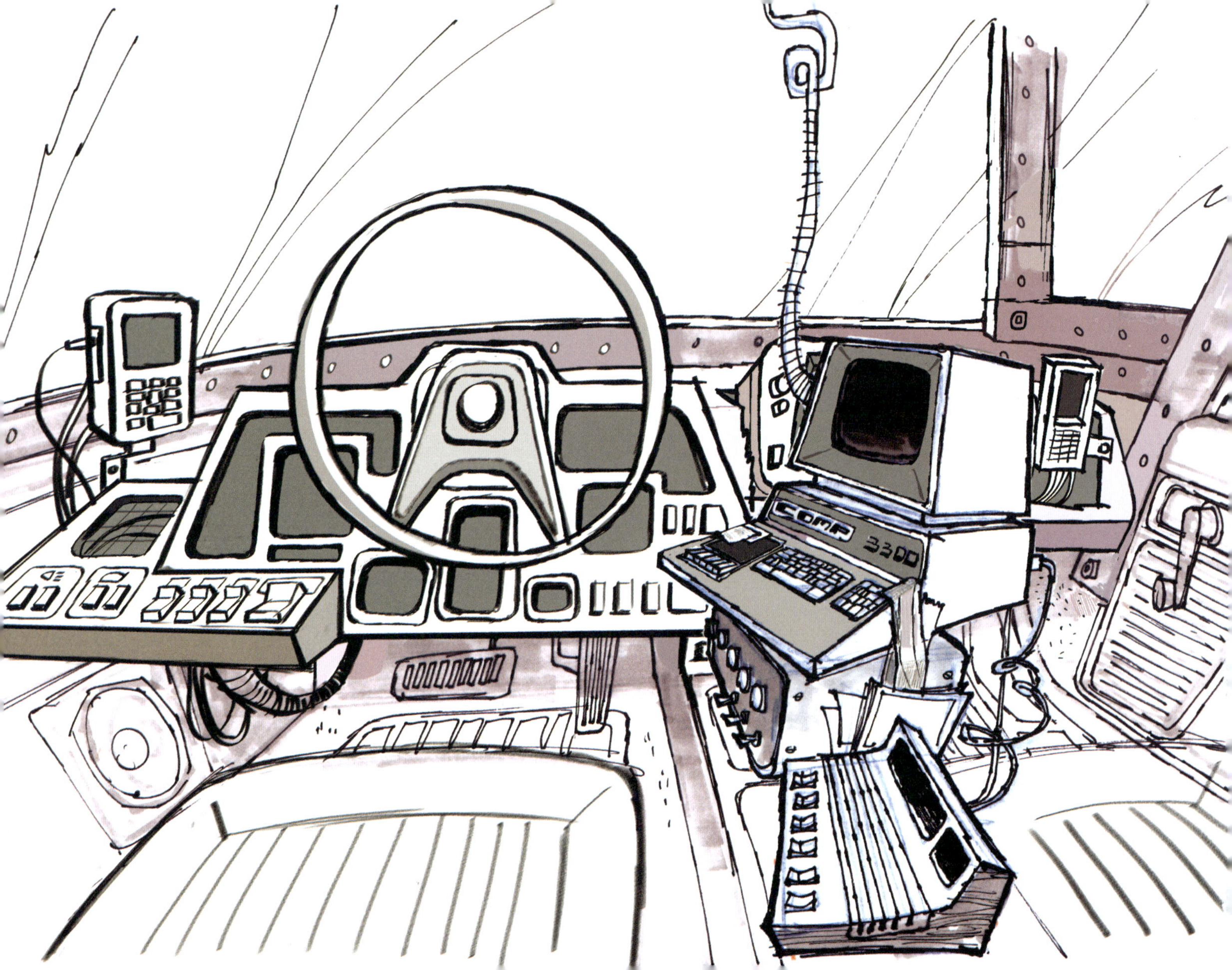
COMP
3300

← Flint's Car Interior ★ Chris Reccardi
↓ Flint's Car Interior ★ Dean Gordon

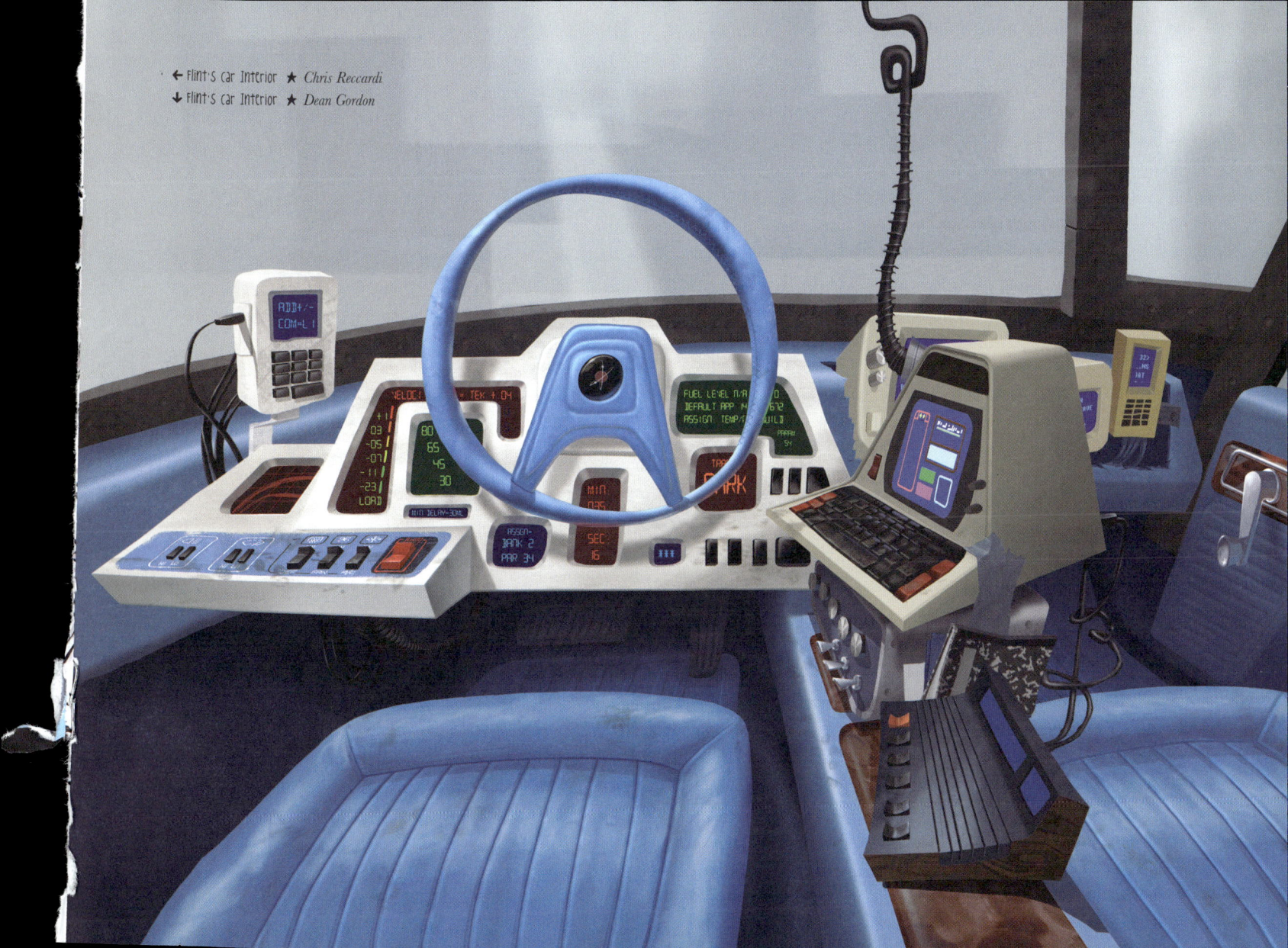

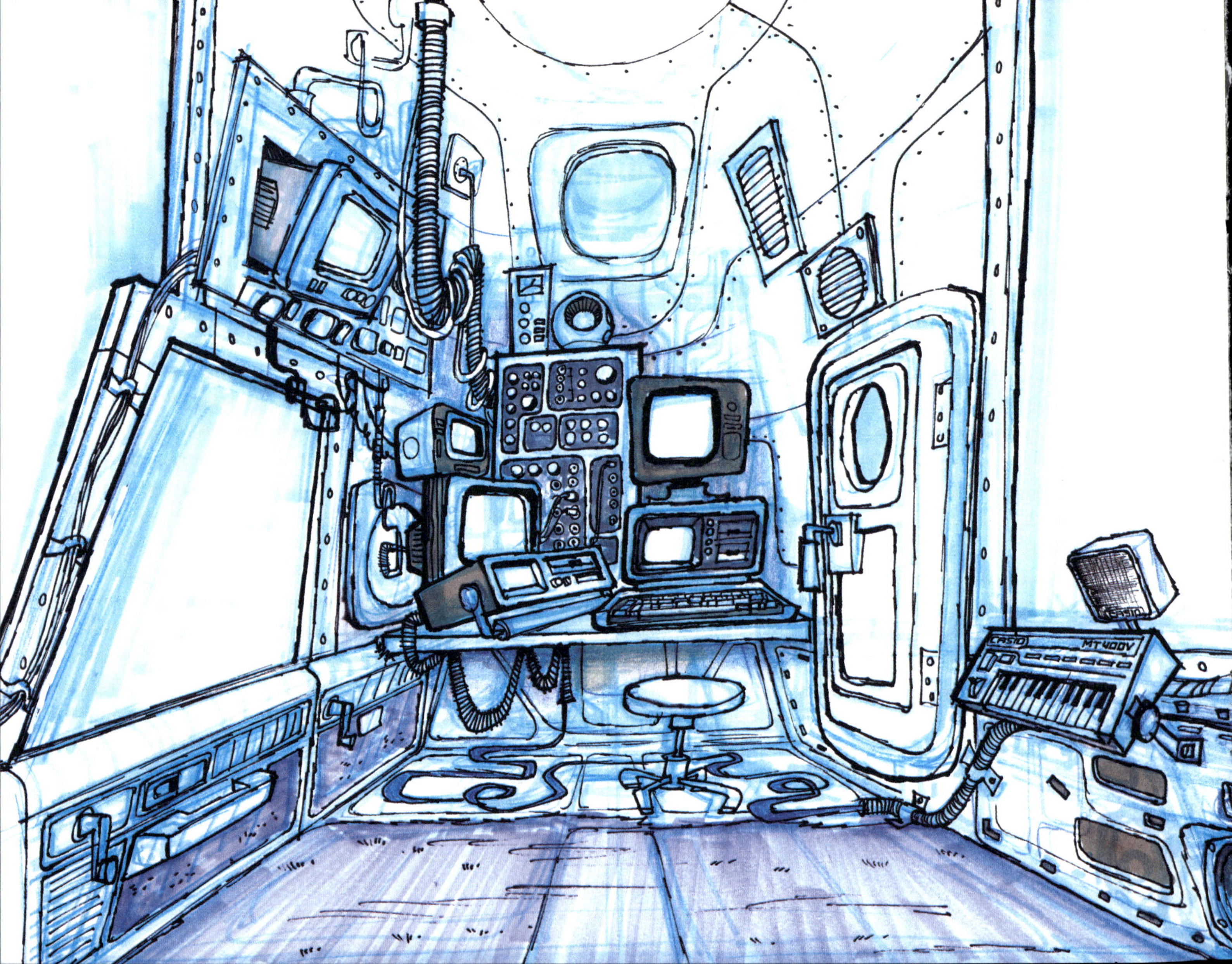
CASIO
MT400V

← Flint's Car Interior ★ Chris Reccardi
↓ Flint's Car Interior ★ Dean Gordon

↑ Storyboards ★ Chris Mitchell
← Flint's car/plane ★ Chris Reccardi

FLYING CAR

↑ Flint's Plane: Wing  ★ *Dean Gordon*
↗ Flint's Plane takes off

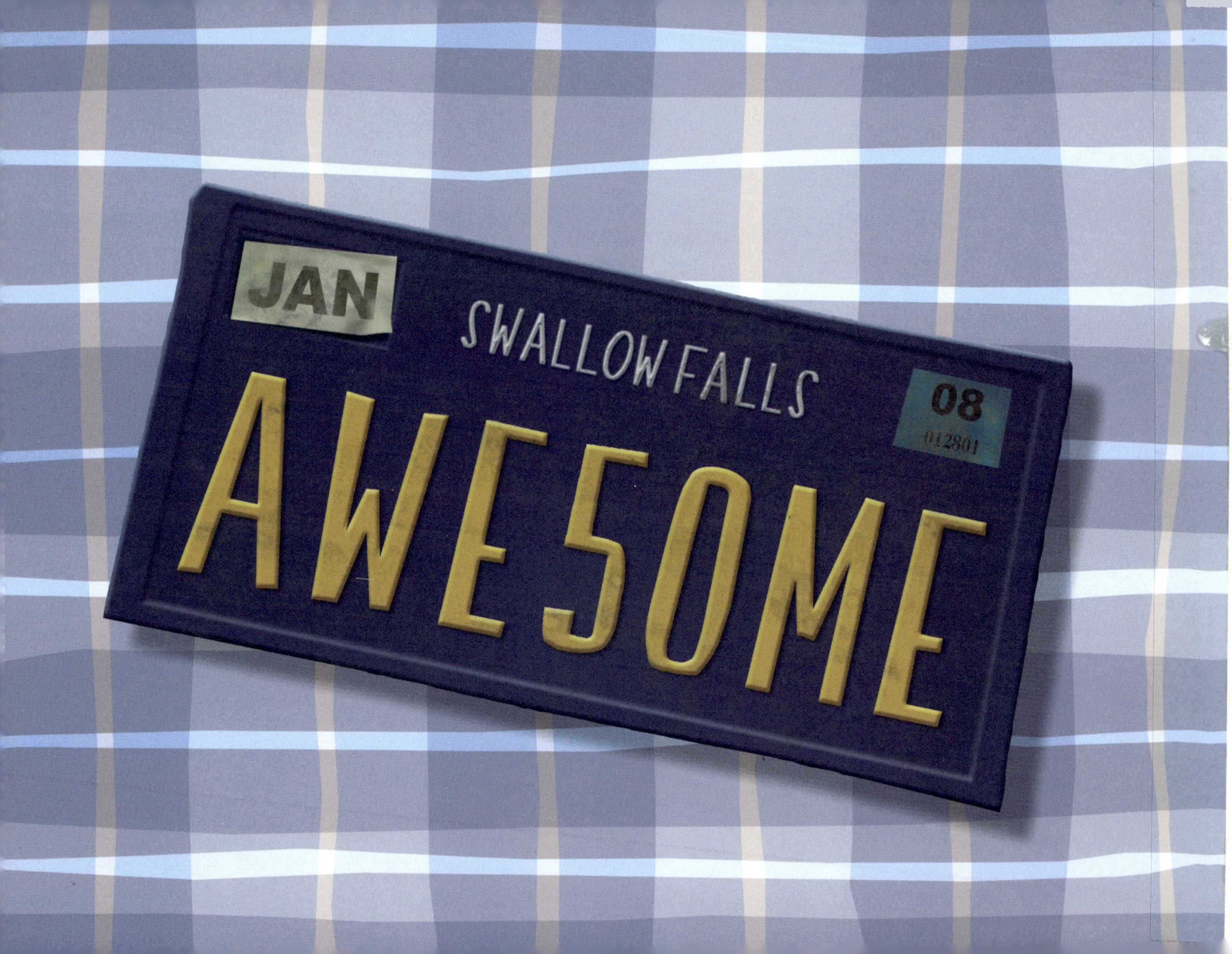
JAN
SWALLOW FALLS
08
012801
AWESOME

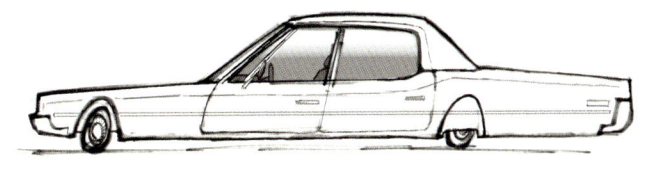

← Police Car ★ Simon Rodgers
← Generic Car ★ Cristy Maltese
← Taco Truck ★ Michael Kurinsky

↑ Generic Car ★ Chris Reccardi
↓ Flint's Car ★ Design: Chris Reccardi, Paint: Michael Kurinsky

# the cannery

The Baby Brent Sardine Cannery may have closed years ago, but its presence still looms large upon the town of Swallow Falls. It stands as the largest building in town and the most glaring reminder of what once was the livelihood of the community. Because of its scale and location, it is an ominous presence "that literally casts a shadow over everything," notes production designer Justin K. Thompson. One particular image by visual development artist Simon Rodgers speaks volumes: The center support beams of the cannery are crumbling and sagging, a poignant reflection on Swallow Falls as it "represents the backbone of the town, broken in the loss of the sardine industry," he explains. Rodgers also subtly brought the rectangular patterning into this structure with his inventive use of galvanized-steel panels and wooden braces, suggesting shoddy repair work that had been done throughout the years and which is consistent with the "upkeep" of all other Swallow Falls structures. Although the cannery is merely a shell of its former self, one can still sense the grandeur and energy that once emanated from its walls and still lives in the hearts and collective memory of the townsfolk of Swallow Falls, fueling their sense of pride and unwillingness to let go of the past.

While art director Michael Kurinsky created the color palette for the cannery, he credits director Christopher Miller's personal knowledge of canneries for his influence. Several members of Miller's family worked at canneries over the course of their lives, and through photos and stories from their experiences, Miller learned that cannery walls were "usually painted a rusty red color to hide all the blood that splashed on them," a deliciously graphic yet informative detail indeed.

↑ cannery ★ *Bruce McCall*

→ cannery ★ *Dave Bleich*

98

↑ cannery ★ *Simon Rodgers*

↑ ↘ Cannery Studies & Cannery Destroyed by Candy Corn ★ *Simon Rodgers*
→ Sardine Cannery & Surrounding Town ★ *Dan Quarnstrom*
↓ Cannery Destroyed by Watermelons ★ *Justin K. Thompson*

100

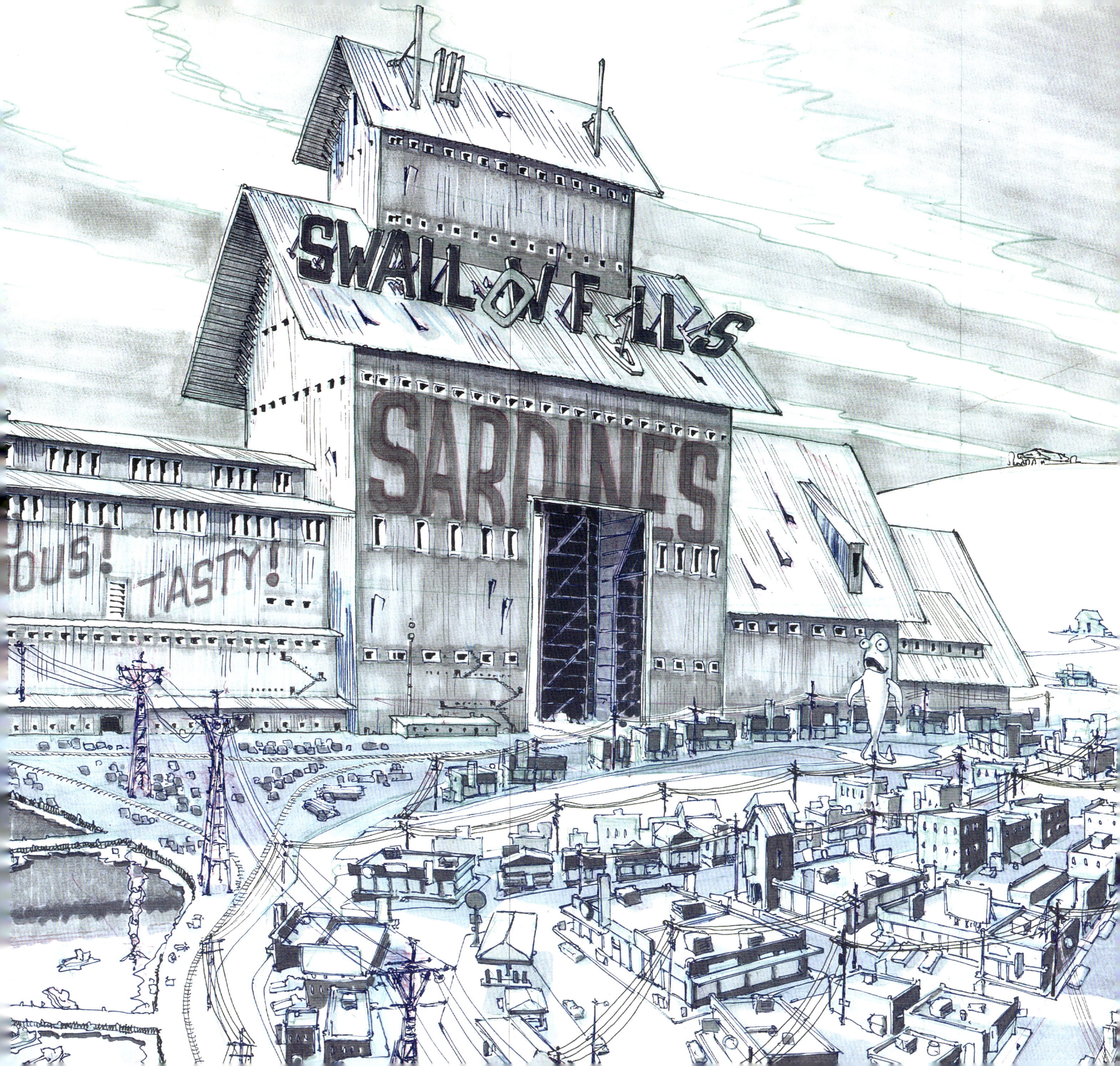
SARDINES
TASTY!

# The Docks

The docks were designed to be the dingiest location in the film so that they would set the stage for Flint's darkest hour, right after his invention causes great destruction in Swallow Falls. "We layered in numerous textures to create the grittiness that comes with rust, mold, mildew, and bird droppings in this location in order to convey the crudeness and ugly truth of Flint's realization that he is truly 'a fish out of water,'" says production designer Justin K. Thompson. The docks' disrepair highlights Flint's despair but also serves as a nice contrast to the magical glow that comes with the falling of the burger rain, when the skies clear and Flint is given new hope, courtesy of his newfound success and his introduction to Sam.

This location offers the audience its first close-up look at the breathtaking water effects created by Imageworks artists. "We knew we didn't want the water to look hyperreal, as that wouldn't fit in with the simple dock architecture or the town in general, so we asked Imageworks to turn down the high-frequency information in the water effects. That way, we still got movement and wave patterns that were realistic, but there was less visual noise, which complemented our world," explains Thompson. Even more challenging than the ocean was the giant rolling fishbowl that comes crashing through this part of town, and this difficult fluid effect was brought to reality through the use of "a smooth-particle hydrodynamic solver that Imageworks developed in-house to integrate with the Houdini software used in effects work," notes effects animation supervisor Matt Hausman.

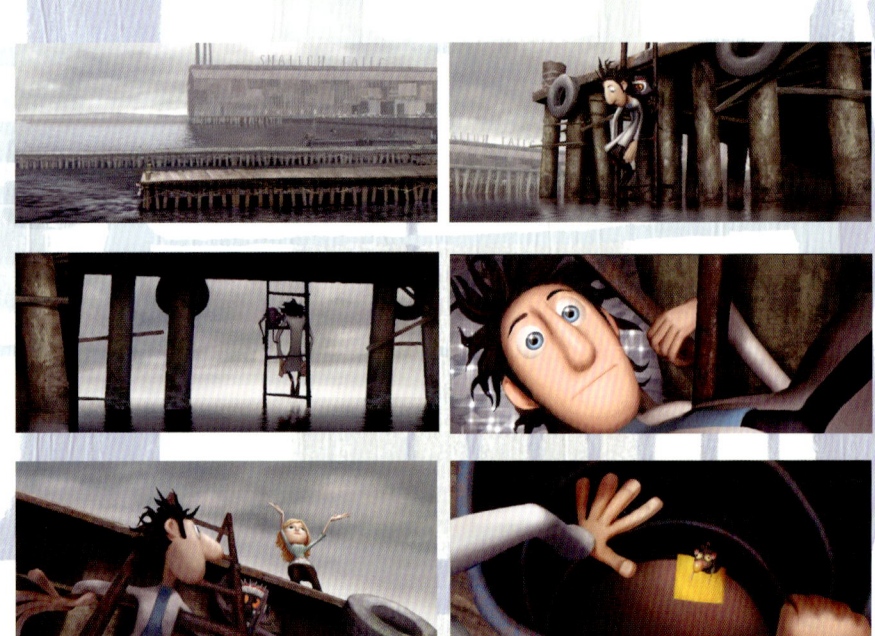

↑ Color Keys ★ *Michael Kurinsky*
→ Docks ★ *Design: Simon Rodgers, Paint: Dave Bleich*

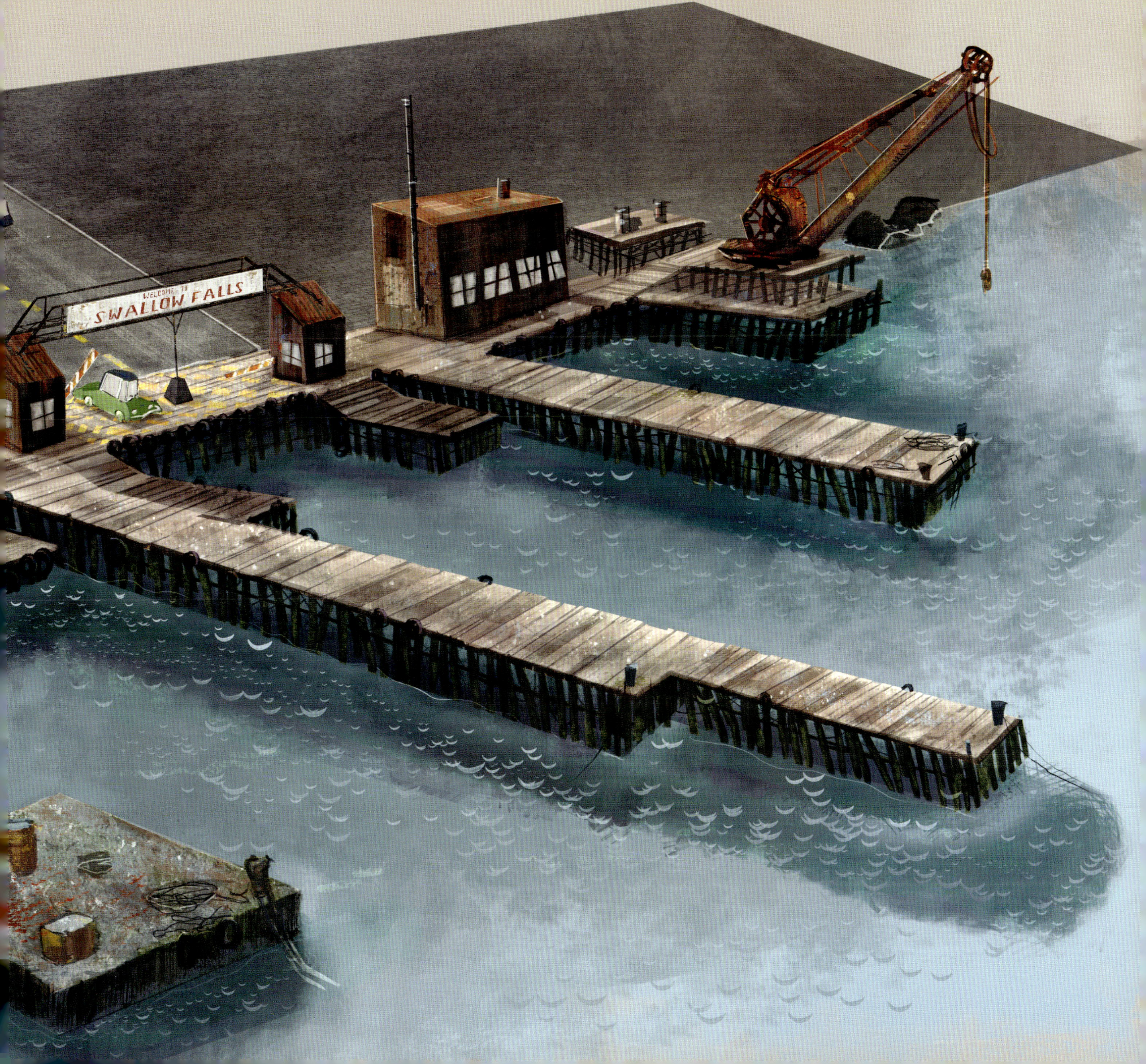
WELCOME TO
SWALLOW FALLS

33
POST NO BILLS
POST NO BILLS
POST NO BILLS
PRIVATE PROPERTY NO TRESPASSING
POST NO BILLS
POST NO BILLS

"[Visual development artist] Dave Bleich was a master at creating convincing texture illusions by combining the watercolor textures with very 'painterly' mark making. His application on the docks stands as some of the directors' favorite instances of texture work."
– Michael Kurinsky, *Art Director*

↑ Docks Overview ★ Justin K. Thompson
↖ Storyboards ★ Kris Pearn
↓ Docks Siding Texture ★ Dave Bleich

# Sardineland

Just blocks away from the defunct cannery, Mayor Shelbourne demonstrates how he is still trying to push the sardine theme by setting up an amusement park called Sardineland, hoping to draw visitors to Swallow Falls to help resurrect the local economy and his own career. When visual development artist Marcelo Vignali was asked to create an icon for this location, he was told to think of this job going to one of the local townsfolk, so he imagined that a statue of a sardine wouldn't be hewn out of natural stone, cast in copper, or sculpted in ceramic, but made instead from "corrugated steel attached to a grain silo, kind of like how a child makes something out of the cardboard tubes in toilet-paper rolls," he explains. "There is a simple, unsophisticated purity to it, a raw, tangible statement rather than an artistic concept, that is fitting with the honest, blue-collar tone of Swallow Falls," says production designer Justin K. Thompson.

↗ Sardine Statue ★ Design: Marceelo Vignali

↑ Sardineland ★ Design: Justin K. Thompson, Paint: Dave Bleich

↗ The Virtual Sardine Experience color render ★ Dave Bleich

↑ Storyboards ★ Jack Hsu

↗ Brent Cuts the Ribbon ★ *Final Frame*
→ Color Keys ★ *Michael Kurinsky*

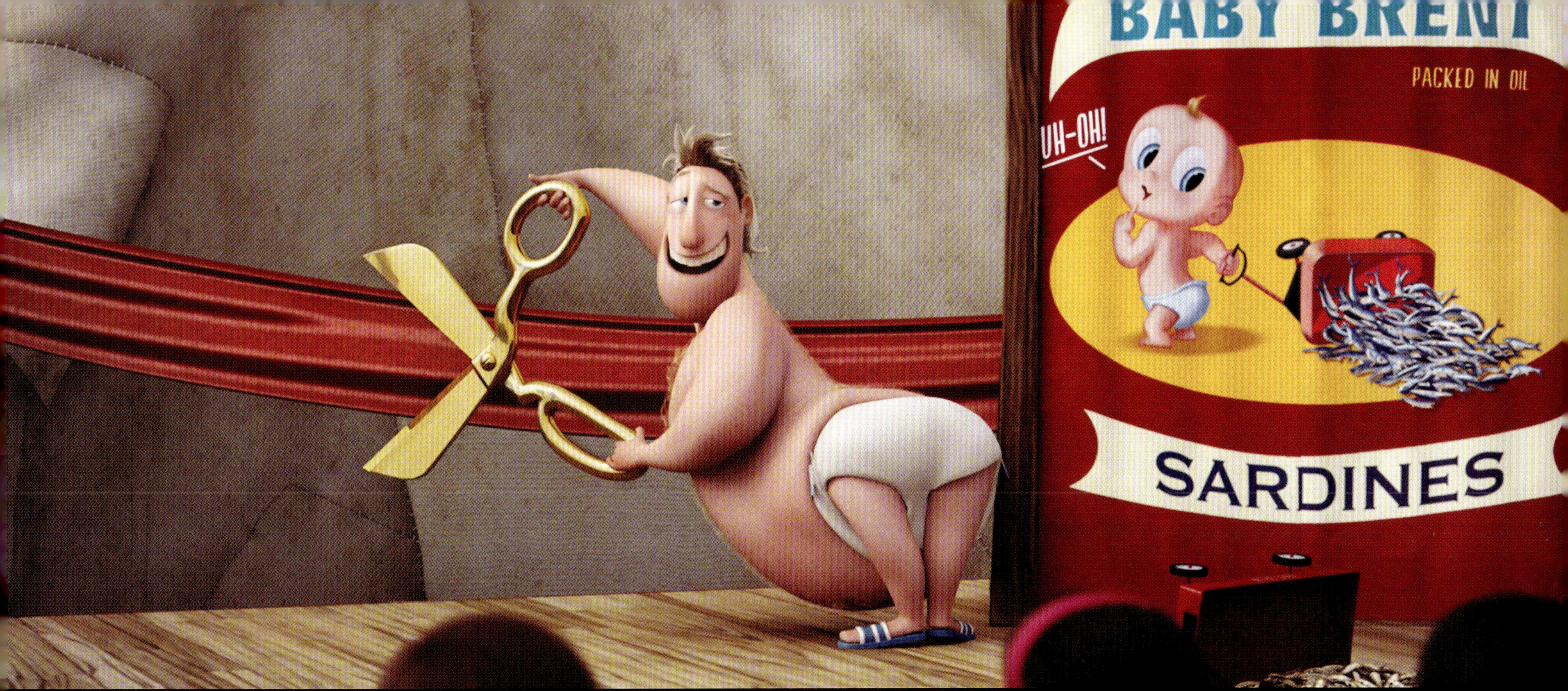
BABY BRENT
PACKED IN OIL
UH-OH!
SARDINES

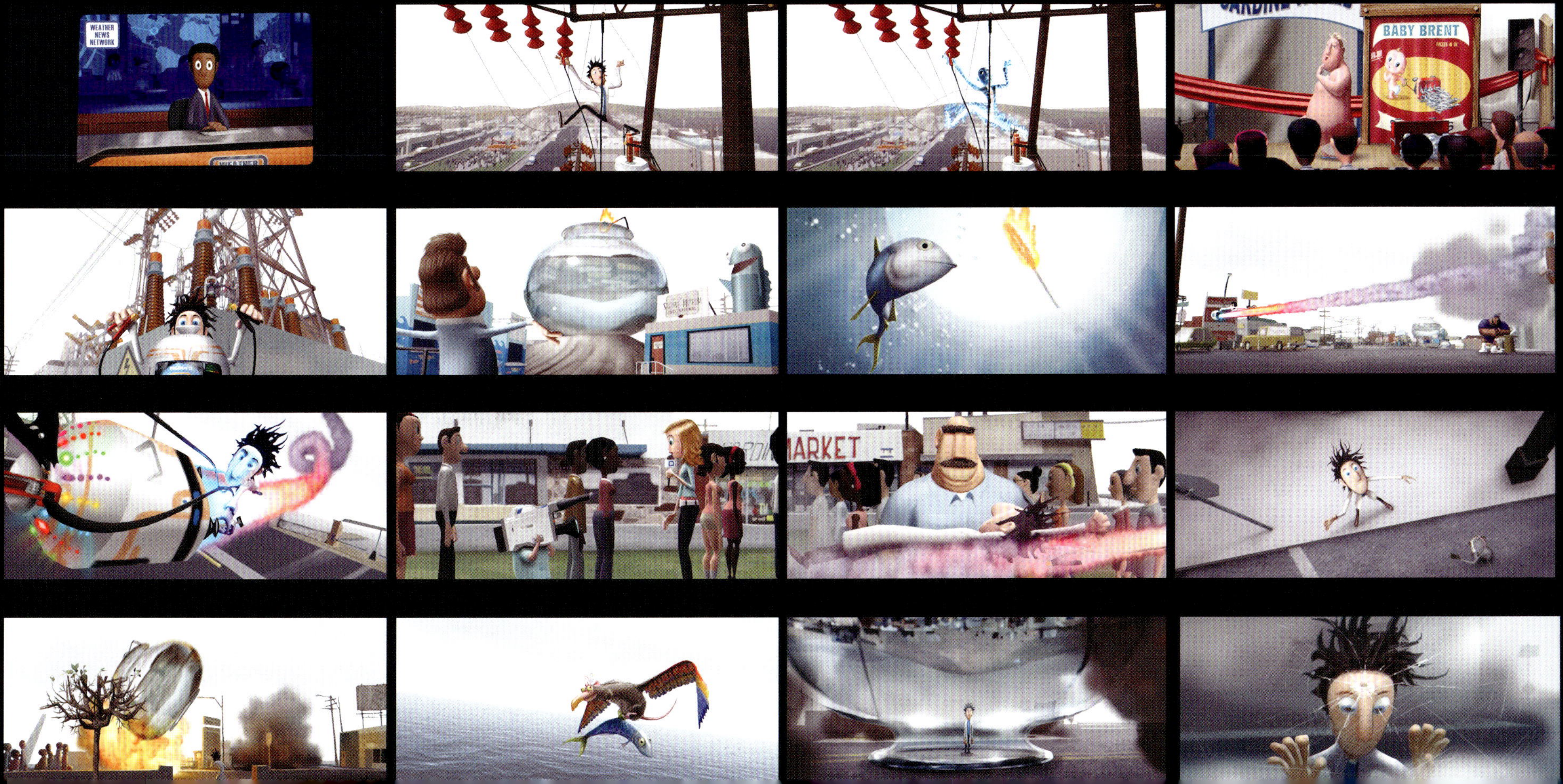

# Elementary School

The elementary school is reminiscent of the brick-façade buildings that compose many public education facilities built across east Los Angeles in the 1970s. Windows, walls, sidewalks, and fencing all effectively continue the rectangle-and-square patterning. In an earlier version of the story, Earl was much more stringent in applying rules to his son, and Cal felt imprisoned by such excessive discipline. To further that character experience, "the school was intended to be a physical extension of that idea for Cal: It was meant to be a dreary place, full of rules and dull class work, so we designed it to feel very Spartan and cold in shape, line, texture, and color," explains production designer Justin K. Thompson. While the mural on the gym wall must have been a fun activity for the children of the school to paint, it was clearly commissioned long ago and now serves as a "faded reminder of happier times in Swallow Falls," he adds.

↑ School Mural ★ *Noelle Triaureau*

↑ Storyboards ★ *Will Mata*
→ Classroom Texture Map ★ *Digital*

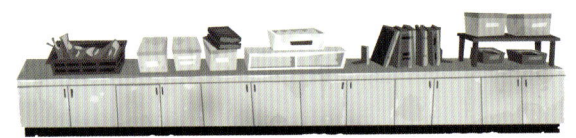

↑ School Props ★ *Armand Serrano*

↑ Elementary School ★ Gaëtan & Paul Brizzi
↓ Elementary School ★ Design: Armand Serrano, Paint: Michael Kurinsky

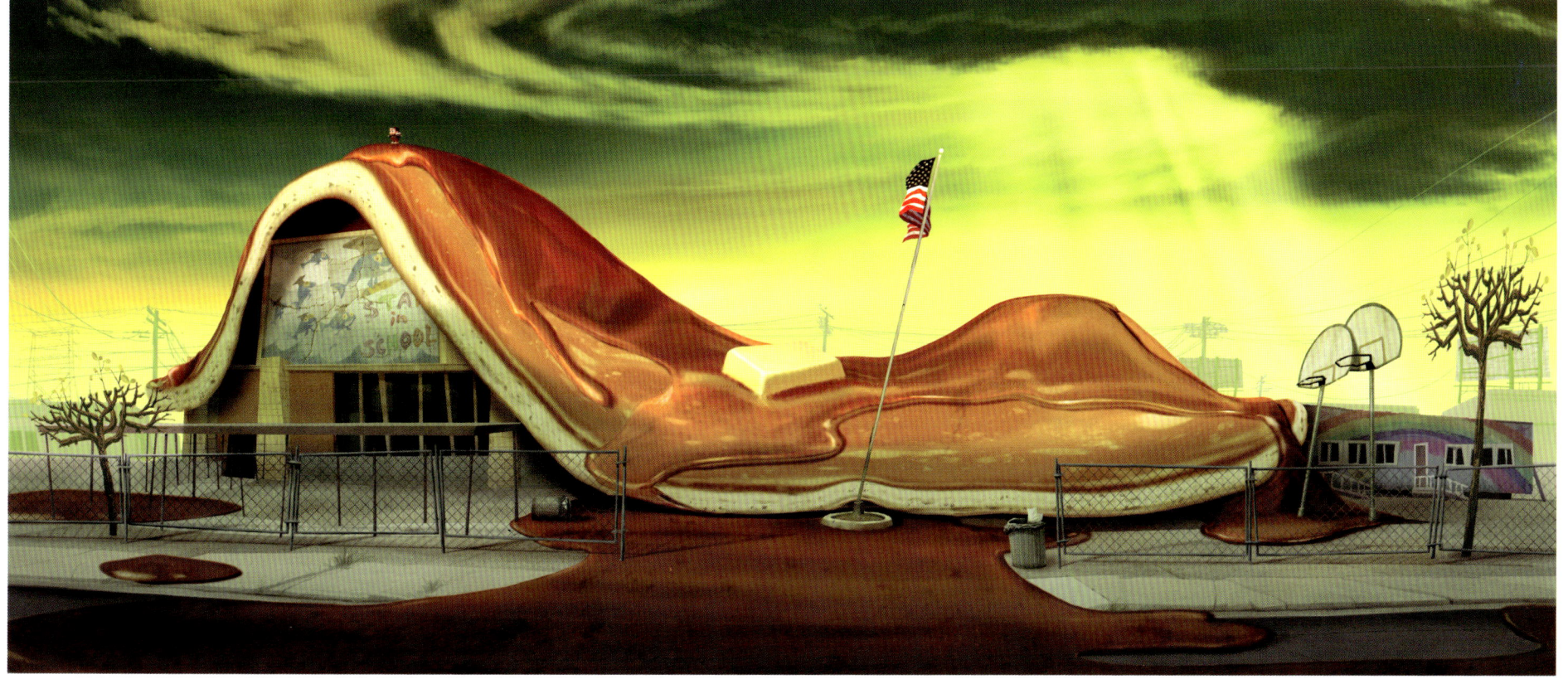

# the Lockwood Residence

"There are three unique house models that are repurposed throughout the neighborhood, sometimes mirrored, and with very different look treatments applied," notes visual effects supervisor Rob Bredow. Flint's house is one of these models, and the interior suggests that while there was once a womanly presence in the house, it is now just a serviceable abode for the Lockwood men. "The withered flowers and the dated family portraits show that this home has lacked the motherly touch for quite a while," notes visual development artist Simon Rodgers. This absence resonates in the relationship between Flint and his father, who clearly have not had the benefit of a facilitator to help their communications for years.

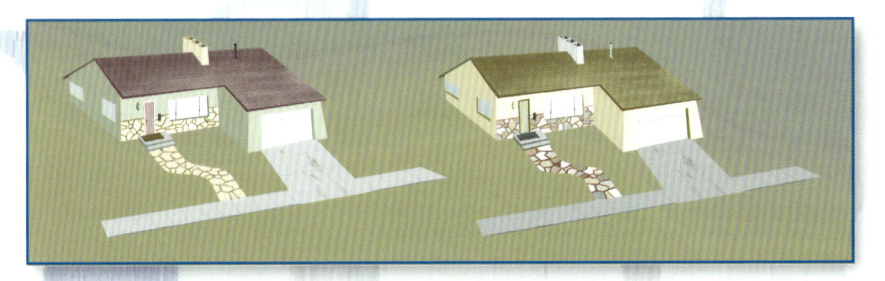

↑ Generic Houses  ★ Design: Justin K. Thompson, Paint: Jerry Loveland

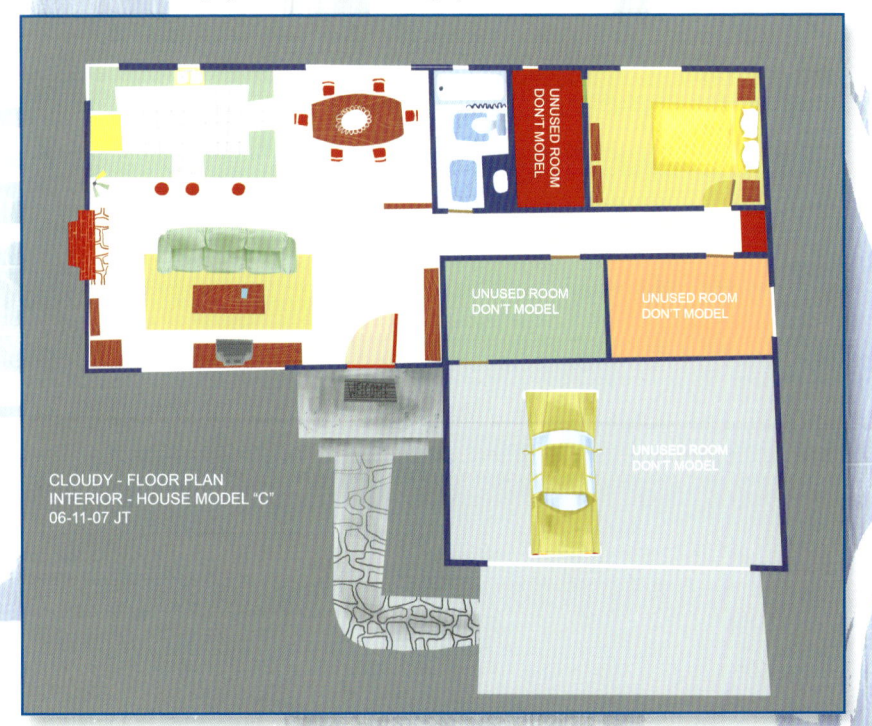

↑ Floor Plan  ★ Justin K. Thompson  → The Front Room  ★ Cristy Maltese

"The posters in Flint's bedroom were all stylized, and I often looked to magazines from the 1960s and 1970s for layout inspiration. All of them incorporate the Sasek feel and a font designed by Justin K. [Thompson]."
— PETE OSWALD Visual Development Artist

↑ Posters ↑ Pete Oswald
↑ Flint's Bedroom ↑ Design: Simon Rodgers; Paint: Dean Gordon

→ Storyboards ★ *Bob Logan*

# Flint's Lab – Exterior

Flint's lab sticks out like a sore thumb when viewed against the backdrop of the rest of Swallow Falls, an analogy which could apply directly to Flint's presence in his hometown as well. What had started as a humble treehouse when Flint was a child has been added onto with found objects—everything from a Porta Potti to telephone poles to an abandoned school bus—until it has reached epic proportions of ridiculousness. Just as Flint's car stands out among the other cars in town because of its curves and components, so does his lab, and this is resonant of a production design theory to highlight the differences between forward-thinking Flint and his backward-looking hometown. "These two competing ideas had to be in strong visual conflict to each other . . . hence, the town is squares, rectangles, flat space, whereas Flint's world is round, curvilinear, and ambiguous space," says production designer Justin K. Thompson.

→ Lab Exterior ★ *Justin K. Thompson*
↓ Lab Exterior ★ *Final Frame*

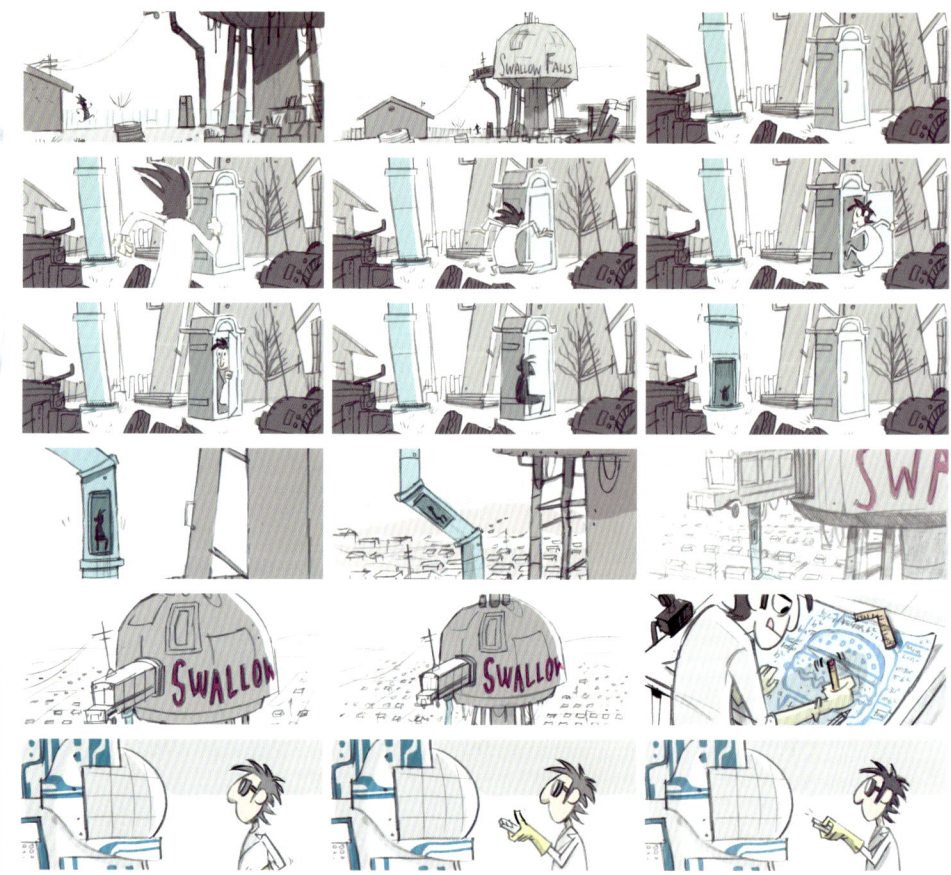

← ↑ Lab Exterior Sketches ★ *Justin K. Thompson*
→ Porta Potti Lab Entry ★ *Design: Todd Frederiksen, Paint: Jerry Loveland*

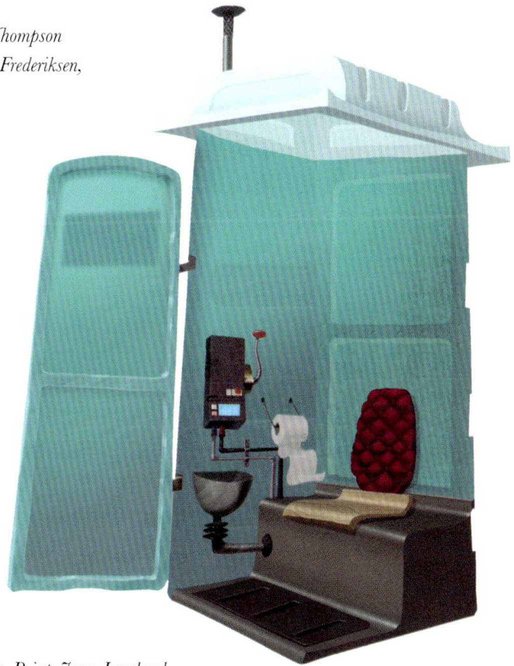

↑ Lab Exterior ★ *Michael Kurinsky*
↓ Lab Entry ★ *Design: Todd Frederikson, Paint: Jerry Loveland*

↑ ↓ Lab Exterior Sketches ★ *Justin K. Thompson*

# Flint's Lab — Interior

> "All the shapes in Flint's lab are asymmetrical to reflect his skewed perspective, as Flint never sees things quite clearly or balanced."
> —**JUSTIN K. THOMPSON** Production Designer

The difference in shape and space configuration is even more pronounced and palpable when comparing the interiors of typical Swallow Falls buildings to Flint's lab. To contrast the impression of being "boxed in" when inside the tackle shop or the Lockwood living room, Flint's lab has ceilings elevated so high that they seem almost infinite. Cinematography also plays into this sense of space: As layout supervisor Dave Morehead describes the moment in which Sam is brought into the lab for the first time, she "enters the lab following a long, locked-off elevator scene in which you are meant to feel confined to strongly contrast to the wide openness of the lab." Thompson further explains, "the freedom of movement, depth, and time in an ambiguous space creates an environment that gives Flint a more appropriate and believable space within which to create such unbelievable, almost magical, contraptions."

To understand what happens in Flint's lab, it is important to grasp a few pieces of backstory. As previously established, the town has fallen on hard times due to the lack of demand for sardines, the former financial lifeblood of this community. Combine that with the fact that this town exists on a rather isolated island, and therein lies the logic behind everything in Swallow Falls appearing to be stuck in the past, with no new commerce or technology coming in, "as if shipments of new things stopped a long time ago," elaborates Thompson. "If the world Flint grew up in were as contemporary as our own, he could just order things from the Internet. Instead, Flint is forced to be inventive and find creative solutions to the massive computational efforts that he undertakes in his lab. Through his own self-taught brilliance, he has figured out how to wire together all of the early '80s–style technology that could be found inside the town," Thompson continues. Thus his lab is a hodgepodge of speakers, monitors, synthesizers, and hi-fi units, which align to form a mesmerizing electronic pattern of lights and circuitry—things that basically look cool more than anything. And yes, the handprint security entry system is nothing more than a painted curtain preceded by a portico encased in egg cartons, but it all comes together in an inspiring setting that looks nothing like the reality outside of the lab, and it's all Flint needs to create his own world of possibilities.

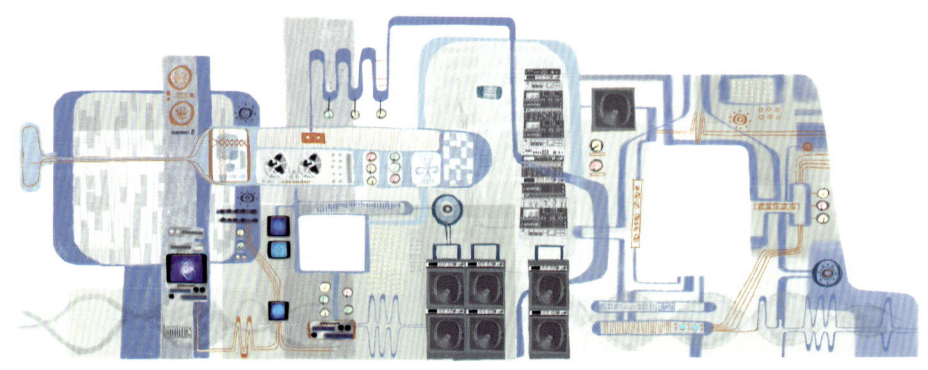

↓ ↑ Tech Walls ★ *Design: Justin K. Thompson, Paint: Dean Gordon*
← The Button ★ *Michael Kurinsky*

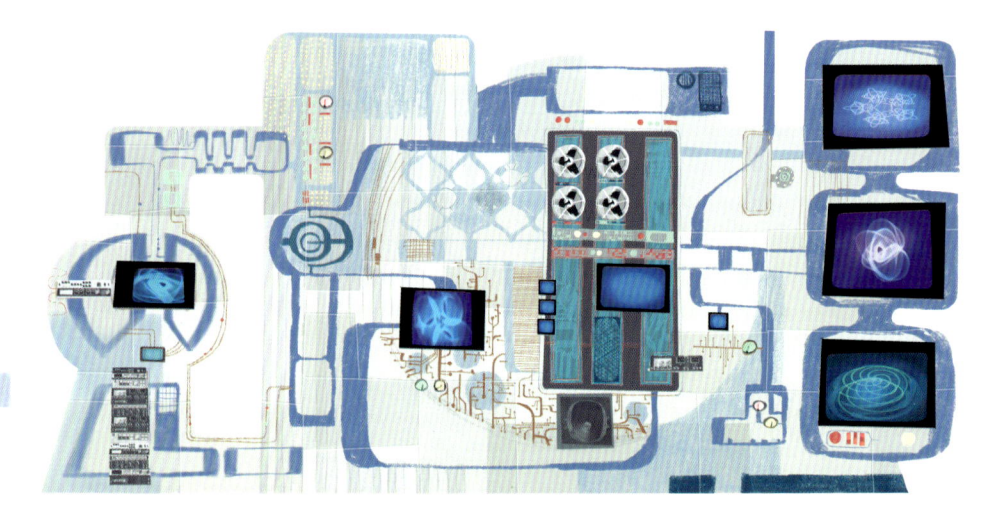

→ Flint's Lab Interior ★ *Final Frame*

114

*"Flint is obsessed with how things look, often to the detriment of their functionality. This is in stark and direct contrast to the town, which has no zoning, no attention paid to how things look or feel, and no aesthetic appreciation at all."*
—PHIL LORD Director

SFL COLORKEYS

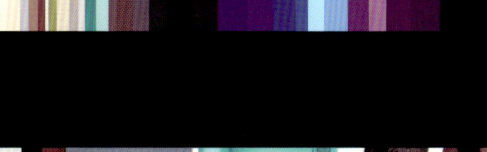

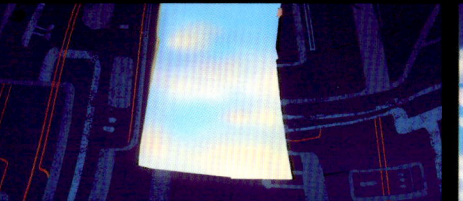

↖ Lab Interior ★ Justin K. Thompson
↑ Lab Interior ★ Andy Gaskill
↙ Color Keys ★ Michael Kurinsky
Overleaf Lab Interior ★ Michael Kurinsky

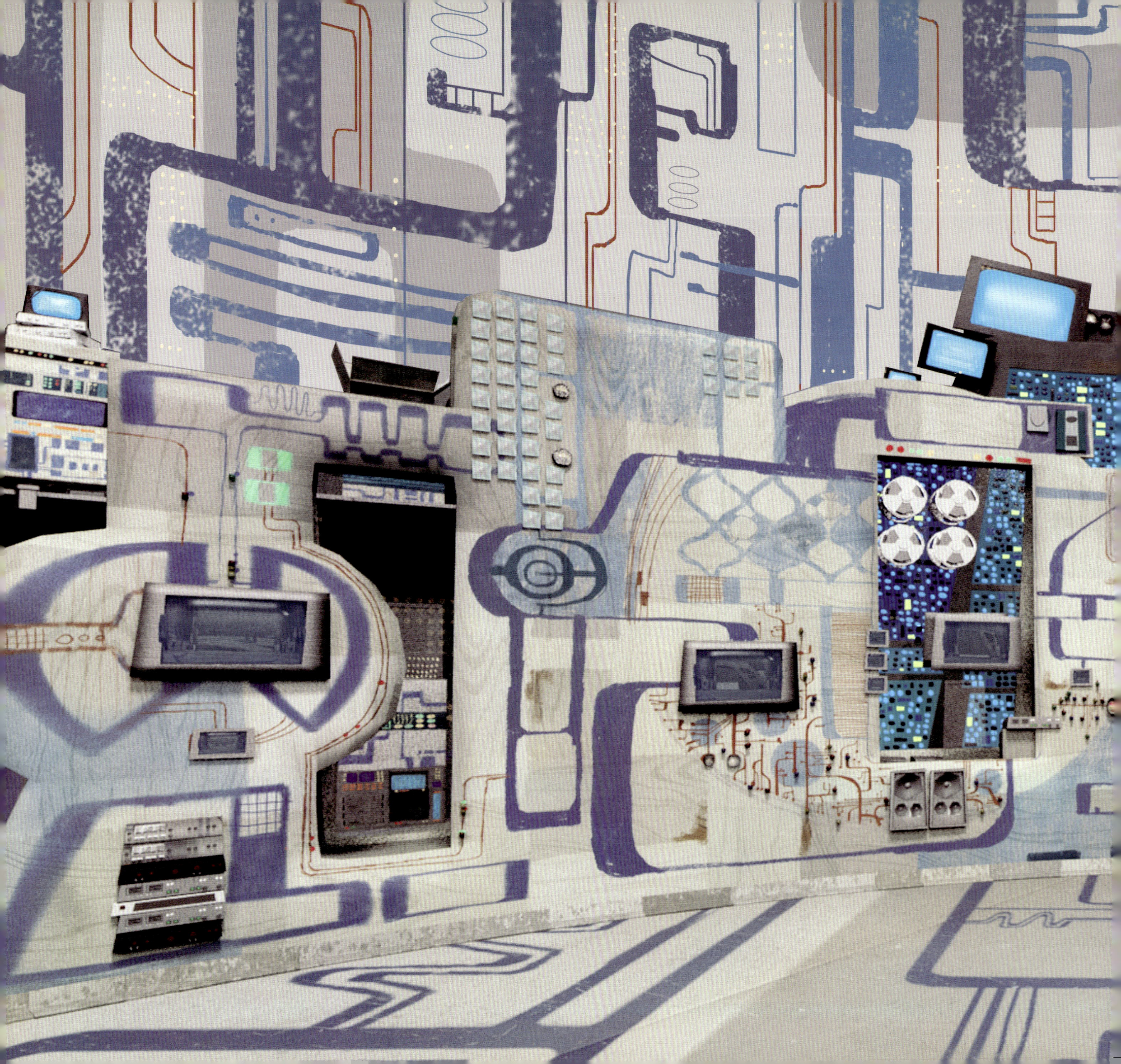

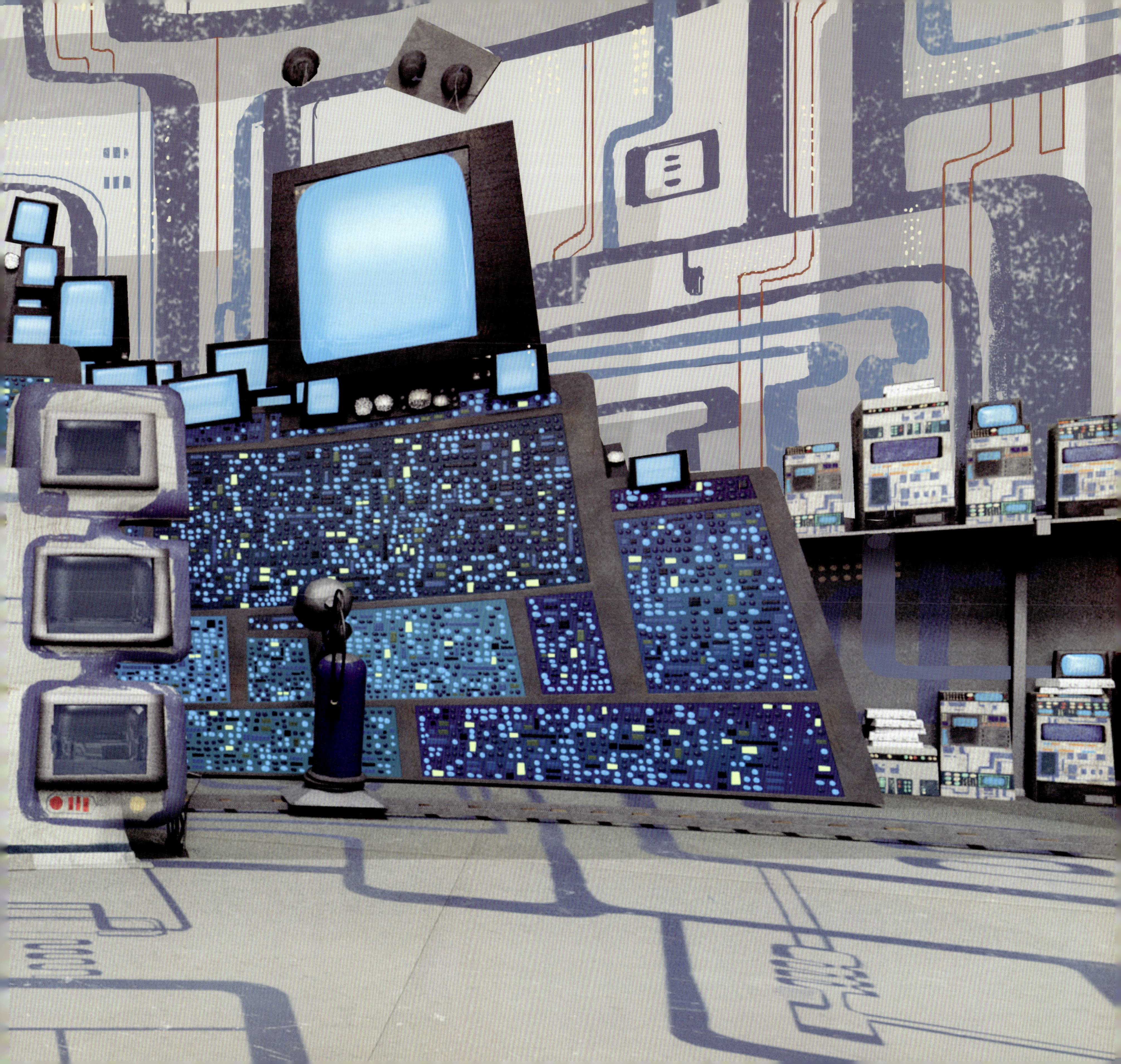

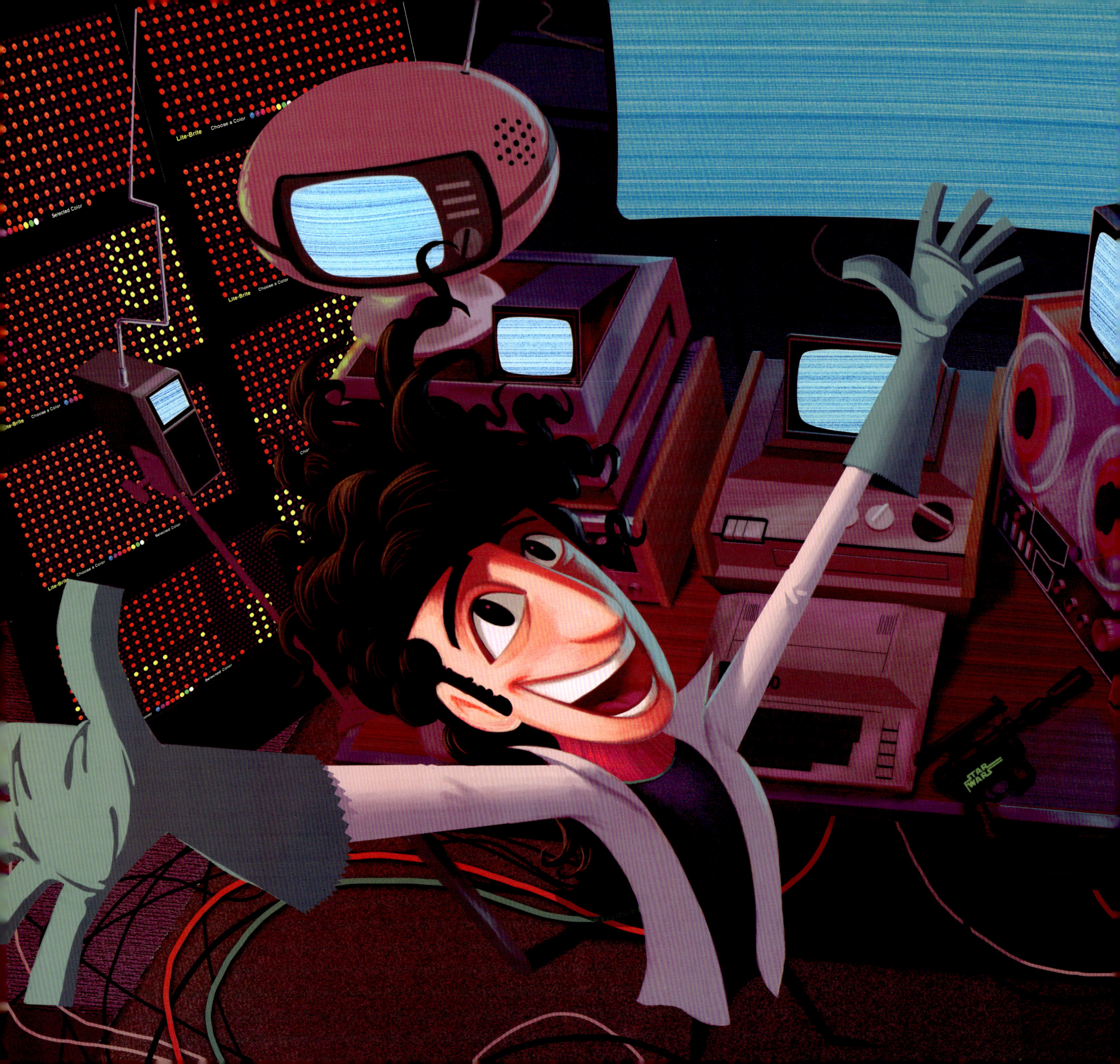
Lite-Brite
Choose a Color
Selected Color
STAR WARS

↖ ↑ Lab Interior ★ *Andy Gaskill*

*"The lab is lit with blue light, giving it a mysterious but cold feel, until Sam enters it, and then the light becomes warmer. We consciously left the curtain to the portico open to let in that light, but it was more about her effect on Flint than anything."*
— **MICHAEL KURINSKY** Art Director

← Lab Monitors ★ Design: Justin K. Thompson, Paint: Dean Gordon
→ Flint's Bed ★ Dean Gordon
→→ Lab Interiors ★ Andy Gaskill
↘ Lab Monitors ★ Justin K. Thompson

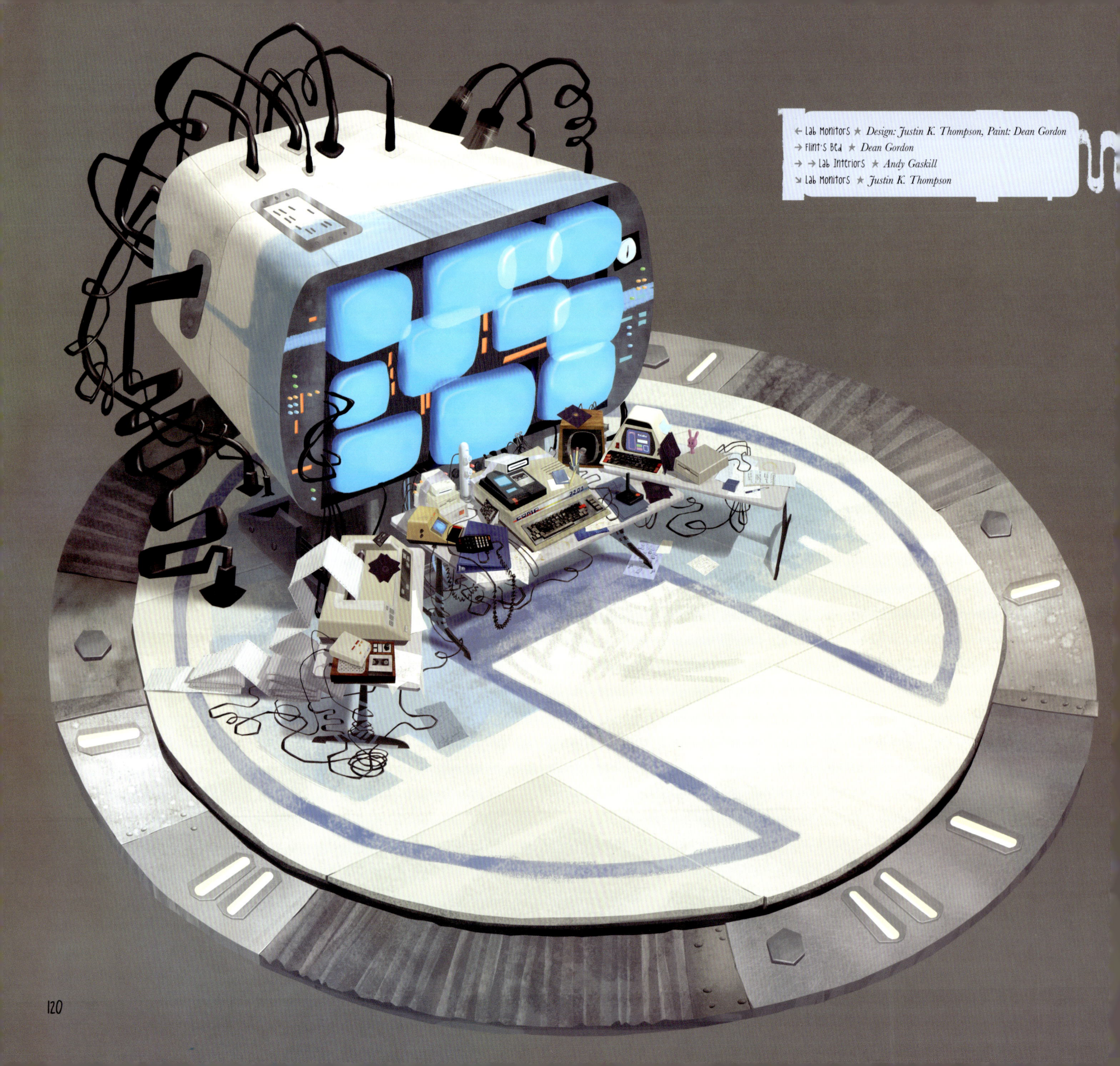

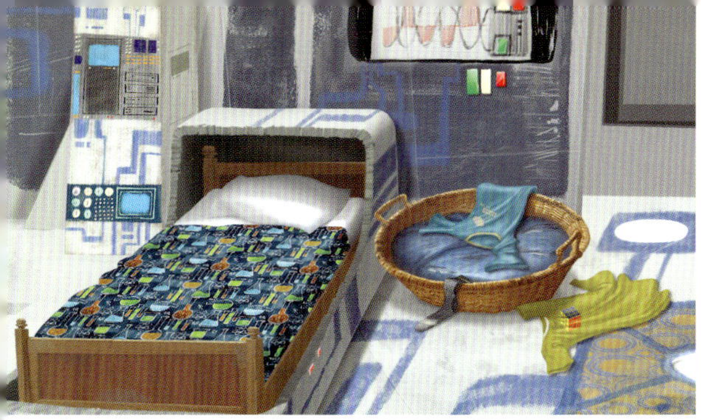
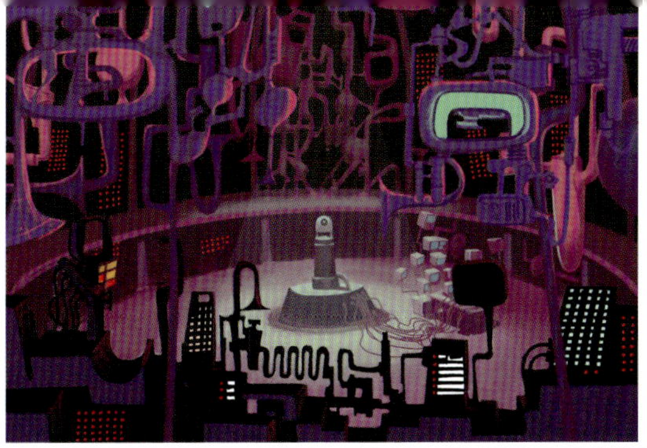
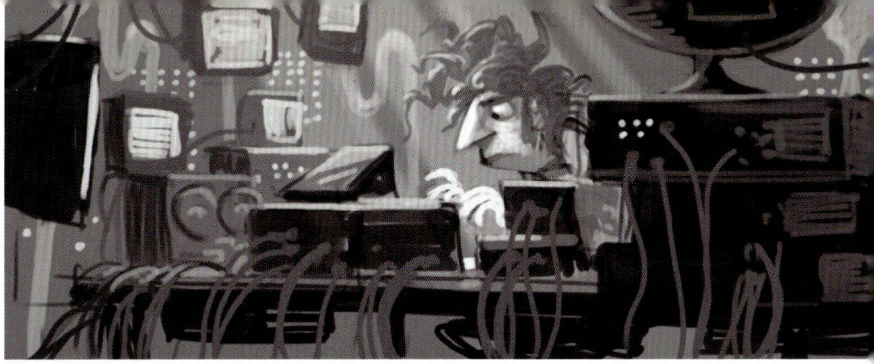
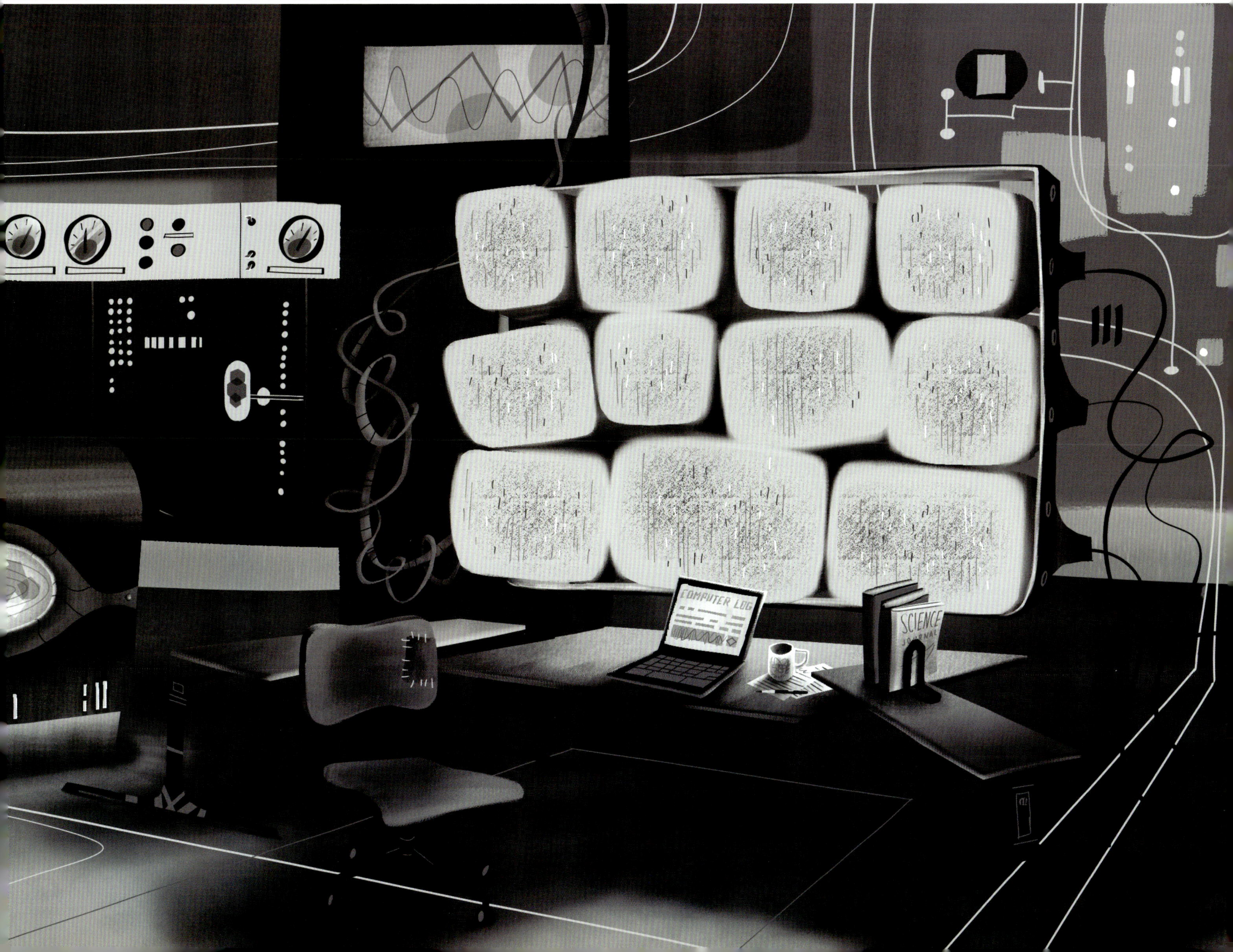
COMPUTER LOG
SCIENCE
JOURNAL

# the food machine/FLDSMDFR

**T**he one invention by Flint that finally gets the town's attention and respect is his food machine, which has a technical mouthful of a name: It's called the Flint Lockwood Diatonic Super Mutating Dynamic Food Replicator, or in its equally difficult to say acronym, it is known as the FLDSMDFR. The concept of how it works is simple, if one casts aside logic and allows cartoon chemistry to take over: "Water goes in the top and food comes out the bottom" is Flint's basic explanation. By virtue of its design, the FLDSMDFR gives the impression that Flint is a *Star Wars* fan, as it has "a touch of droid combined with a kitchen appliance," notes visual development artist Chris Reccardi. This prop was the first hard surface built by the modeling department, and "it really helped establish the style for our team, plus it involved the building of a number of buttons and details that we were able to reuse throughout other sets and props," recalls modeling supervisor Marvin Kim. Most importantly, it is the means of propelling the story into hyperspeed and the look of the film into hypercolor.

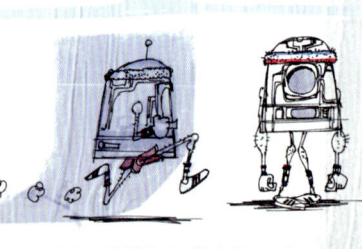

↑ ↗ Food Machine ★ *Chris Reccardi*
↙ Food Machine ★ *Digital*
↘ Food Machine ★ *Michael Kurinsky*

↑ Food Machine ★ *Chris Reccardi*

↑ Motion Graphic ★ *Design: Justin K. Thompson, Paint: Michael Kurinsky*

> *"I wanted to make the rainbow colors of the machine a theme because it reminded me of late 1970s science fiction movies like Star Trek: The Motion Picture. It wound up representing the idea that Flint's goal was to bring color to his dull, grey town."*
> – Phil Lord, *Director*
>
> *"The FLDSMDFR was an unusual challenge because we had to design a prop that became a character that became an environment, affecting everything and dominating the entire world by the end of the movie."*
> – Justin K. Thompson, *Production Designer*

← Food Machine ★ *Chris Reccardi*  ↓ Food Machine ★ *Final Frame*

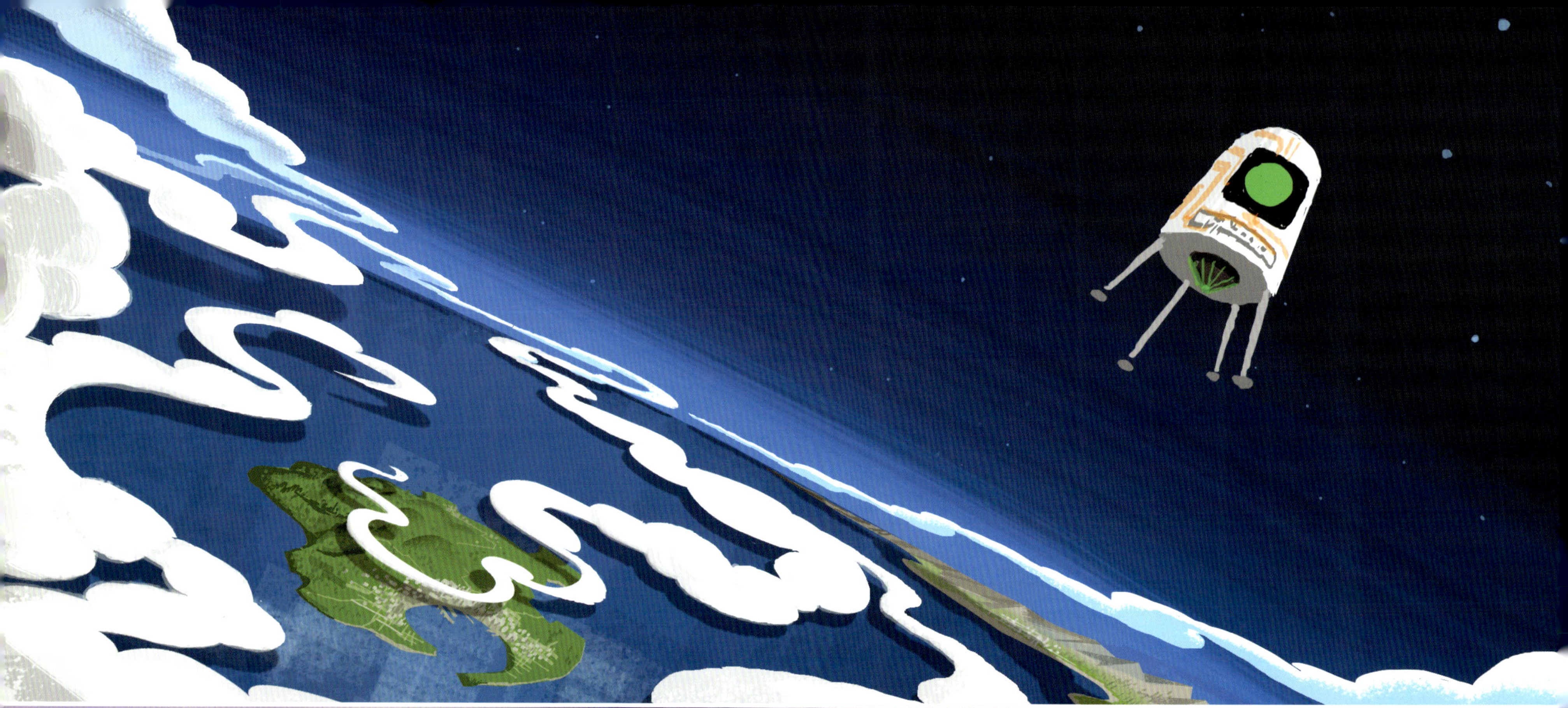

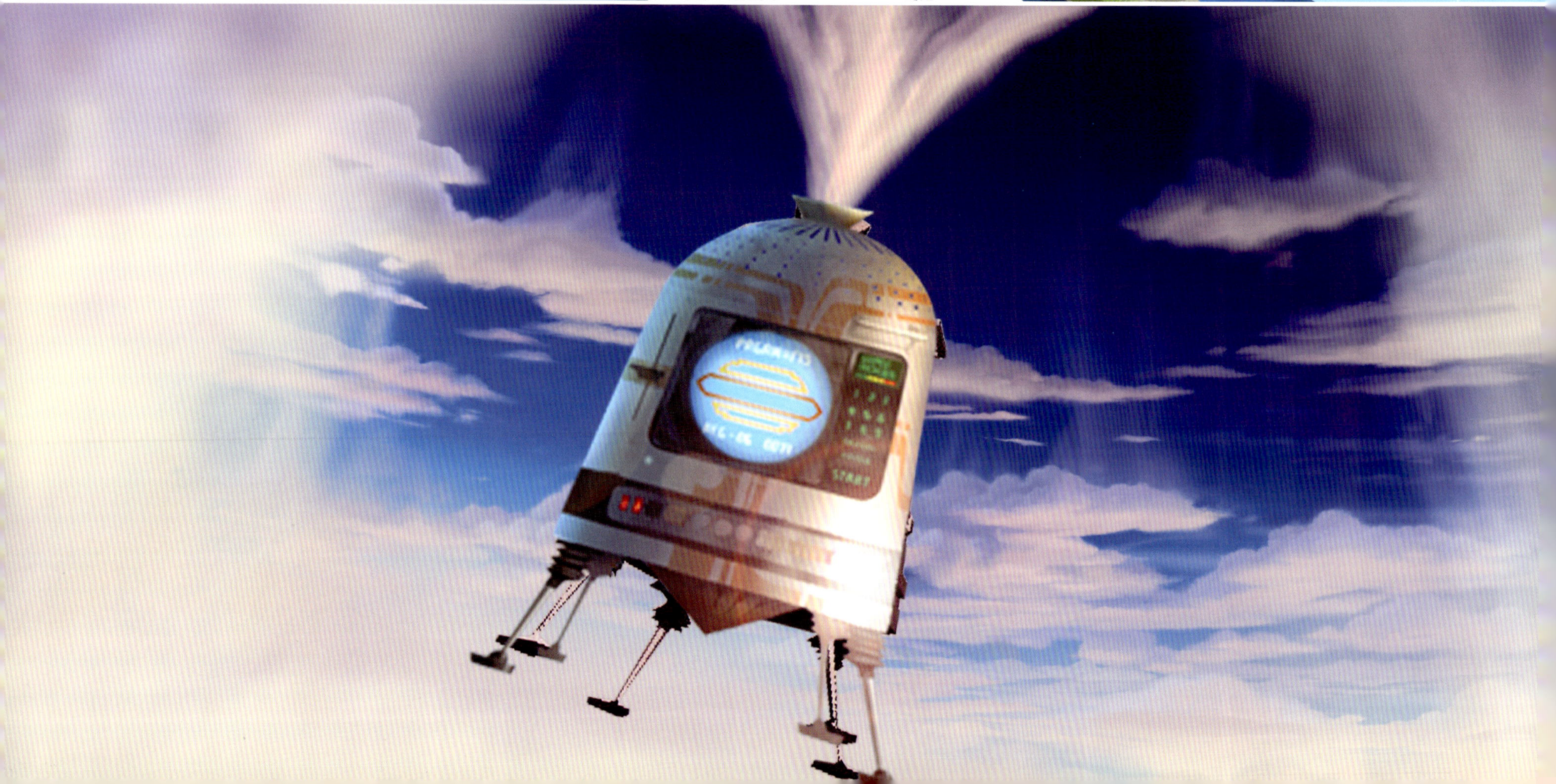

| INITIALIZING | MEATBALL | GARLIC BREAD | ASPARAGUS | SHRIMP | CELERY | SPAGHETTI |

- ↑ FLDSMDFR Screen Graphics ★ *Digital*
- ↘ Food Machine & Food ★ *Dean Gordon*
- ← Food Machine Launch ★ *Chris Reccardi*
- ↙ Food Machine ★ *Dean Gordon*

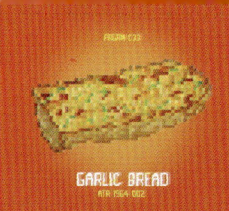

PRGRM=
PG-06  0077

125

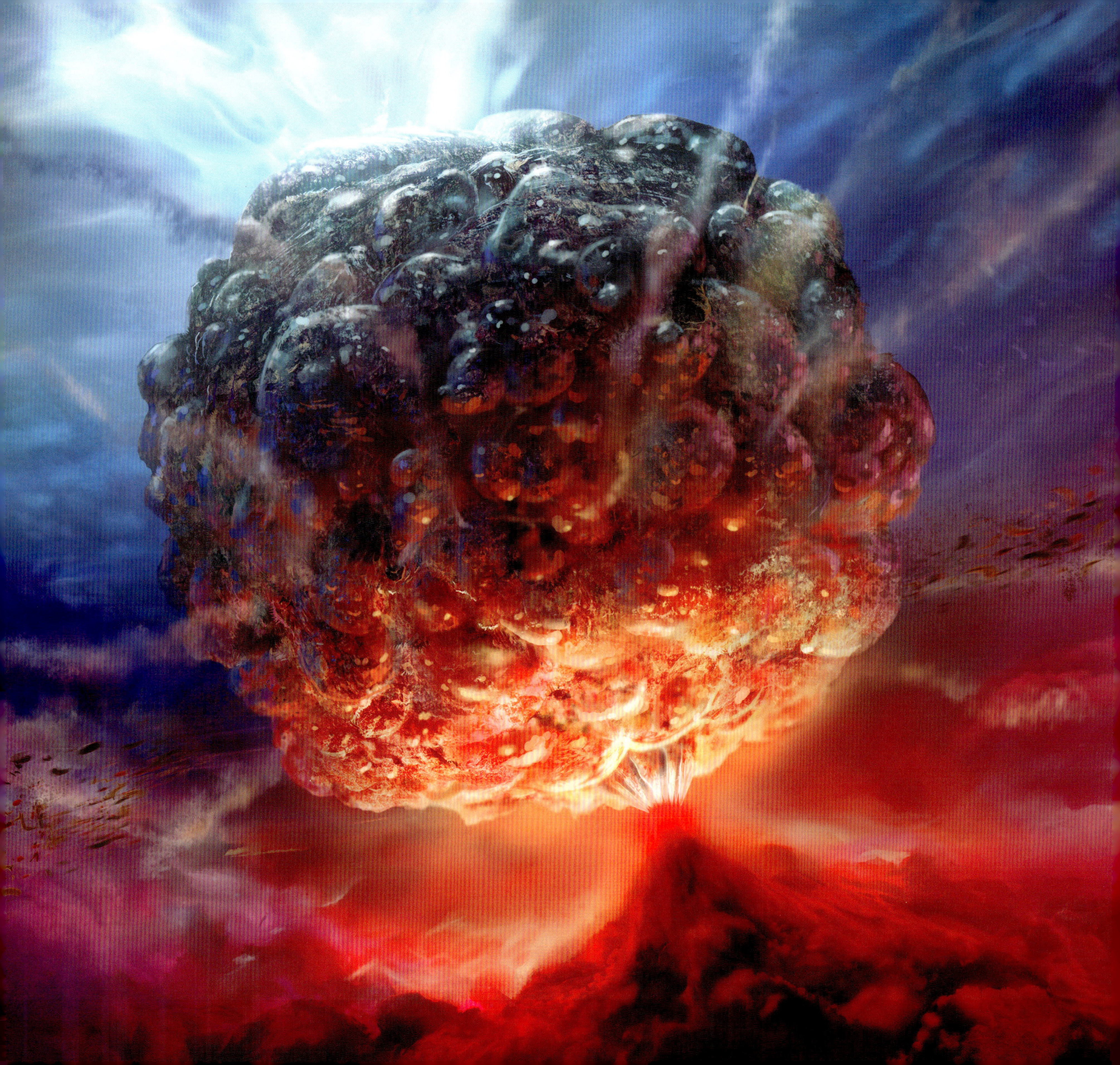

# Production Design
## The Many Flavors of Revitalization

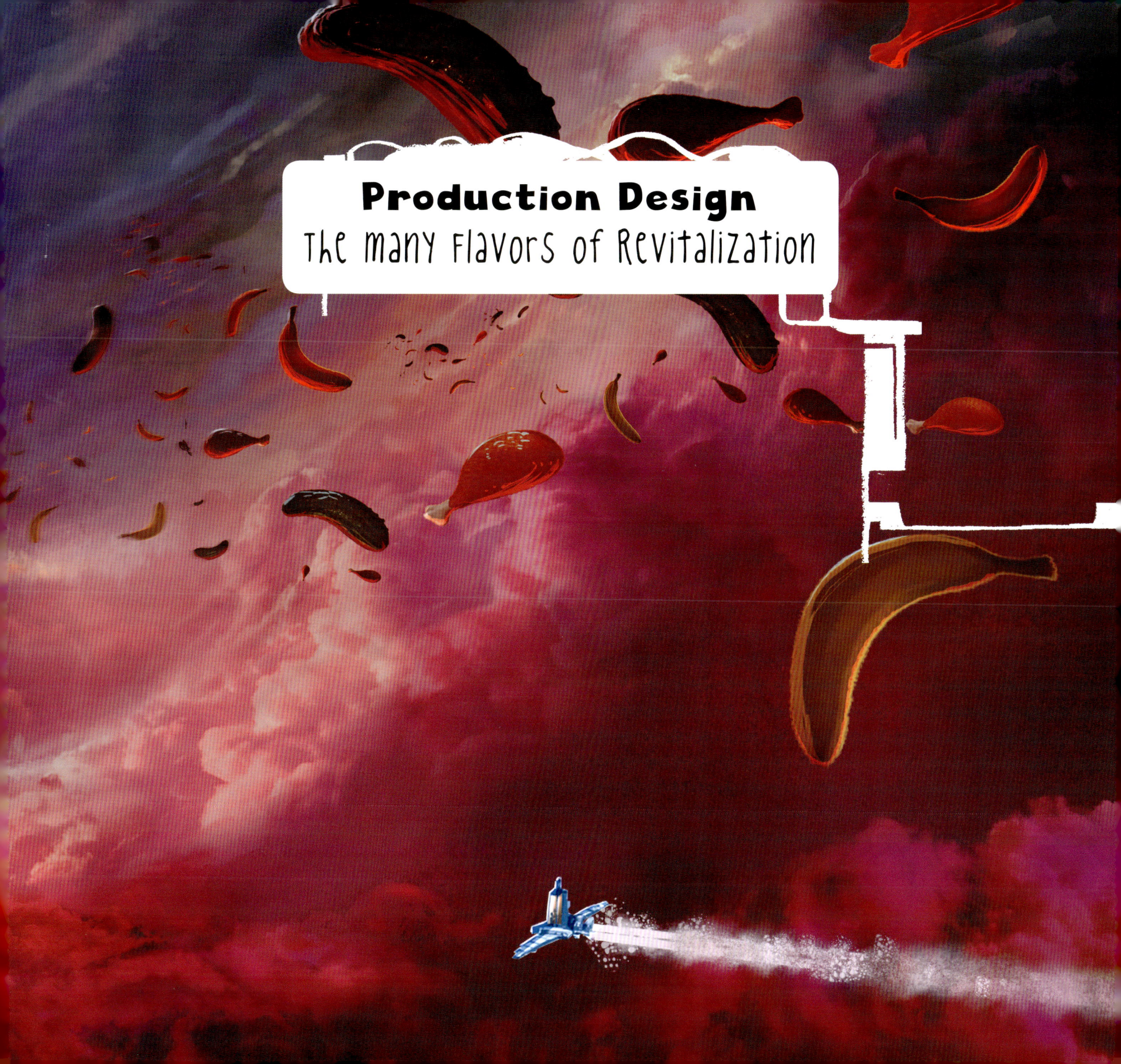

# Clouds

As suggested by the title of this film, clouds are an important part of this very weather-minded project. There was a vast amount of shape, texture, and color exploration, and the effort was great because the visual development team knew they had to find the perfect cumulus construct to serve as a beacon for story progression, providing visual cues to enhance good or bad turns of events. "We wanted the clouds to be less complex texturally so that they are believable for the look of this world, but depth, strength, and volume remained more realistic because the lighting is so rich," explains production designer Justin K. Thompson. To achieve this look, the matte painters blended texture with a wide range of colors, and then the Imageworks team put its dynamic SVEA volume rendering software and its photorealistic ARNOLD lighting system to the test.

When the film begins, the clouds are naturalistic in shape and color, acting as something of a damper to reflect the depressed state of the town. Then as Flint's invention starts to work, the clouds clear and let the blue sky show through as if heralding happier times to come. As things progress in the realm of falling food, the clouds take on more magical and whimsical shapes. Later, when things get out of control, the clouds look ominous and scary to add tension to the story. In fact, the clouds play an important role in creating this tenuous situation, as they mask the corrupt machine that hovers above, disseminating its light and presence while fueling its power.

It's obvious that this crew's cloud efforts were well spent, not just some "pie in the sky" attempt at special effects.

Previous Spread APPROACHING THE MEATEROID ★ Design: Simon Rodgers, Paint: Noelle Triaureau
↓ Weather News Network ★ Final Frame

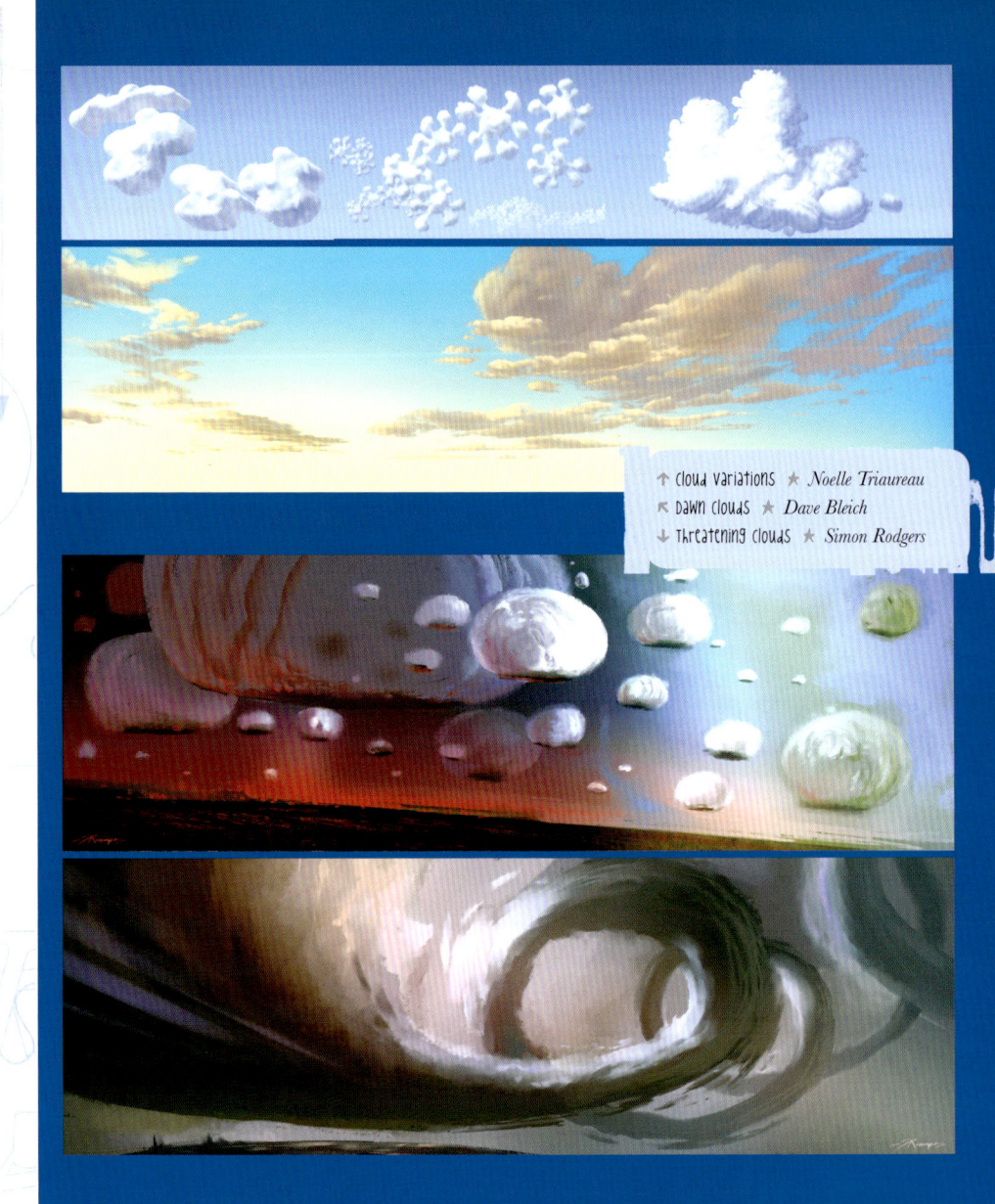

↑ Cloud Variations ★ Noelle Triaureau
↖ Dawn Clouds ★ Dave Bleich
↓ Threatening Clouds ★ Simon Rodgers

→ Violent Clouds ★ Noelle Triaureau

128

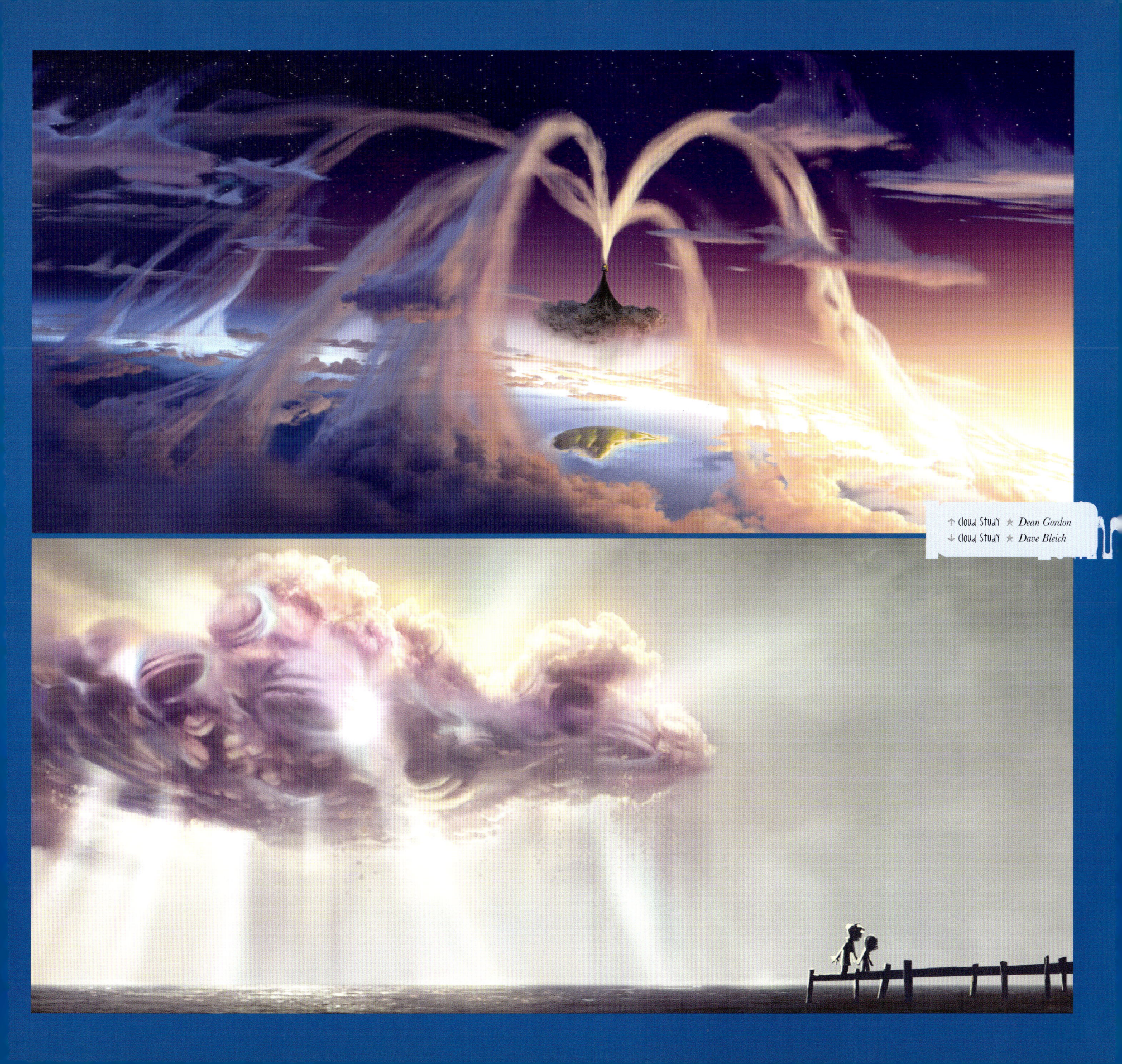

↑ Cloud Study ★ *Dean Gordon*
↓ Cloud Study ★ *Dave Bleich*

# Burger Rain

The FLDSMDFR proves its power with the downfall of a burger rain upon Swallow Falls. After its unintentional launch into the stratosphere, the machine pulls moisture from the skies, or in Sam's geek speak, it works by "inducing a molecular phase change of the vapor from the cumulonimbus layer" and thus creates massive amounts of food. Its effect upon the town is immediate, in more ways than the obvious one of raining burgers. Primarily, it is this occurrence that produces mutual fascination between Sam and Flint: Flint has finally impressed someone with an invention and feels validated by this connection, and Sam has finally let down her guard enough to allow her brainy side a voice in expressing her excitement about this scientific phenomena. It is also the impetus for the Mayor to ramp up his self-promotion, kicking his greed into high gear because "This is big," and, coincidentally, he had just stated that "This town's too small for me. . . . I want to be big!"

Speaking of big, the task of editing the "burger rain" sequence was a huge undertaking unto itself. It was important for the story team to build in small indicators to foreshadow what was coming, and it was vital to roll these out with the proper pacing to build the maximum tension and anticipation worthy of such a momentous event. "There is a balance between taking too much time and making an event anticlimactic, or rushing to the moment and not making the payoff feel as rewarding as it should," notes editor Bob Fisher, who brought years of live-action experience to this film. "I wanted to keep the audience in Flint's perspective to truly appreciate how big of a moment this is," and in doing so, Fisher deftly found the perfect timing to make the burger rain a wondrously jaw-dropping reveal.

Visually, the burger rain launches the second act of art direction for the film. A new, brighter color language is immediately obvious in the changing skies over the town, shifting from drab greys and tans to the more magical combination of pinks, magentas, yellows, and violets. Inspired by the palette of *Edward Scissorhands*, art director Michael Kurinsky explains that he "wanted to go from a very desaturated palette, which represented Flint's state of mind as he lost control of his invention, to the most warm, saturated, vibrant colors to show his unexpected triumph and to herald the beginning of good times for the town." The FLDSMDFR serves as a source of illumination as well, casting a faint version of its "rainbow disco ball" component's light through the clouds and into the spectrum. The clouds begin to take on a less natural shape, and the camera takes the audience on an imaginative ride by working on the diagonal, going into deep space, and even going to the point of absurd at times: The long, drawn out "GASP!" scene in response to the falling burgers is pure entertainment and certainly not the expected use of cinematography.

*"I can't tell you how many times I re-boarded the 'burger rain' sequence, but I can tell you that I ate way too many cheeseburgers while working on it. Drawing food really makes you hungry!"*
—**KRIS PEARN** Head of Story

↑ Burger Clouds ★ *Final Frame*
← ↑ Falling Food Effects Animation Tests ★ *Digital*

Technically, the falling-food concept was an appetizing challenge for the Imageworks crew, as it asks so many questions: Do the buns, meat, cheese, and toppings fly apart while in the air, or upon impact, or not at all? What level of bounce do these items have? Does ketchup splatter out when the burger hits the ground? These questions had to be answered even before the first patty of meat could be modeled, as the crew needed to know if each ingredient would be built as a separate element or if the entire burger would be a single piece of geometry. The decision was made to model each element separately, "then to bind them as if they are held together by an invisible string, courtesy of the Rigid Body Dynamics (RBD) system," explains visual effects supervisor Rob Bredow. "A lot of work went into the Soft Body Collision extension of RBD, figuring out how to make burgers bounce, break apart, and still look appealing," recalls digital effects supervisor Daniel Kramer. "Without RBD, we would have had to spend infinite hours animating each piece of falling food individually and we would never have gotten the movie done," adds co-producer Chris Juen. RBD FTW!

↑ Beatboard ★ Jerry Loveland

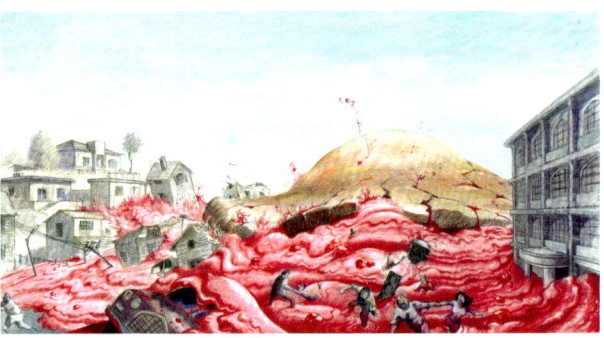

↑ Falling Pie & Soda ★ Gaëtan & Paul Brizzi

↑ Falling Candy Corn ★ Ted Blackman
→ Storyboards ★ Jeff Ranjo
↘ Pizzas ★ Michael Kurinsky

PUDDING.

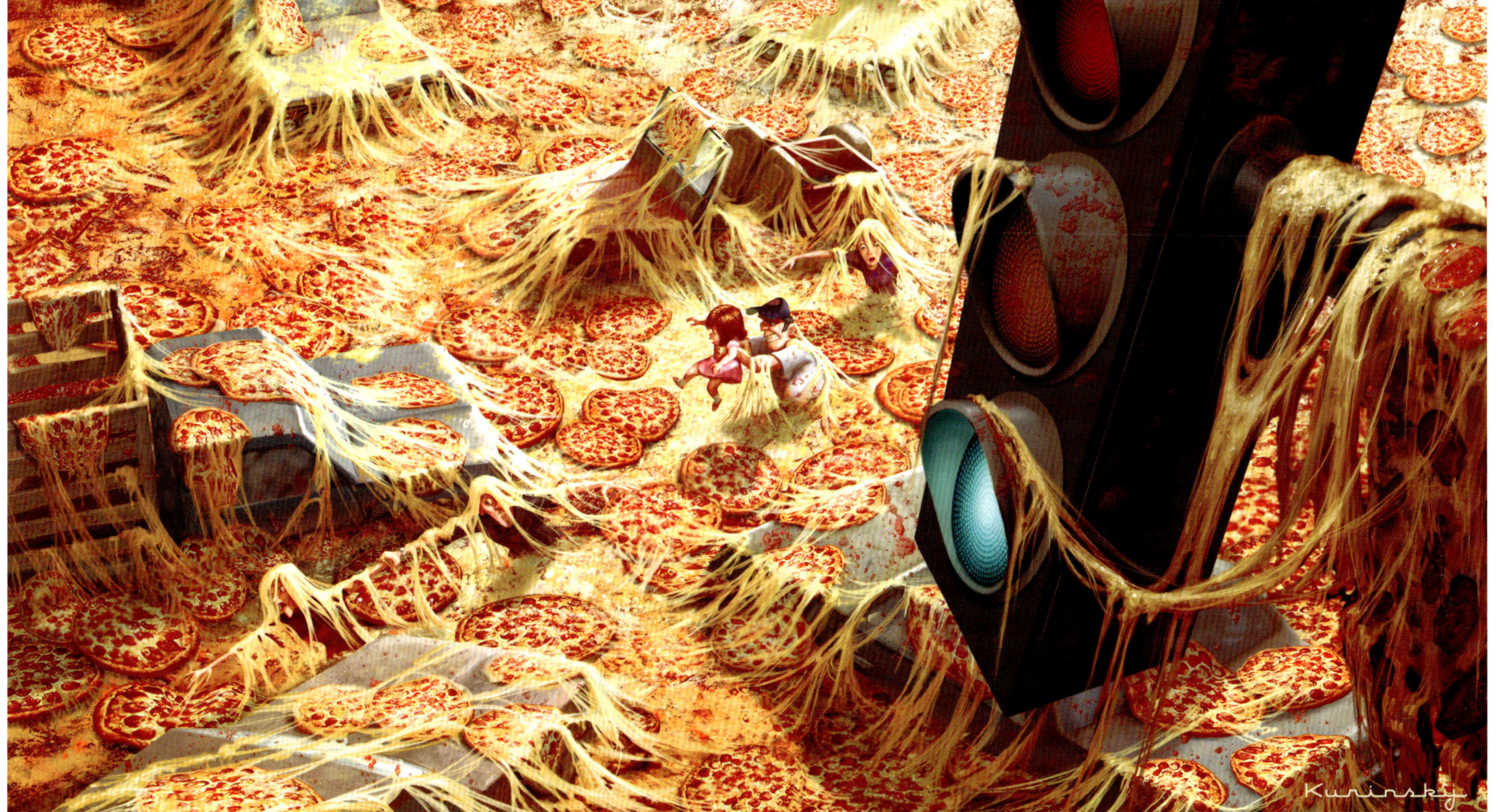

BALONEY.

CHICKEN TIKKA

CORN DOGS

BABAGANOUSH.

PANCAKES.

CRABCAKES

CHEESE BALLS

FUNNEL CAKES.

GUMBO

MU GU GAI PAN.

CHICKEN PAD THAI

KIELBASA.

BUTTER FUDGE

MEL, MORE GUAC.

# Food Props

The food items themselves bring a whole new sense of color and vitality to the town. "The food is designed to resemble perfect little gems, based on the illustrations often used in ads and menus from the 1950s," notes production designer Justin K. Thompson, and these idyllic representations were carefully grounded to blend into the look of the world by "adding realism to a simple cartoon shape, such as the cracking glaze on the donuts," adds Kurinsky.

*"Who knew getting broccoli to look good was so hard and expensive?"*
—**MICHAEL KURINSKY** Art Director

↑ ↗ Watermelon & Ham  ★ Cristy Maltese
↑ ↗ Donut & Cherry Pie  ★ Noelle Triaureau
↗ Pretzel & Hot Dog  ★ Michael Kurinsky

Swallow Falls undergoes a mouthwatering makeover as food begins to fall from its skies. "The simplicity of the town was like having a fresh canvas for each act, allowing me to easily create new lighting and color scenarios as the story progressed," explains art director Michael Kurinsky. Blossoming from drab, grey tones to at least thirty-one flavors of color, the town reemerges as Chewandswallow, a vibrant community full of energy and hope.

↓ Top Images Swallow Falls ★ Design: Antonio Canobbio & Justin K. Thompson, Paint: Dave Bleich, Dean Gordon & Michael Kurinsky
↓ Bottom Image Swallow Falls ★ Design: Armand Serrano, Paint: Noelle Triaureau

↘ Top Images Chewandswallow ★ Design: Simon Rodgers, Armand Serrano & Justin K. Thompson, Paint: Dave Bleich, & Dean Gordon
↘ Bottom Image Chewandswallow ★ Design: Armand Serrano, Paint: Noelle Triaureau

MARSHMALLOW WAREHOUSE
GET YOUR PICTURE TAKEN WITH FOOD
parsley's
CHEW AND
SWALLOW
CITY HALL
XXXXXXL T-SHIRTS
INTERNATIONAL HOUSE OF CUMIN

FLINT LOCKWOOD NAPKINS
NECKBUCKETS
LIKE A BUCKET ... ... BUT FOR YOUR NECK!
HANDS FREE EATING !
THE OPEN TROUGH
YOUR NAME ENGRAVED ON A BANANA
JUST HAM
Mouth funnels
spicemarket
MICROSURGICAL STOMACH STAPLE REVERSAL
BEFORE
AFTER
www.stomachstaplereversal.com
PAPER TOWEL SUITS
HAND-TAILORED DISPOSABLE CLOTHES

Bibs
FORKS FORKS FORKS
KNIVES KNIVES KNIVES
SPOONS
31
flavors of SALT
HOUSE of PEPPER
ANTI-GAS tablets

SARDINES

# welcome to chewandswallow

**W**ith this miraculous event, Mayor Shelbourne is inspired to use this phenomena to draw attention and even more tourists to his island community, and he propels the town into complete food-centric makeover mode, all the way down to renaming it Chewandswallow, which readers of the original children's book will recognize. Establishments including the Marshmallow Warehouse and the International House of Cumin open for business, and the growing needs of the town are satisfied by purveyors of gadgetry such as mouth funnels, neck buckets, and, inevitably, XXXXXXL T-shirts.

↑ Chateau Mignon ★ *Michael Kurinsky*

↑ Welcome to Chewandswallow ★ *Chris Mitchell*

↑ World's Largest Lazy Susan ★ *Ted Blackman*
← Chewandswallow Theme Park ★ Design: *Simon Rodgers*, Paint: *Noelle Triaureau*

← Marshmallow Warehouse ★ Design: *Simon Rodgers*, Paint: *Dean Gordon*

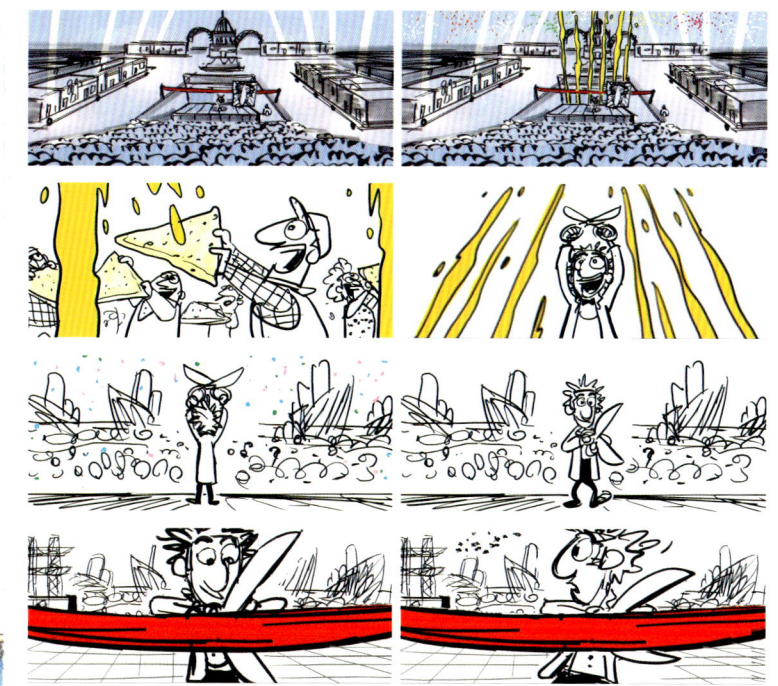

## CHE COLORKEYS

▸ Billboard ★ Bruce McCall
▸ Storyboards ★ Jack Hsu
▸ Color keys ★ Dean Gordon

This sequence portrays the first time Flint has ever been heralded for his inventions. The worldwide attention and excitement bring new color and life to both the town and Flint's perspective.

# Roofless Restaurant

The Sardiner is renovated into the posh Roofless Restaurant, which is swankier than anything the town has ever seen, replete in all of its stainless steel, neon, and plate-glass glory. The materials chosen for this model portray a subtle but effective shift in art direction: "As the town finds success, its constructs become less handmade and more synthetic," explains production designer Justin K. Thompson. The restaurant almost glows with its less textured, more polished look than anything in the former version of town, reinforcing to the audience how new and cool it is. It's also symbolic of Flint's state of mind, characterizing all the glamour and fame that Flint has never experienced before this moment, shining so brightly that it blinds him to reality.

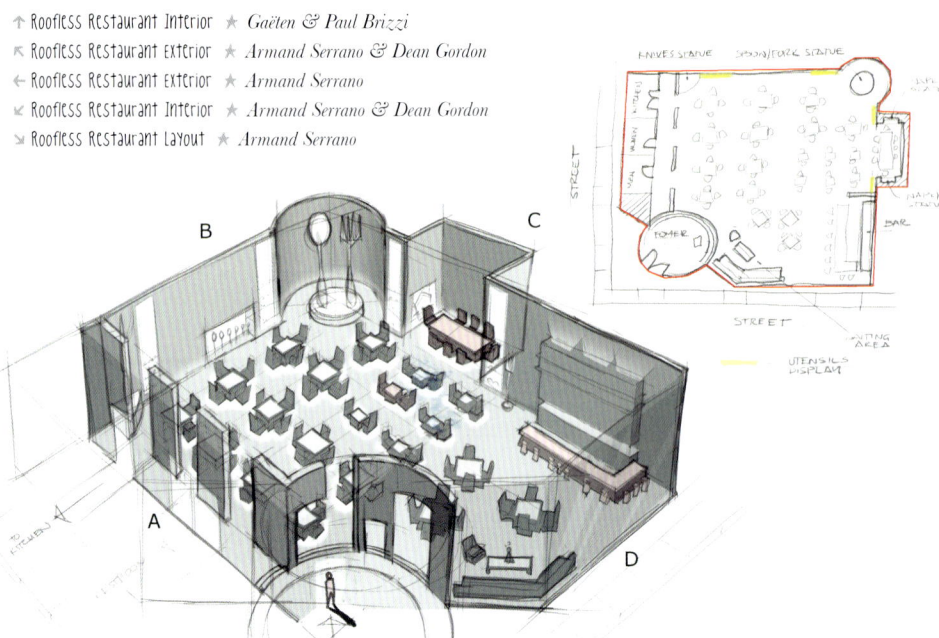

↑ Roofless Restaurant Interior ★ Gaëten & Paul Brizzi
↖ Roofless Restaurant Exterior ★ Armand Serrano & Dean Gordon
← Roofless Restaurant Exterior ★ Armand Serrano
↙ Roofless Restaurant Interior ★ Armand Serrano & Dean Gordon
↘ Roofless Restaurant Layout ★ Armand Serrano

# RES COLOR KEYS

"The relationship between Flint and Tim shows that even when father and son are two very different people, they can still find common ground and mutual respect. At an early screening, the kids in the audience easily picked up on the idea that no matter how out of place you feel as a kid, everyone finds his place in the world when he grows up."
– Hannah Minghella, *President of Production*

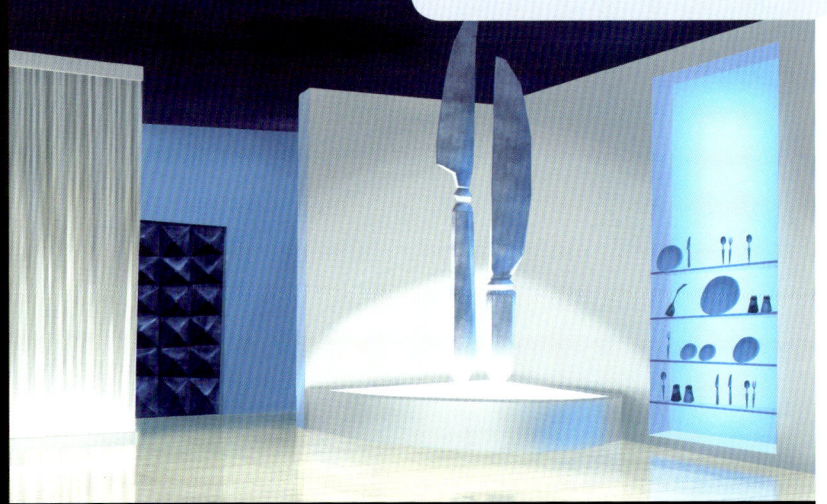

↑ Color keys & Roofless Restaurant Interior ★ *Dean Gordon*
↑ Roofless Restaurant Interior ★ Design: *Armand Serano*, Paint: *Dean Gordon*
← Roofless Restaurant Interior ★ Digital

# The Outtasighter

↓ Outtasighter ★ Chris Reccardi

**A**nother of Flint's inventions makes its debut after a few showers of hot dogs, pizza, waffles, and more—the Outtasighter, which could be best described as a street sweeper with oversized utensils and an awesome pitching arm. "It's a clever solution that's practical yet whimsical and it seemed like something Flint would create," says director Christopher Miller. Visual development artist Chris Reccardi explains that the vehicle is based on the cab of the generic pickup truck, but then it gets "ridiculous, in a good way." Reccardi recalls that he started to design a powerful, heavy-duty Caterpillar-looking construction vehicle, but Miller refocused those efforts by sketching what he had in mind, namely "a truck with a fork and spoon attached by arms with big elbows, more reminiscent of what is in the original children's book." The purpose of the Outtasighter is to clear leftovers out of town, simply by scooping them up and catapulting them "out of sight, and therefore, out of mind," as Sam explains in her telecast. While the concept of taking care of pollution and waste is respectable, this particular solution proves to be not as well thought-out as it should have been, later delivering a message on what happens when "the eyes are bigger than the stomach" thinking takes hold and gluttony takes over.

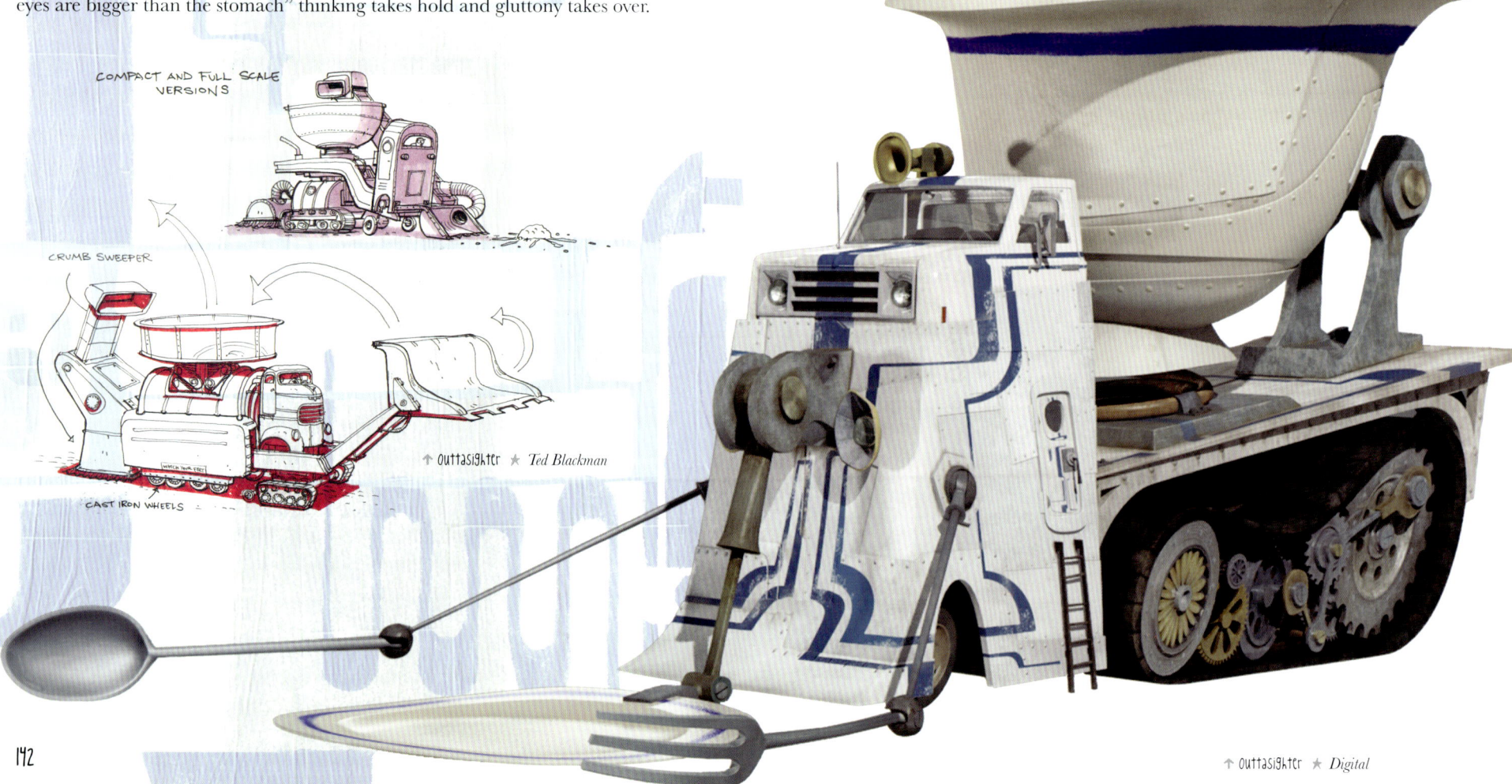

↑ Outtasighter ★ Ted Blackman

↑ Outtasighter ★ Digital

↑ Outtasighter ★ *Bruce McCall*
↖ Storyboards ★ *Michael Lester*

The food dam is located just outside of Chewandswallow proper, and it is the point of collection for all of the Outtasighter's leftover-wrangling efforts. Mountains of food have ended up in the dam, due to the townfolks' eyes becoming bigger than their stomachs: Although their midsections did stretch, their ever-expanding desire for more, more, and more food created simply too much to be eaten. Not to spoil the story line with all this spoiled-food talk, but it is worth noting that when the town's overactive appetite overruns the capacity of the dam, it's a thoughtful lesson to see the devastating effects of their gluttony come crashing down upon them, literally.

→ Dam Side Profile ★ *Simon Rodgers*
↓ The Dam ★ Design: *Simon Rodgers*, Paint: *Dave Bleich*

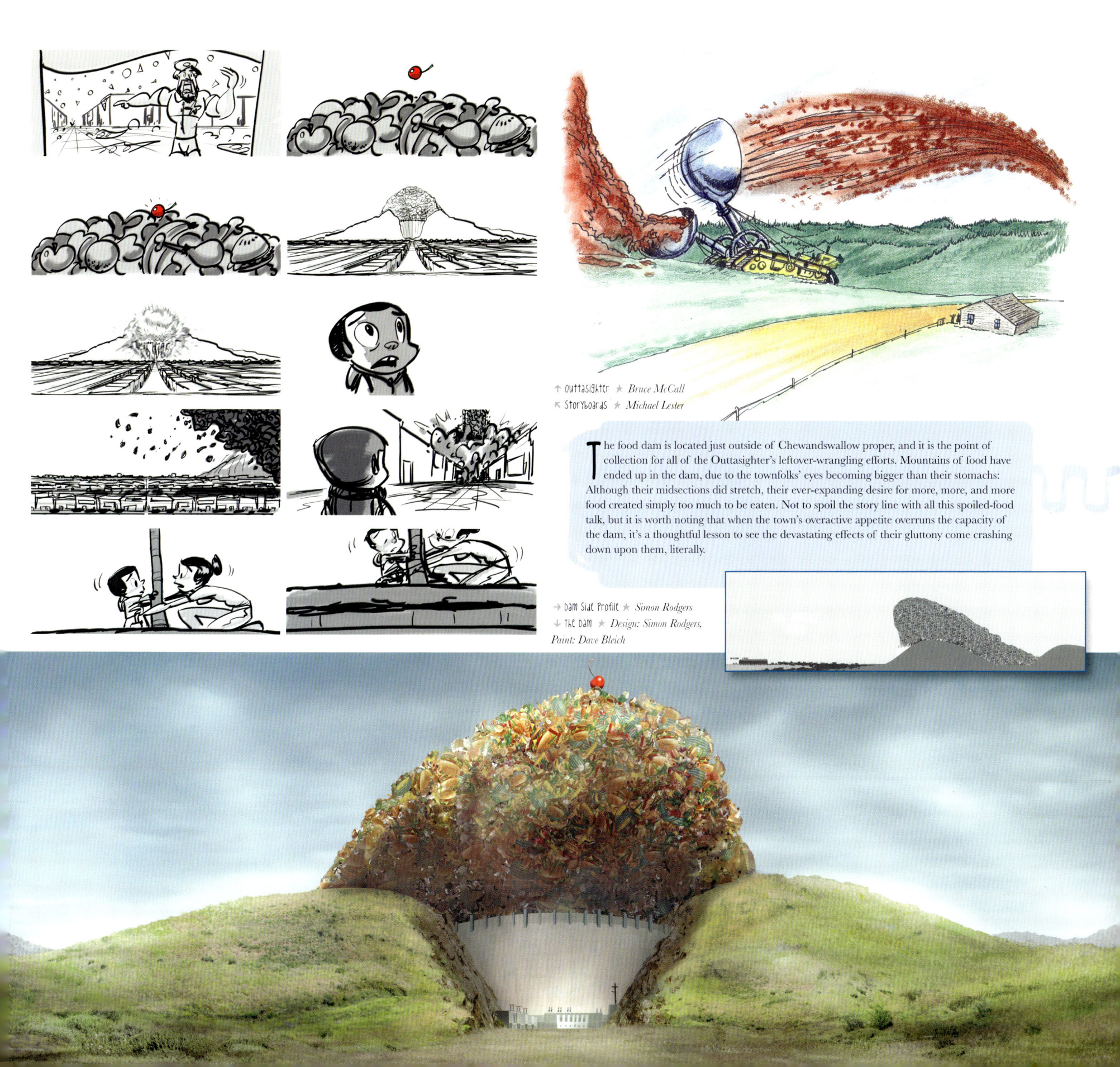

↓ Outtasighter ★ Ted Blackman

↑ Outtasighter ★ Chris Reccardi

↑ → Outtasighter ★ Gaëtan & Paul Brizzi

← ↓ ↑ Outtasighter ★ Ted Blackman

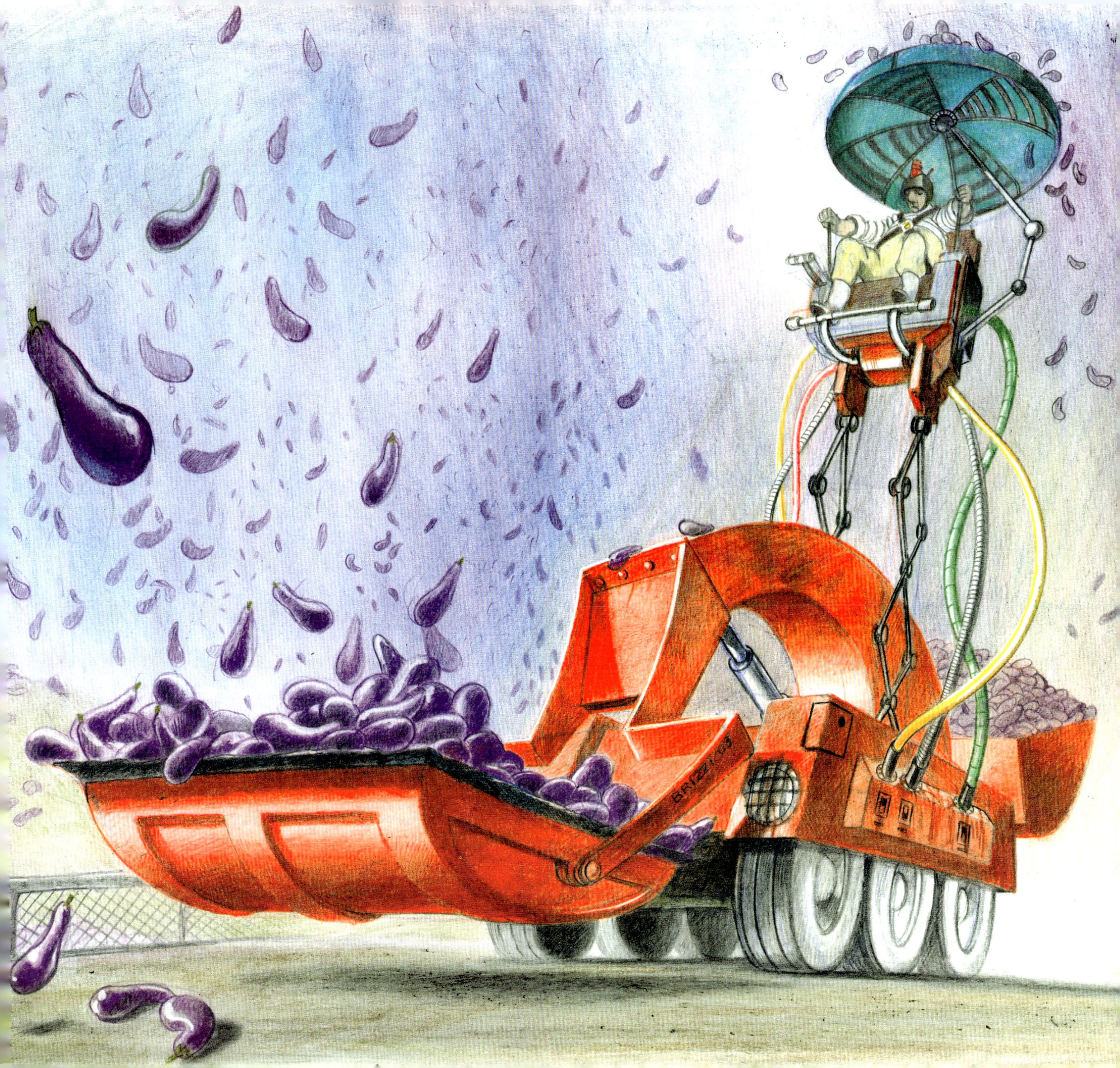
BRIZZI '03

→ Snow Day ★ *Final Frame*

# Snow Day

One of the most breathtaking scenes in the film comes with the dawn of "ice cream snow day," on which the neighborhood is transformed into a pastel winter wonderland. The design team pondered what could differentiate ice cream drifts from a snowfall for quite a while, much longer than the time it takes a visitor to Baskin-Robbins to decide which flavor to choose. "After all that exploration, we came back to the iconic scoop shape, even though the scale of the scoop was notably larger than we had previously used on the falling food," recalls visual development artist Armand Serrano. To paint such a fantasyland, art director Michael Kurinsky was inspired by the palette of Disney artist Mary Blair (*Alice in Wonderland*, *Cinderella*, and *Peter Pan*), and the array of cheerful colors bring an innate sense of joy to the setting.

An important story point sets up the snow day, in that Earl loves his son so much that he is willing to beg the very source of his civic frustration for assistance in creating the special event in honor of Cal's birthday. While this humble act by Earl reminds Flint that his father would probably never think to do something so unexpected for his son, the snow day frivolity distracts Flint from this downer thinking and reminds him that it is good to try to connect with people, an activity for which he is clearly out of practice. Once he realizes how fun a snowball fight can be, Flint's animation really utilizes his Muppet-like movements: "His muscles don't react in a human way, so his floppy limbs support the concept of reckless abandon, showing that he is free of social constraints," notes senior animation supervisor Pete Nash. As if anyone surrounded by mounds of ice cream could be expected to act calmly and rationally. . . .

↓ ↑ Snow Day ★ *Gaëtan & Paul Brizzi*

↑ Ice Cream Man ★ *Noelle Triaureau*

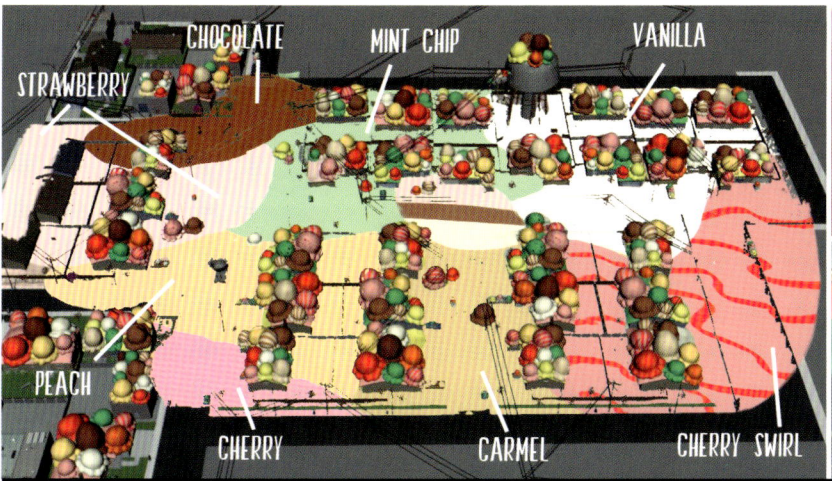

STRAWBERRY · CHOCOLATE · MINT CHIP · VANILLA
PEACH · CHERRY · CARMEL · CHERRY SWIRL

Ice cream topography was well thought-out to create an appealing arrangement of colors. Snowball-fight effects also took color combinations into consideration to ensure that the explosion fallout was a clean visual read.

← ↑ Snowball tests ★ Digital
↖ ↓ Flavor callout Layout & Color Keys ★ *Michael Kurinsky*

# SNO COLORKEYS

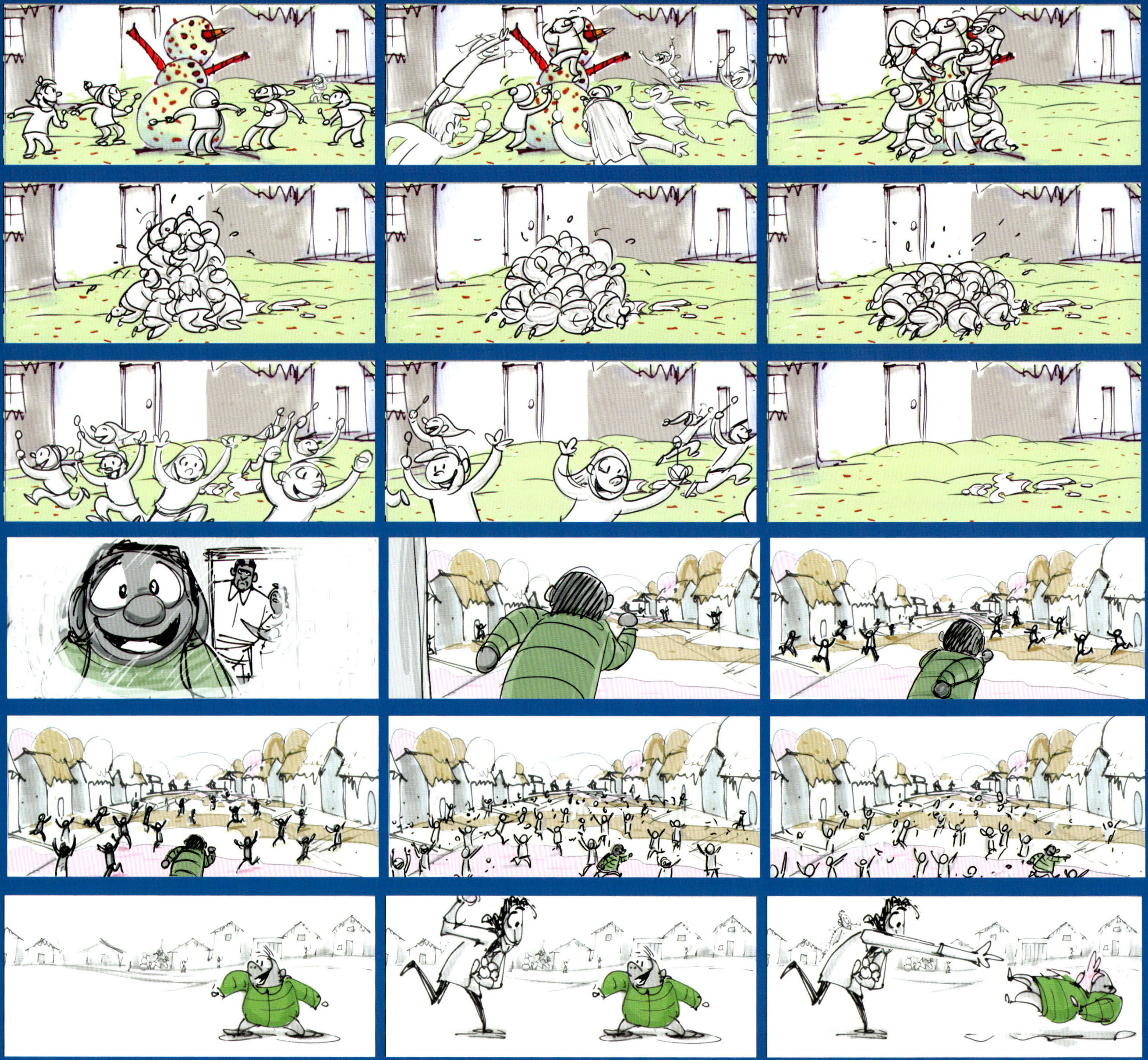

"The pastoral beauty of this sequence really conveys a sense of pure joy in this moment of wish fulfillment." – Kris Pearn, *Head of Story*

"We loved the Handycam approach to the snowball assault, so we just kept telling the animators to make it as awesome as the boards were."
– Christopher Miller, *Director*

Storyboards ★ Cody Cameron

# Jell-O Mold

A nother shiny, happy moment is the unveiling of the gelatin-dessert mold that Flint creates to impress Sam. Oh, sure, Flint says that it was no big deal to "make it rain Jell-O in the middle of the night, then gather it all up with the Outtasighter, then press it into a gigantic custom-carved plastic Tupperware mold" that he made, but the CG crew that actually built this model begs to differ with this statement. "We're told this is supposedly the most complicated set ever built in CG," states director Phil Lord, and visual effects supervisor Rob Bredow explains that it's because this model has to take into account "translucency, refraction, reflection, transmission, and other properties of light and physics."

The directors knew that this location would play a prominent role in their film since it was such a striking image from the original book. "We wanted to make this whimsical design a totally immersive environment," recalls Lord. The action that takes place in the Jell-O mold carries great importance on many levels, and so "I knew we had to make the appearance of the gelatin mold on the horizon a magical moment," recalls editor Bob Fisher. To support this, Fisher made thoughtful pacing and shot choices, but also "did a fantastic job with the temp score, setting the right tone for the scene," notes director Christopher Miller.

In the gelatin mold, Flint finally overcomes his social anxiety and connects with someone, even mustering up the courage to take it even further by going in for the kiss. Sam allows Flint to see some of her nerdy side, and she is transformed by Flint's encouragement to be who she really is and to not hide behind a fake persona. What's fun in this "make-under" is learning that Sam's perspective has been literally and figuratively skewed by her putting on this false self: She is startled when she sees things (namely Flint) much more clearly when she finally puts her glasses back on.

It is also within the Jell-O walls that animation gets to test the film's theory of "concept drives everything." The directors granted their crew the freedom, or rather, the mandate to bend the rules and cheat physics if it supports a character moment, and "here we see that Flint can smoothly walk through the Jell-O wall, but Sam gets stuck," explains digital character animator supervisor Pete Nash. Actual physics would suggest differently, but in the interest of character and comedy, Flint is the expert on Jell-O and other socially strange maneuvers, while Sam is just flustered with the whole situation.

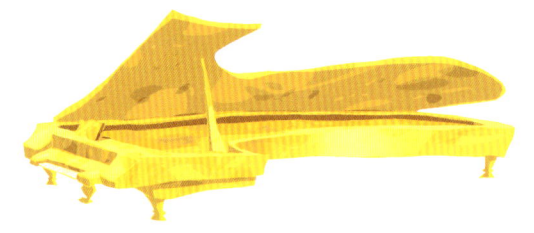

→ Jello-O Mold Path ★ *Cristy Maltese*

↑ ↗ Puppy-Corn & Jell-O Mold Study ★ *Armand Serrano*

↑ ↗ Jell-O Fish Tank and Grand Piano ★ *Cristy Maltese*

→ Jell-O Mold In The Woods ★ *Gaëtan & Paul Brizzi*

↓ Jell-O Mold Establishing Shot ★ Design: *Armand Serrano*, Paint: *Dave Bleich*

← → Early Jello-O Test  ★ *Digital*

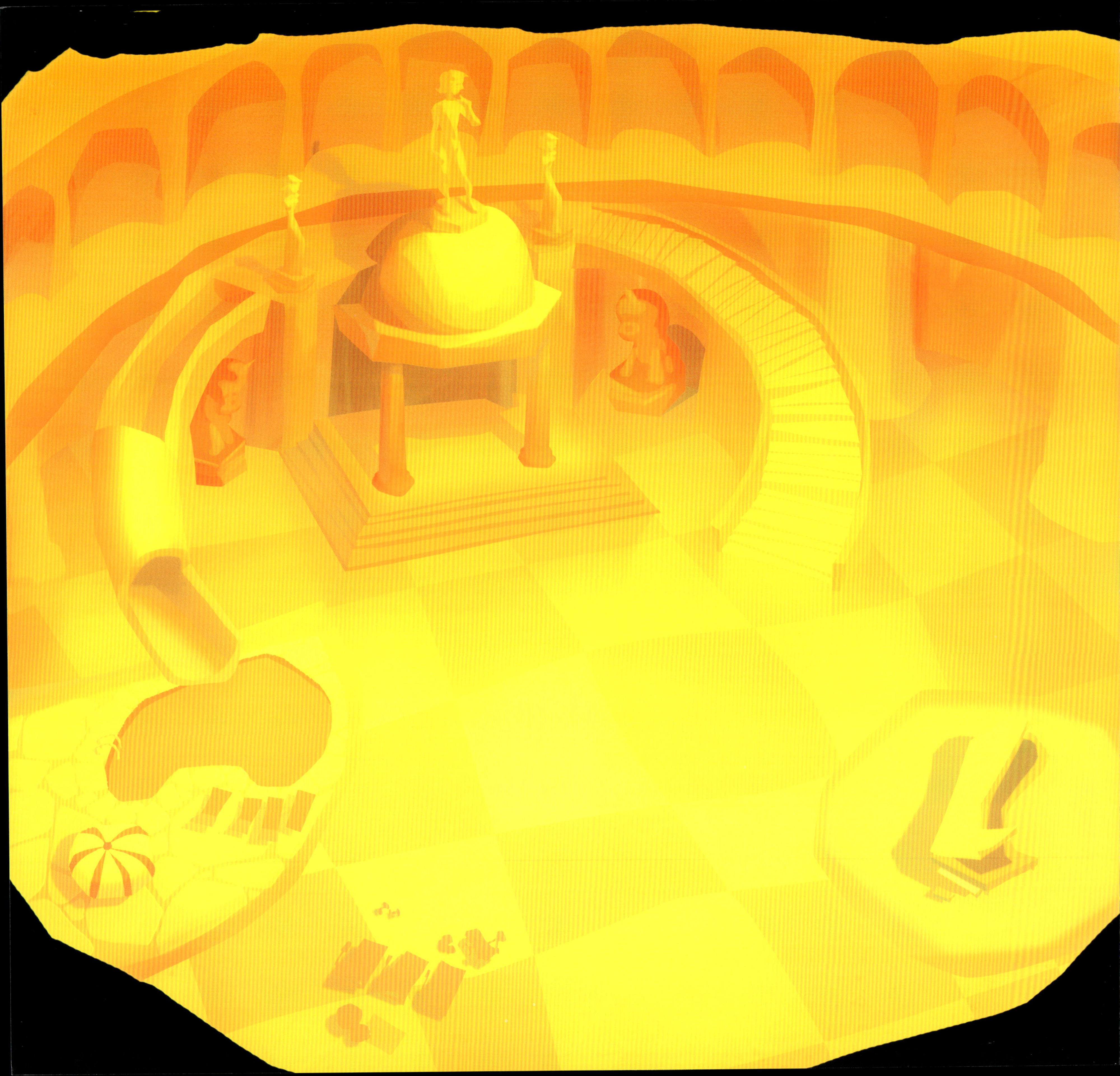

## GDM COLORKEYS

Storyboards ★ John Norton
Color Keys ★ Michael Kurinsky
Jell-O Mold Interior ★ Design: Armand Serrano, Paint: Cristy Maltese

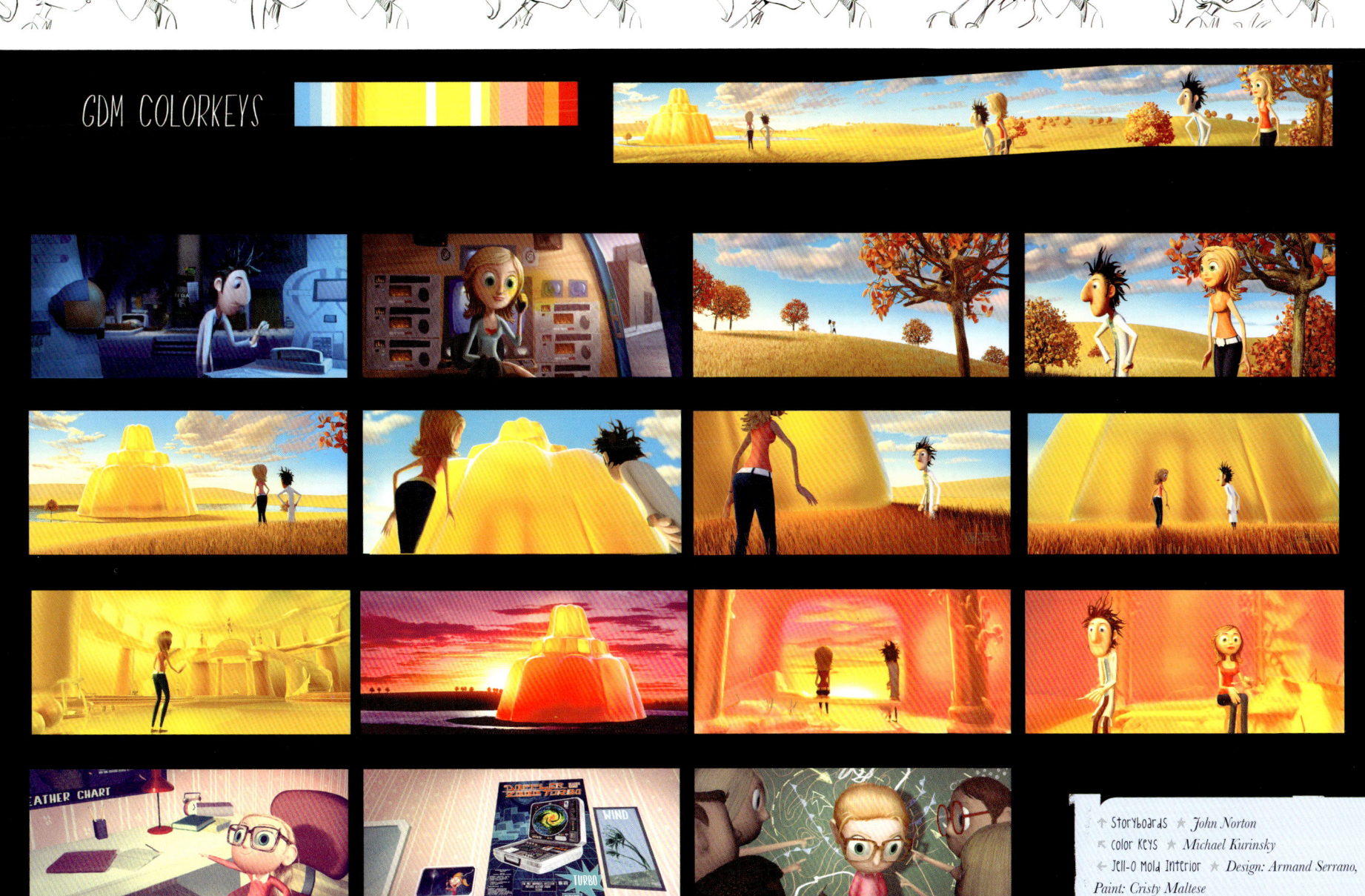

→ Final Frames ★ Digital

# Lighting

An even more subtle but effective tool used in establishing the world of *Cloudy* is lighting. Swallow Falls is initially presented in a very natural, flat light, once again relying on the familiar to welcome the audience into this community.

This realistic lighting is created through Imageworks' custom version of ARNOLD, a system that "uses ray tracing to create more natural, beautiful lighting situations than previously possible in computer-generated animation," explains CG supervisor Danny Dimian. This render technology was first used on the film *Monster House* to calculate lighting, shadows, and reflections, and the *Cloudy* crew couldn't be more thrilled with its progress since then. "The audience can really be distracted by shadows that fall incorrectly, but with ray tracing, it's always done right," adds Dimian.

↑ Test Renderings of Town Square at Midday and Sunset ★ *Digital*

*"In the spirit of food theme, we even named our lighting teams appropriately: We had Team Donut, Team Nacho, Team Sardine, and Team Tomato."*
—ROB BREDOW Visual Effects Supervisor

154

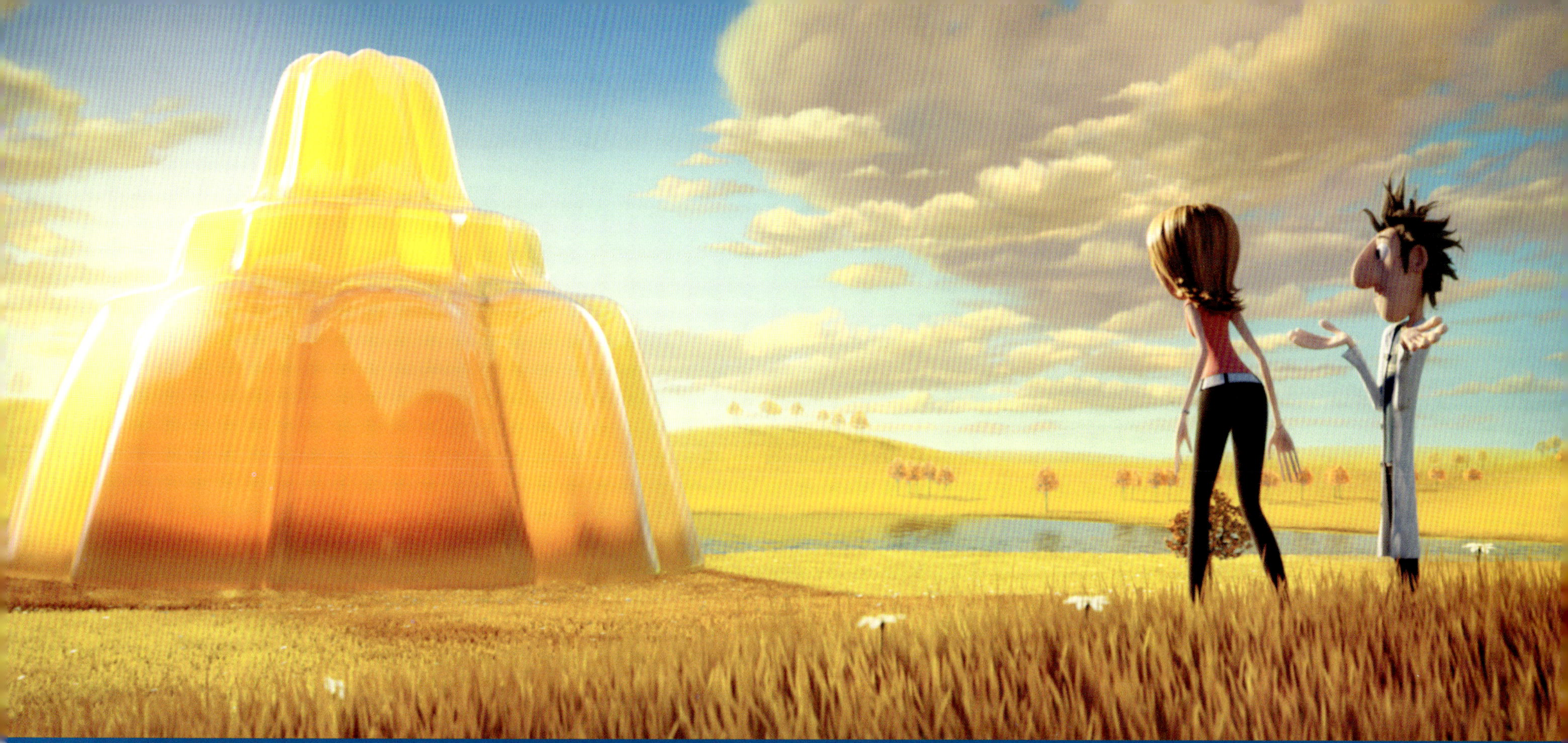

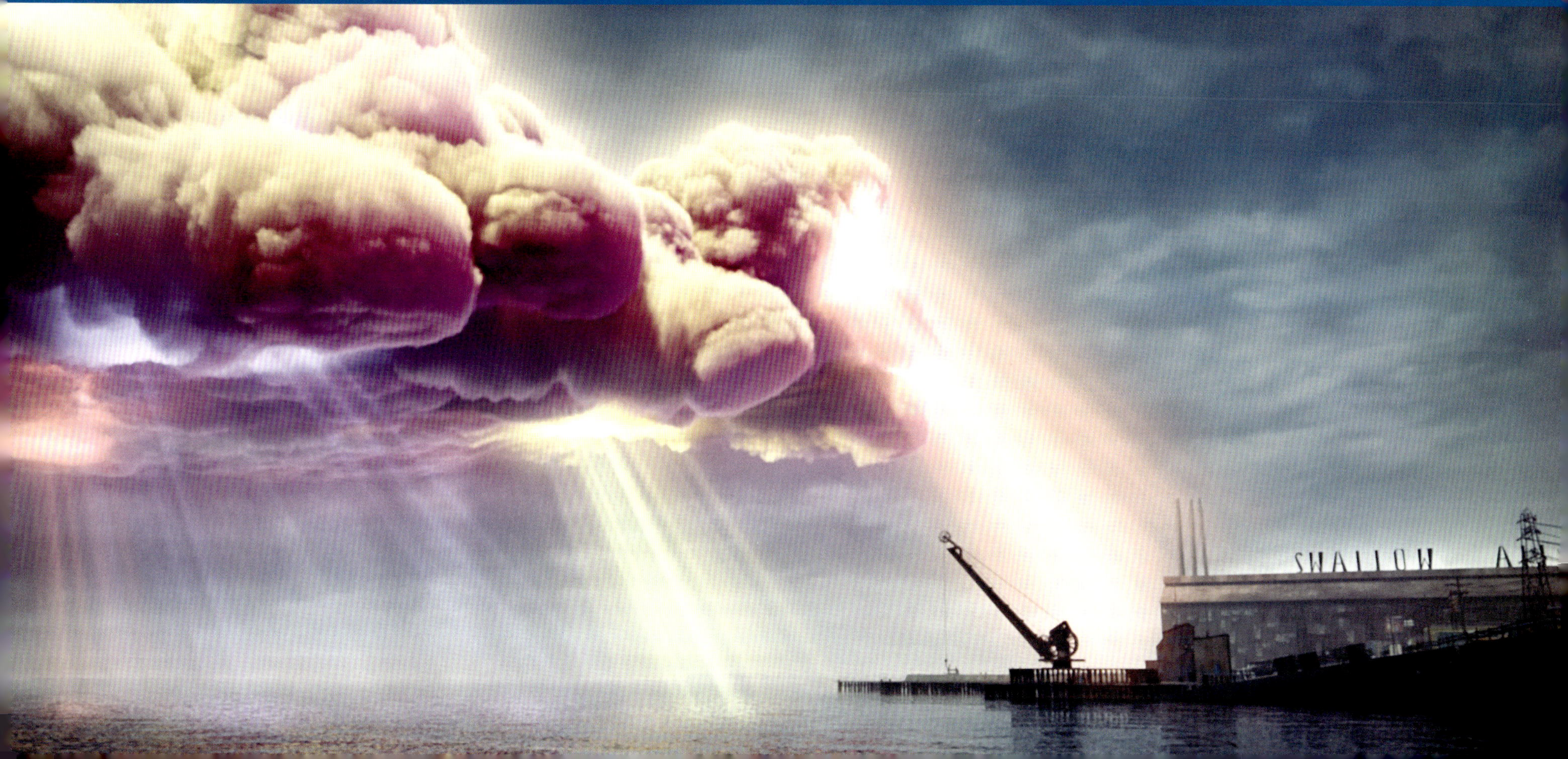
SWALLOW

# Spaghetti Twister

As time passes and the FLDSMDFR starts working in overdrive, the falling-food experiences aren't nearly as happy and cheery as the ice cream and Jell-O moments. Just as things seem to be peachy, the winds of change (and salt and pepper) hit Chewandswallow with the force of a tornado in the form of a spaghetti twister. The first visual cue that something is awry comes with an art-direction shift toward a more Technicolor look, where "saturation and value become more dynamic, and harsher colors and blacks appear," notes art director Michael Kurinsky. The sky fills with orange and red light, the clouds swirl in a frighteningly unnatural way, and, finally, a funnel cloud appears, "which was a challenge to design to show how the strands spin around and don't tangle," recalls visual development artist Chris Reccardi.

The aftermath of the twister was more than a mouthful for the CG team to chew on. "We spent many hours deciding where to put spaghetti splatters, knowing that it would take five days of work to put it on one location versus one day if we put them on another," recalls visual effects supervisor Rob Bredow. "The sheer quantity of art needs that went into having environments, props, and characters all affected by the food destruction was the biggest challenge for look development," says CG supervisor Karl Herbst. Because of the time-intensive work that destruction efforts such as shattering, exploding, and fire effects needed, the CG team eventually learned "to not destroy stuff too early in the process, due to story changes that might render those efforts useless," adds Bredow.

↓ Spaghetti Twister ★ *Marcelo Vignali*   ↗ Storyboards ★ *Fergal Reilly*

*"Because the lighting and shadows are very real, it was a challenge to find the balance between menacing and scary with the twister scenes."*
—**CHRIS JUEN** Co-producer

↑ Early Twister Simulation ★ *Tom Kluyskens*
← Spaghetti Twister ★ *Richard Chavez*
↙ Spaghetti Twister ★ *Gaëtan & Paul Brizzi*
Overleaf Spaghetti Twister damage ★ *Design: Simon Rodgers, Paint: Dave Bleich*

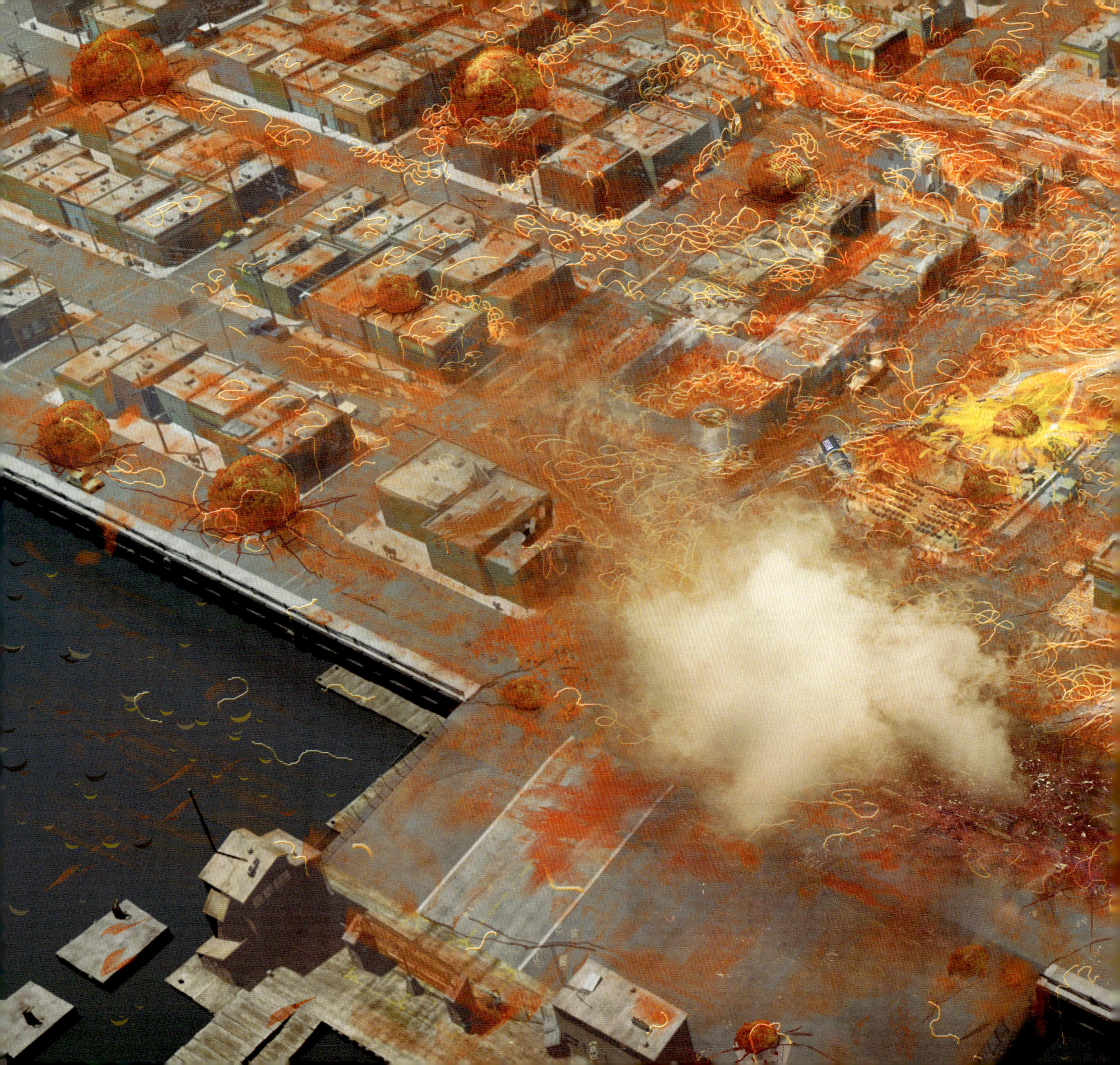

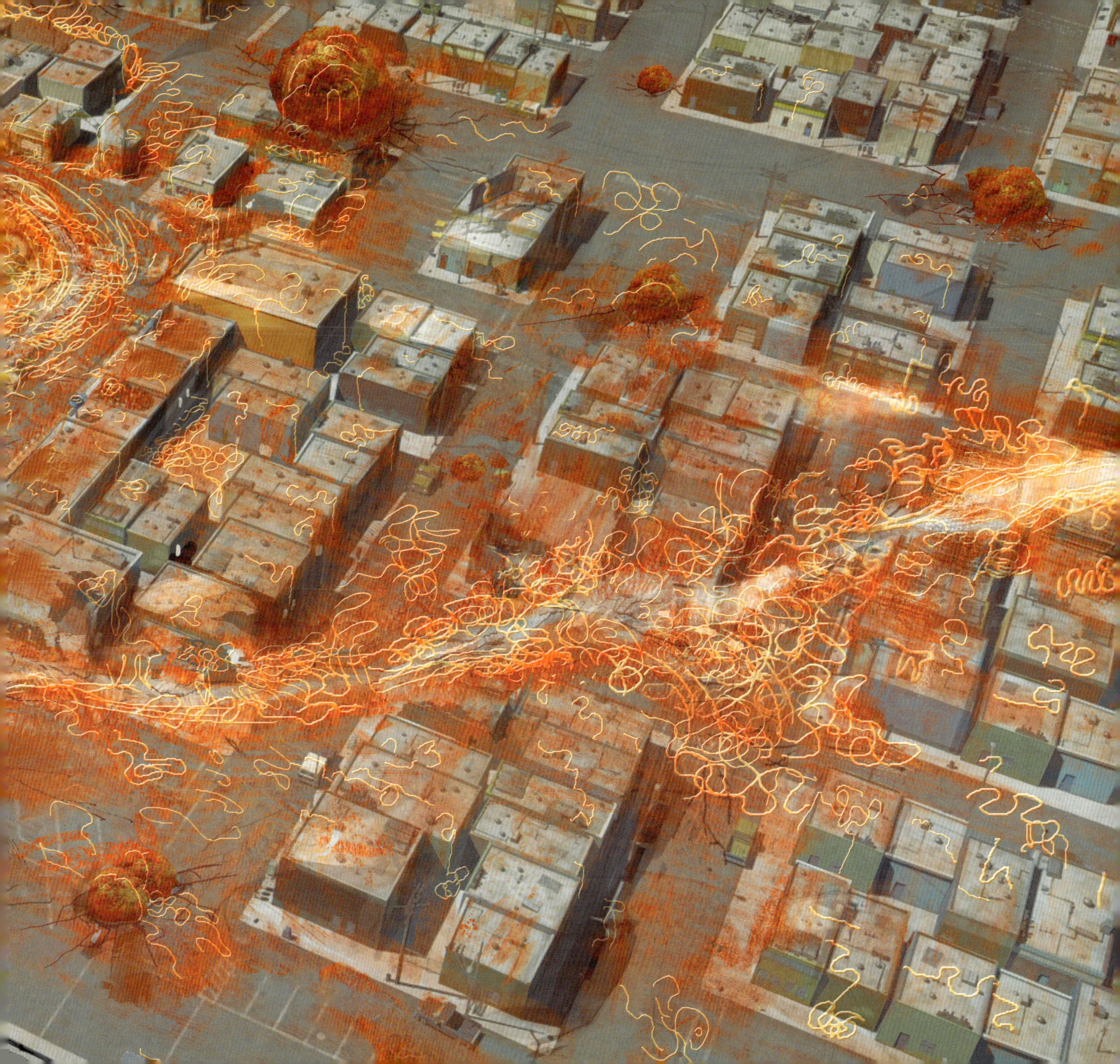

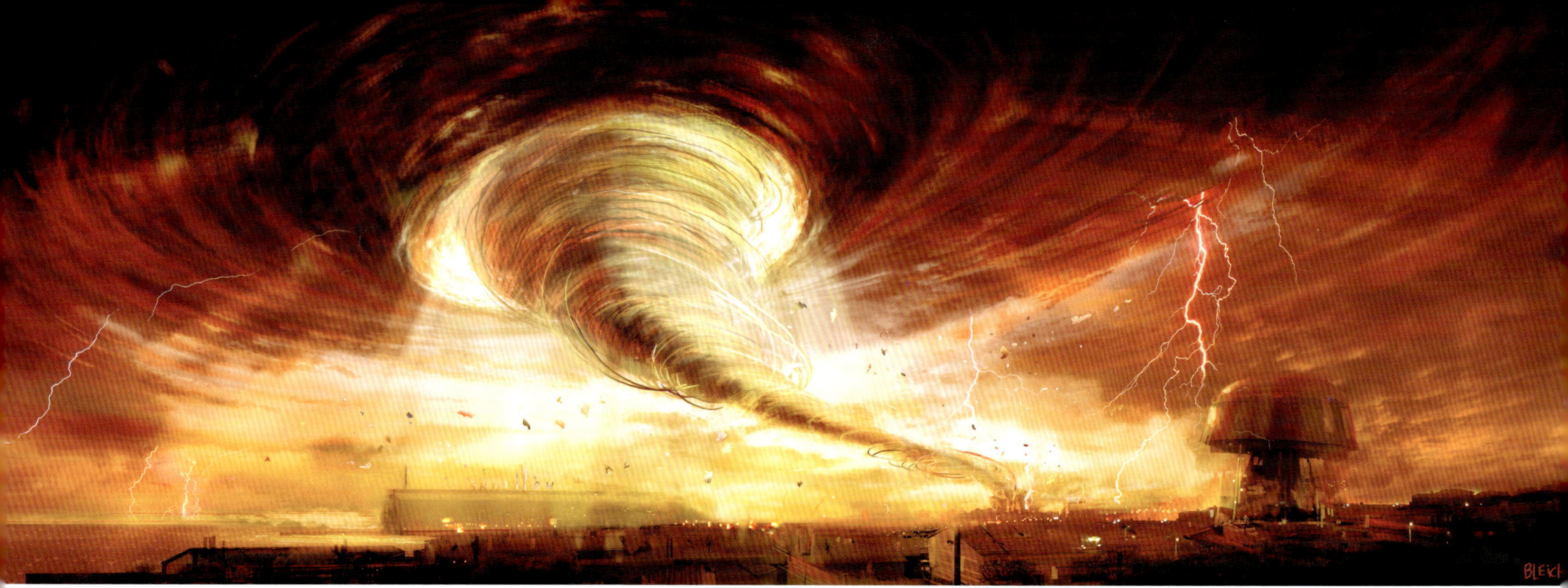

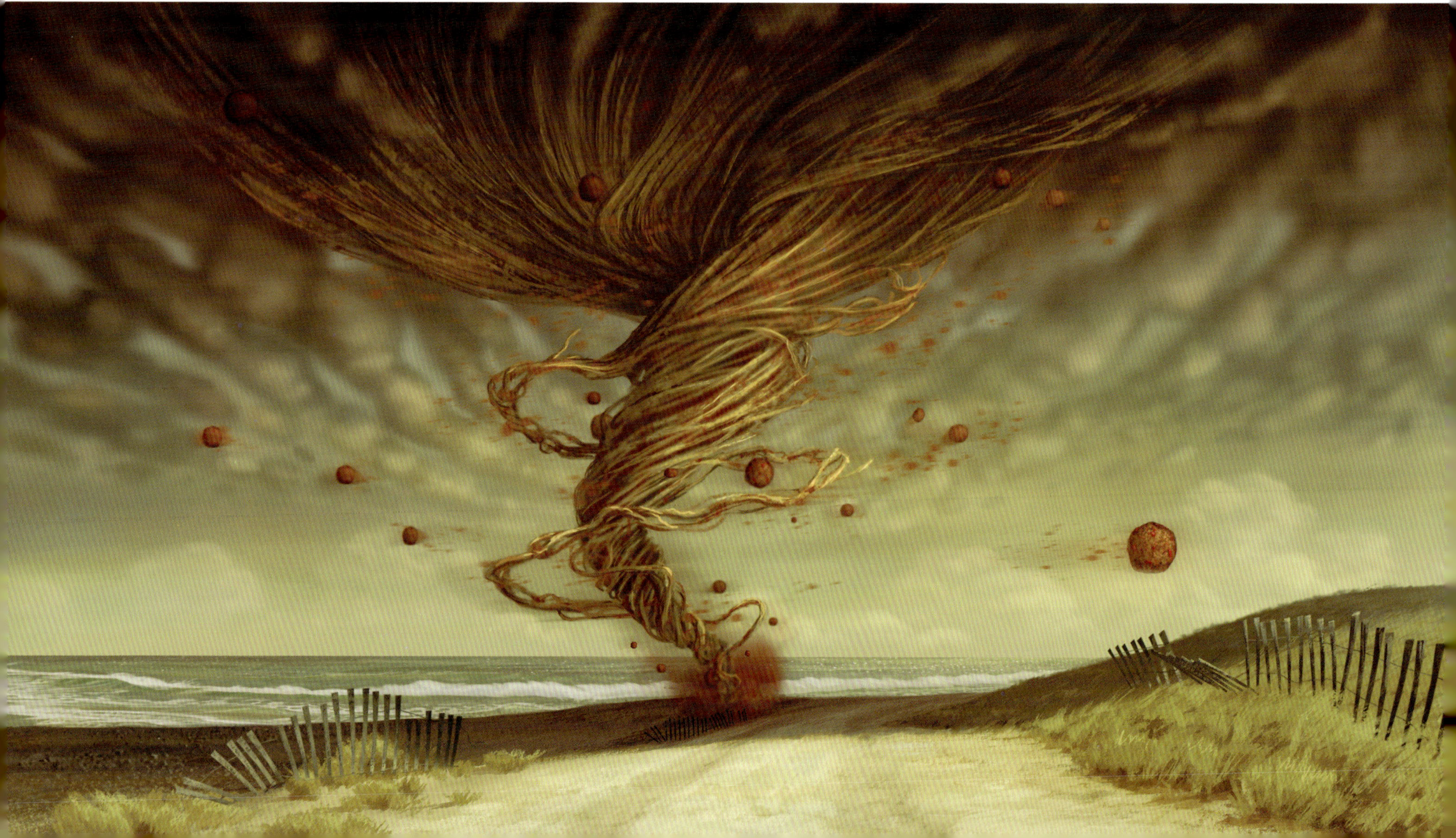

← TWISTER ★ *Design: Simon Rodgers, Paint: Dave Bleich*
↙ TWISTER ★ *Michael Kurinsky*
↘ TWISTER ★ *Justin K. Thompson*

Who said you shouldn't play with your food? The *Cloudy* crew held a competition to construct the "Most Creative Breadboat" and came up with some delicious contenders. No food was harmed in the making of these breadboats.

↖ ↑ PHOTOS ★
*Carmen Woods*

When the dam finally reaches its breaking point, it was a delicate balance story-wise to keep the sense of peril alive for the characters, but to not frighten the core audience of the film, namely kids. The skies are eerily dark, but there is "a light in the distance, intended to give both the characters and the audience a sense of hope on the horizon in this dramatic challenge," notes art director Michael Kurinsky. Although floods are devastating forces of nature (or antinature, in this case), Flint comes up with a logical but comical evacuation plan—to build escape boats out of toast, pizza slices, and Swiss cheese. While this mode of transportation is an icon of the original children's book, it is also a comical way to temper the scariness of the threatening avalanche.

↙ ESCAPING BREAD BOAT ★ *Boat Design: Armand Serrano, Cloud Design & Paint: Noelle Triaureau*

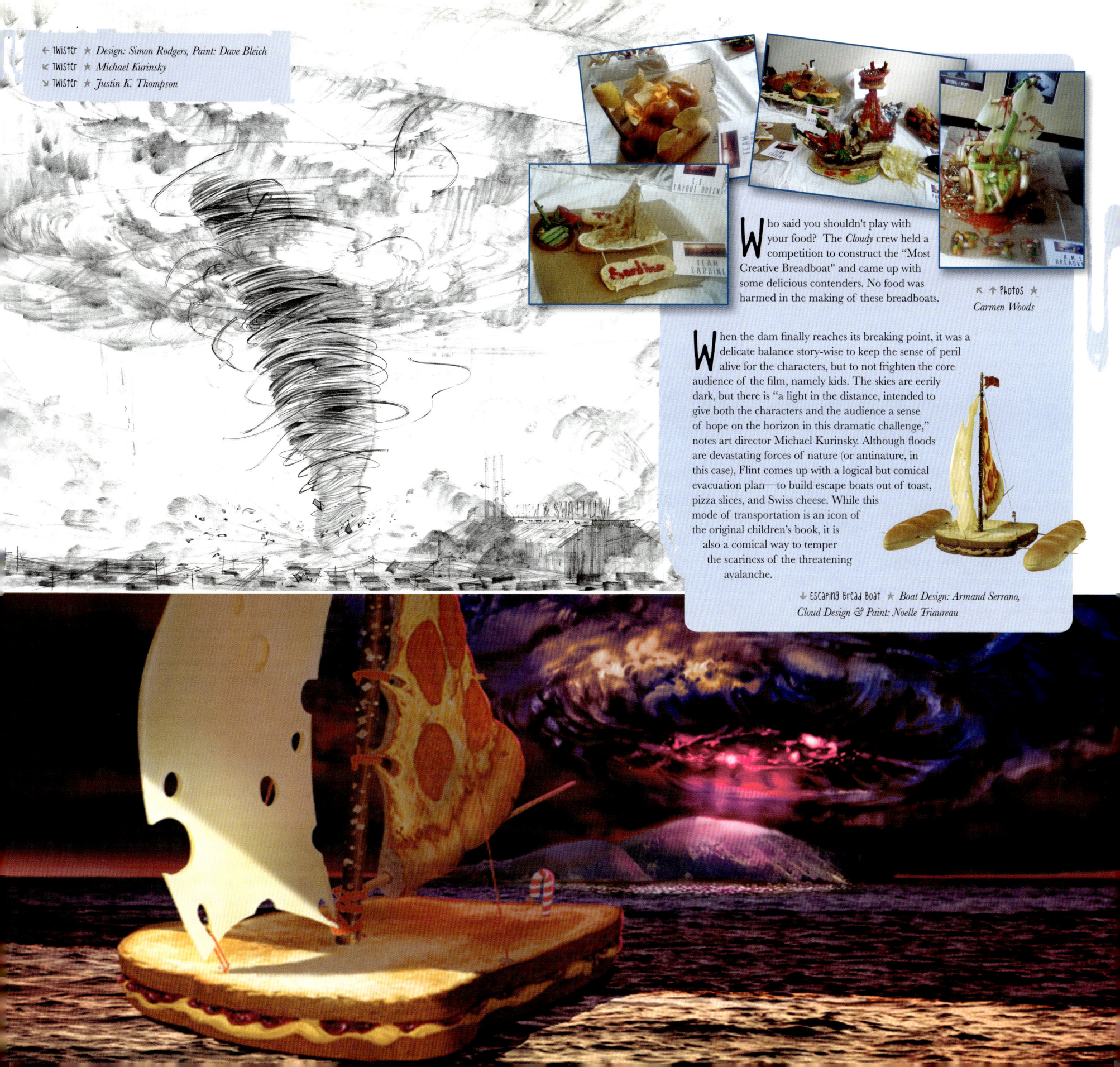

# Million Room Hotel

Prior to the existence of the food dam, Chewandswallow boasted an establishment known as the Million Room Hotel, an upside-down-pyramid building that would catch the food as it falls and then serve it to the millions of tourists who were to flock to Chewandswallow. "It was like the town's Tower of Babel, a symbol of the Mayor's having built the town's future upon a slim foundation," recalls director Phil Lord. "This hotel was modeled and partially textured before that story point became an issue, because building such a grand structure would have taken quite a while, and it made people wonder how long the food had been falling," adds visual effects supervisor Rob Bredow. The dam concept then took over this location, which ended up working better for the function of the Outtasighter anyway.

*"It was like the Death Star meets the Luxor Hotel."*
—**MICHAEL KURINSKY** Art Director

↓ Million Room Hotel ★ *Simon Rodgers*

↑ Million Room Hotel ★ *Justin K. Thompson*

↑ Million Room Hotel ★ *Ted Blackman*

*"It was a giant monument to stupidity."*
—**SIMON RODGERS** Visual Development Artist

↓ Million Room Hotel  ★ *Dan Quarnstrom*

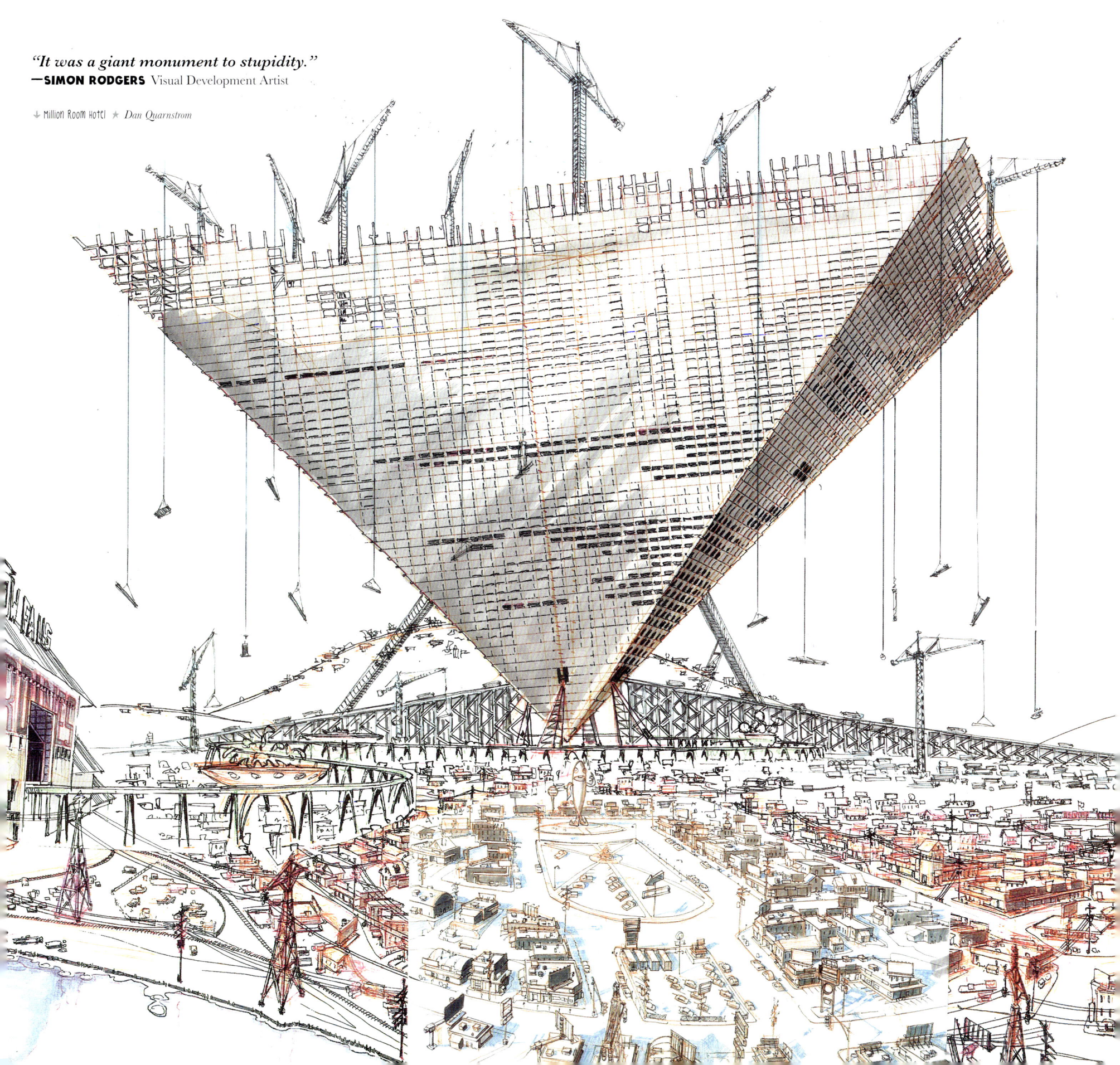

# meet the meateroid

Following the twister, Flint tries to shut down the FLDSMDFR but finds that the Mayor, larger and more gluttonous than ever, has overloaded the machine with even more food requests. Flint's attempts to overtake Mayor Shelbourne are "beet" down in a food fight, so Flint is forced to pull out another invention, Flying Car 2.0, to take to the skies and power down the FLDSMDFR by hand.

Along with a crackpot (or is it a Crockpot?) crew of Sam, Manny, Steve, and Brent, Flint flies into what seems like another world. Art direction cues add to the suspense: Purple skies lead to a cloud layer that thickly veils what lies above it, while lightning flashes of rainbow bursts suggest that the FLDSMDFR is radiating its presence more intensely than ever. Cinematography adds to the otherworldly experience by using a "focus to infinity and tilted angles while shooting action that is perpendicular to the picture plane," explains production designer Justin K. Thompson.

As the flying car breaks through clouds and fog as thick as pea soup, into view comes a massive, spinning orb of food. The FLDSMDFR has apparently been masking itself in some of its products to form a protective outer layer, and it now appears to be, appropriately enough, a mile-wide meatball. "We wanted it to feel wondrous and awesome," explains visual development artist Simon Rodgers, who created the icon that draws in both the characters and the audience. "Plus we wanted to make it gross, the kind of thing that kids appreciate," he adds. To achieve this goal, the crew sought to give the meateroid "a head-cheesy sort of texture, replacing indiscernible bits of meat with a variety of congealed food particles," says art director Michael Kurinsky.

↑ Food Storm ★ *Justin K. Thompson*
↗ Approaching the Meateroid ★ *Design: Simon Rodgers, Paint: Noelle Triareau*
→ Storyboards ★ *Chris Mitchell*

GOOD LUCK SON

OK, SO HERE'S THE PLAN

# Inside the Belly of the Beast

Once inside the giant meateroid, Flint and his crew encounter tunnels paved and caverns plastered with the most disgusting buffet spread imaginable. To complement the unappetizing surroundings, the set is lit with the most unnatural lighting effects, casting a bluish-green tint on the food particles to make them even more repulsive. "We replicated theme-park lighting, like what you see in the Carlsbad Caverns, and we used up-lighting from two or three sources at the same time to create an unsettling environment, along the lines of *Independence Day* and *Alien*," says art director Michael Kurinsky. While in the "belly of the beast," the protagonists must battle a variety of mutated "superfoods," and this multicourse confrontation provides another unspoken but loudly served message on what chaos can arise from genetically engineered foods. It is a food fight like never before seen, as it is truly out of this world.

This gastronomic version of a haunted house involves some imaginative obstacles of food, ranging from an army of gummi bears to a chute of peanut brittle more treacherous than a corridor of broken glass . . . and then there is the matter of the headless chicken bodies. Perhaps the most meaningful scene comes when Flint is rappelling down the peanut-brittle chute on a licorice rope and decides he must do this on his own, not risking Sam's life any more than he already has. "Flint really becomes a hero when he takes responsibility for his actions," notes head of story Kris Pearn.

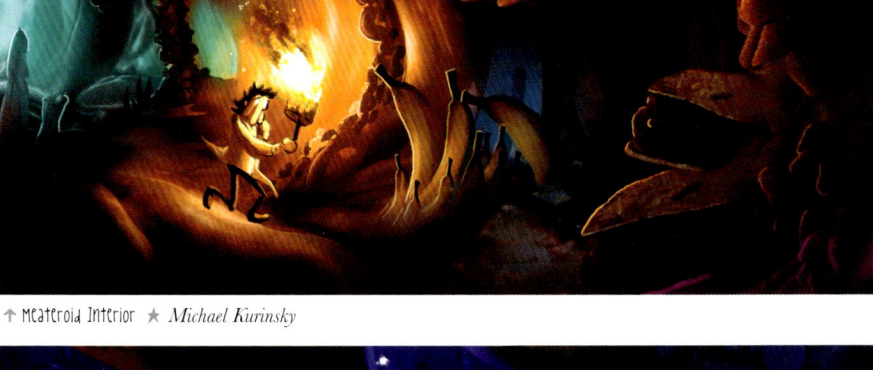

↑ Meateroid Interior ★ *Michael Kurinsky*

← Olive Disguise ★ *Justin K. Thompson*
→ Overleaf Meateroid Interiors ★
Design: *Justin K. Thompson*, Paint: *Dean Gordon*

166

↑ Meatcroid Interior ★ Chris Reccardi

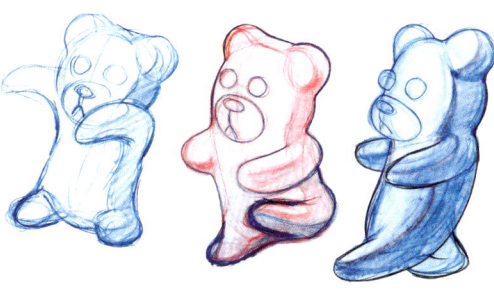

"It was fun to work on the gummi bear models, because how often can you snack on your reference materials?"
—**MARVIN KIM** Modeling Supervisor

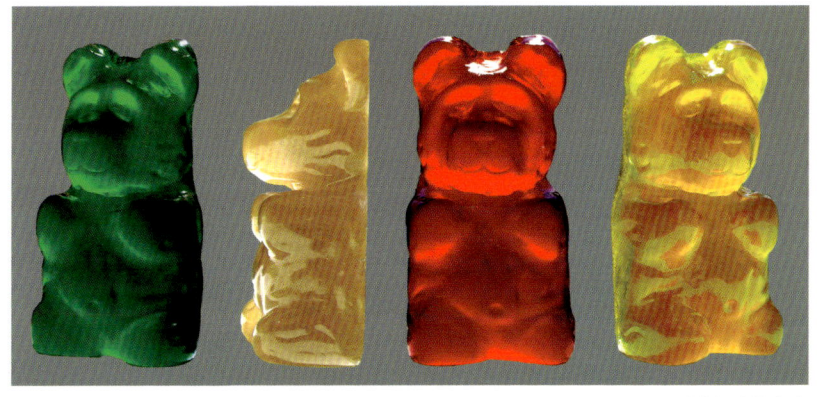

↖ Gummi Bears ★ Mark Colangelo          ↑ Gummi Bears Turnaround ★ Michael Kurinsky

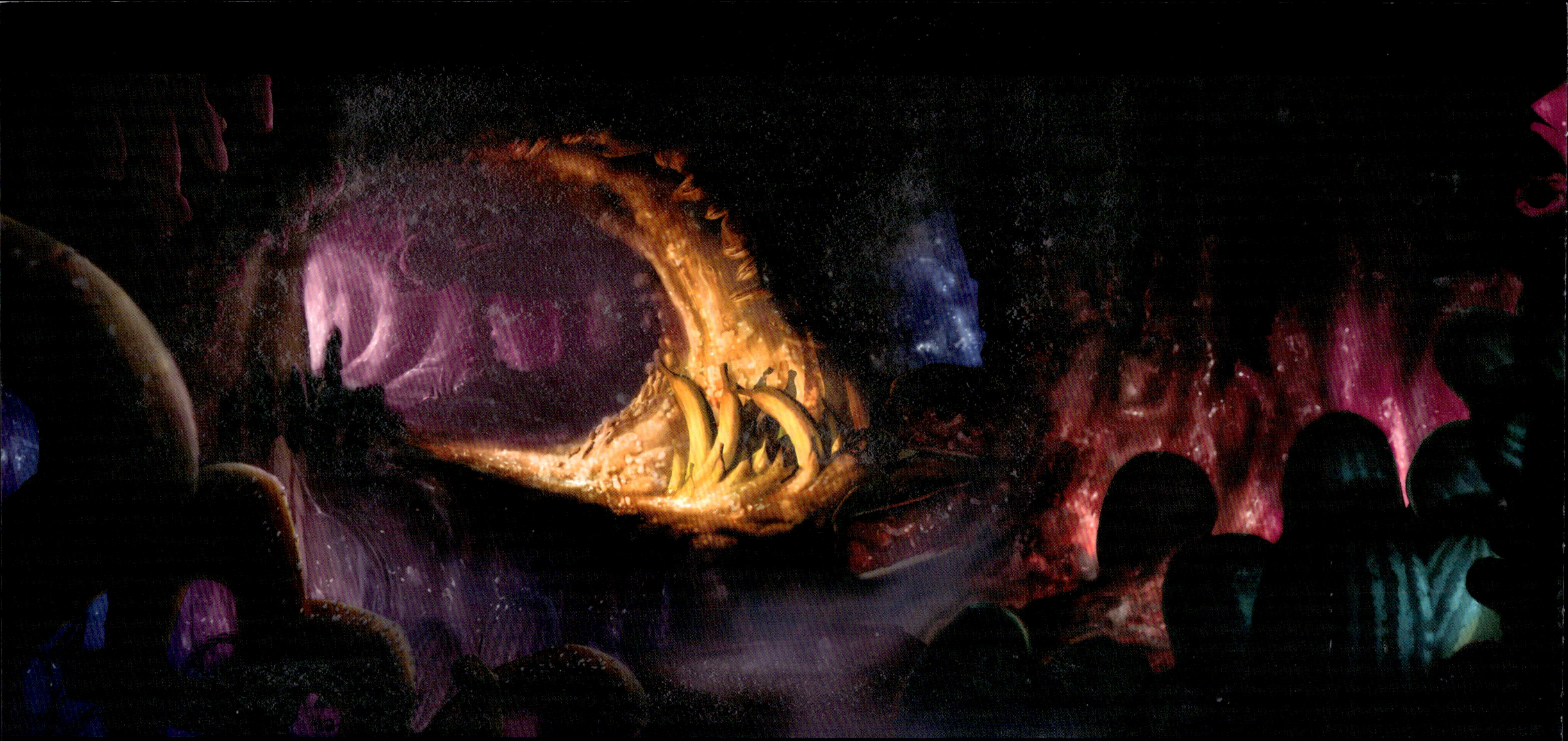

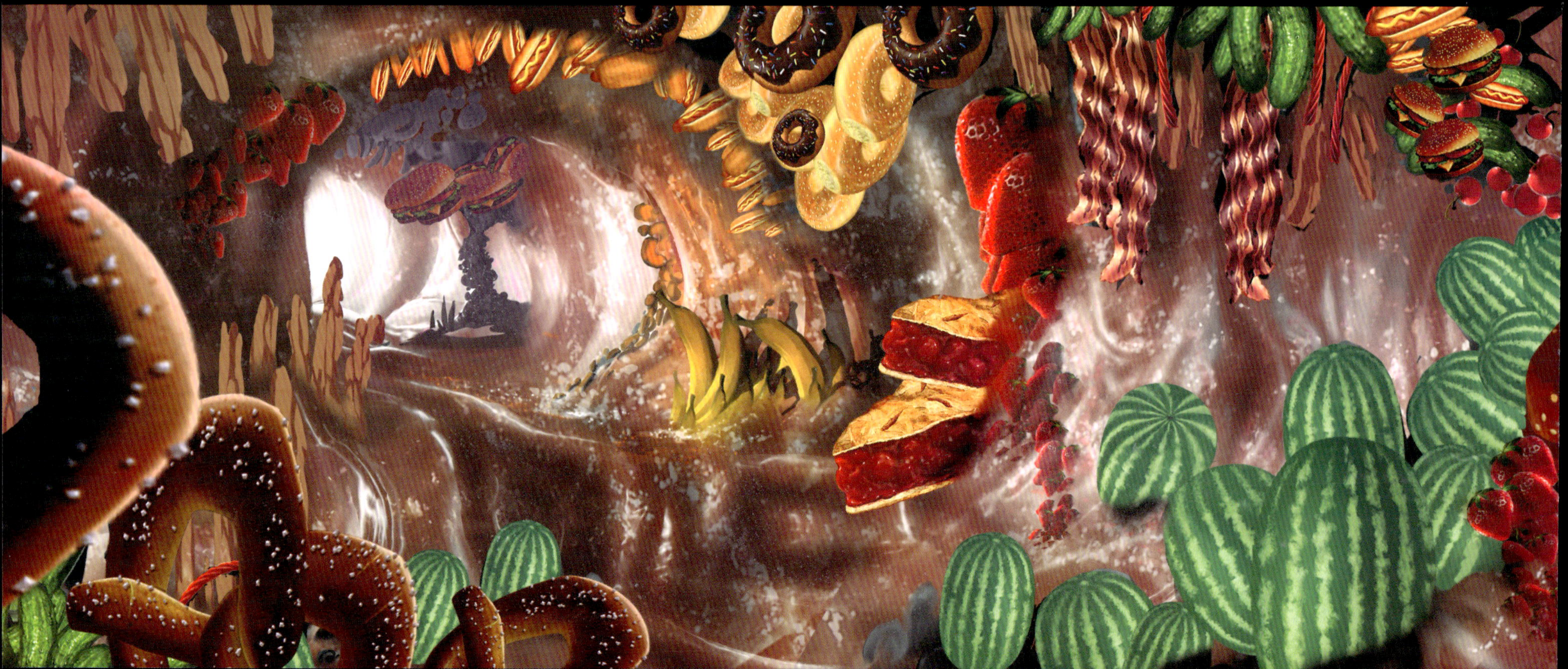

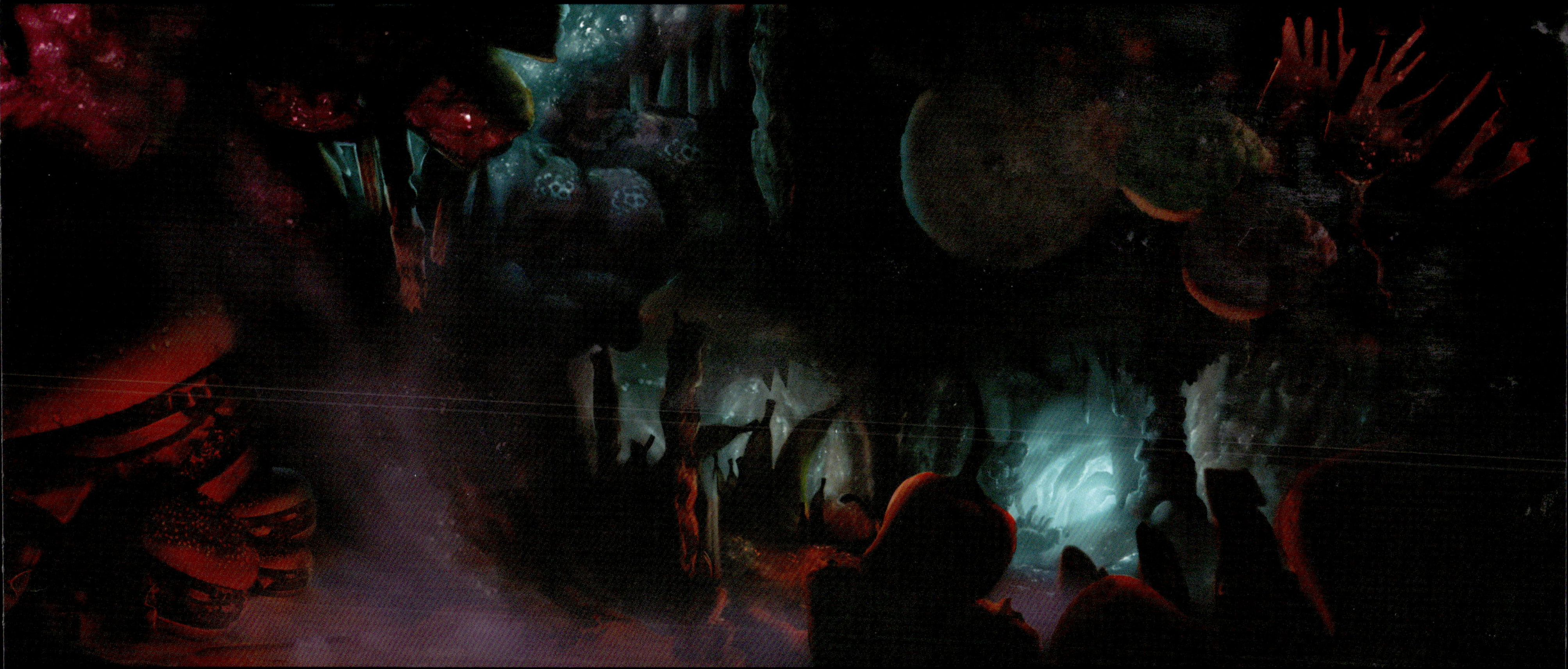
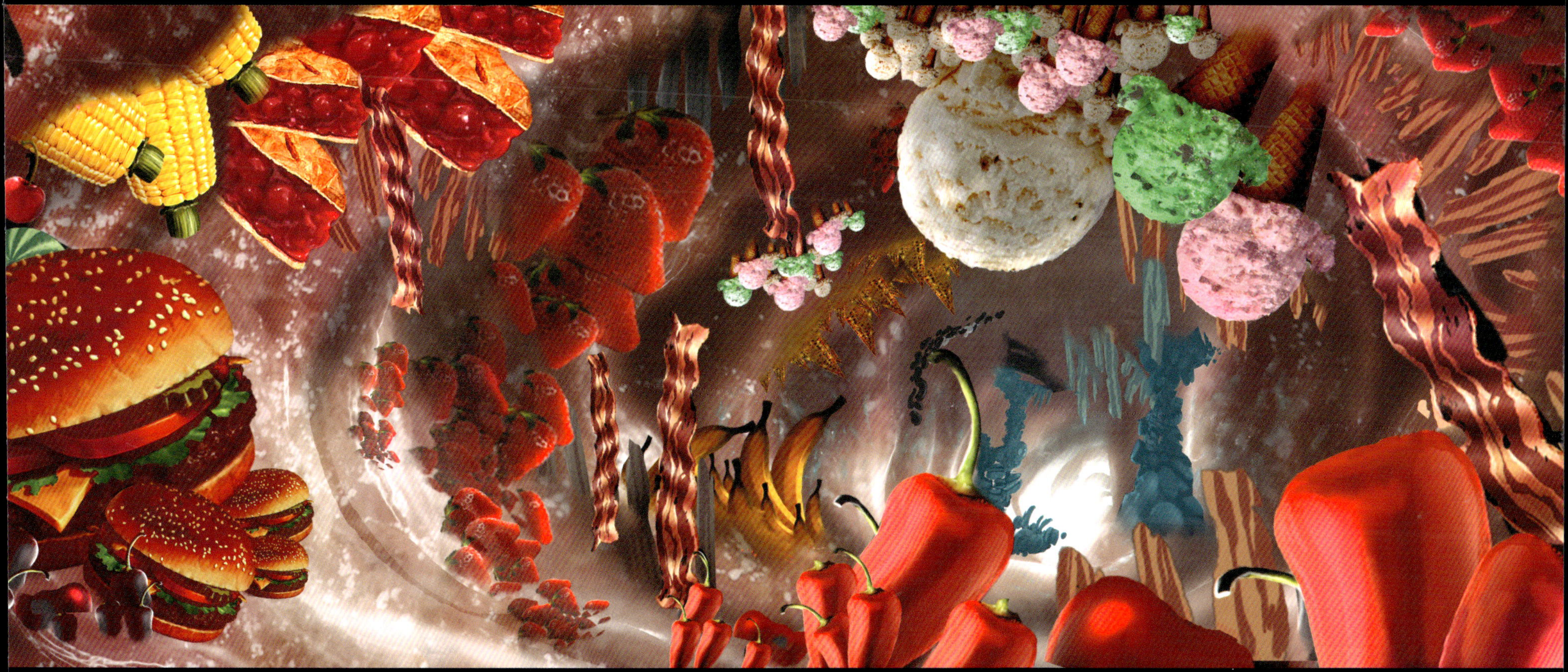

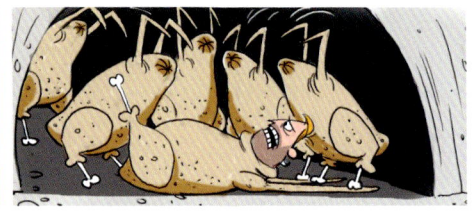

↑ Storyboards ★ Kaan Kaylan

↘ Fighting Chicken ★ Digital

↑ Fighting Chicken ★ Pete Oswald

"I love that the bananas and pickles that line the 'throat' inside the meateroid look and act like cilia.... it adds to the creepiness of the environment."
—**MICHAEL KURINSKY** Art Director

170

↑ Meateroid Surface ★ Simon Rodgers  → Color Keys & Downshaft ★ Dean Gordon

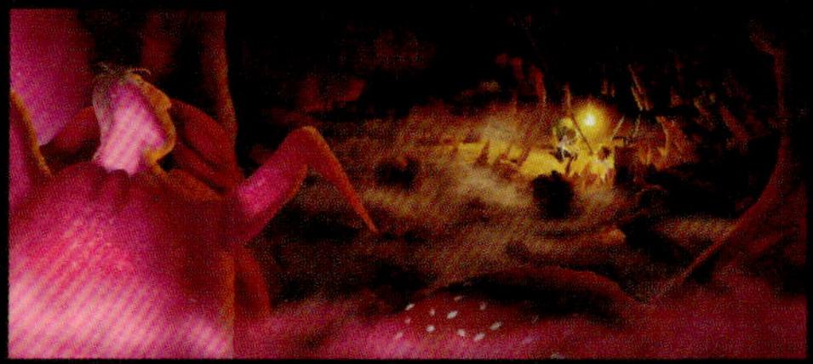
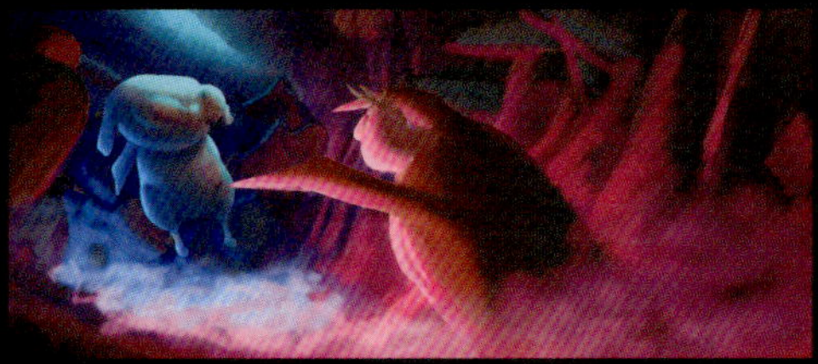
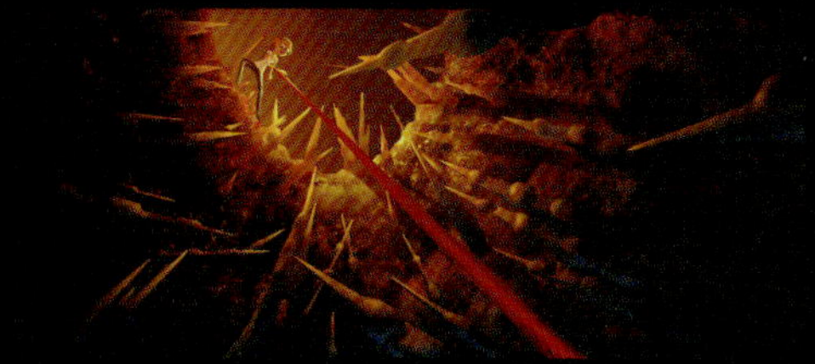
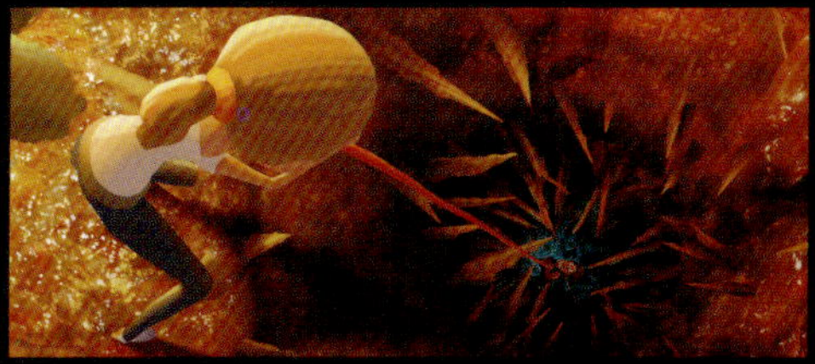
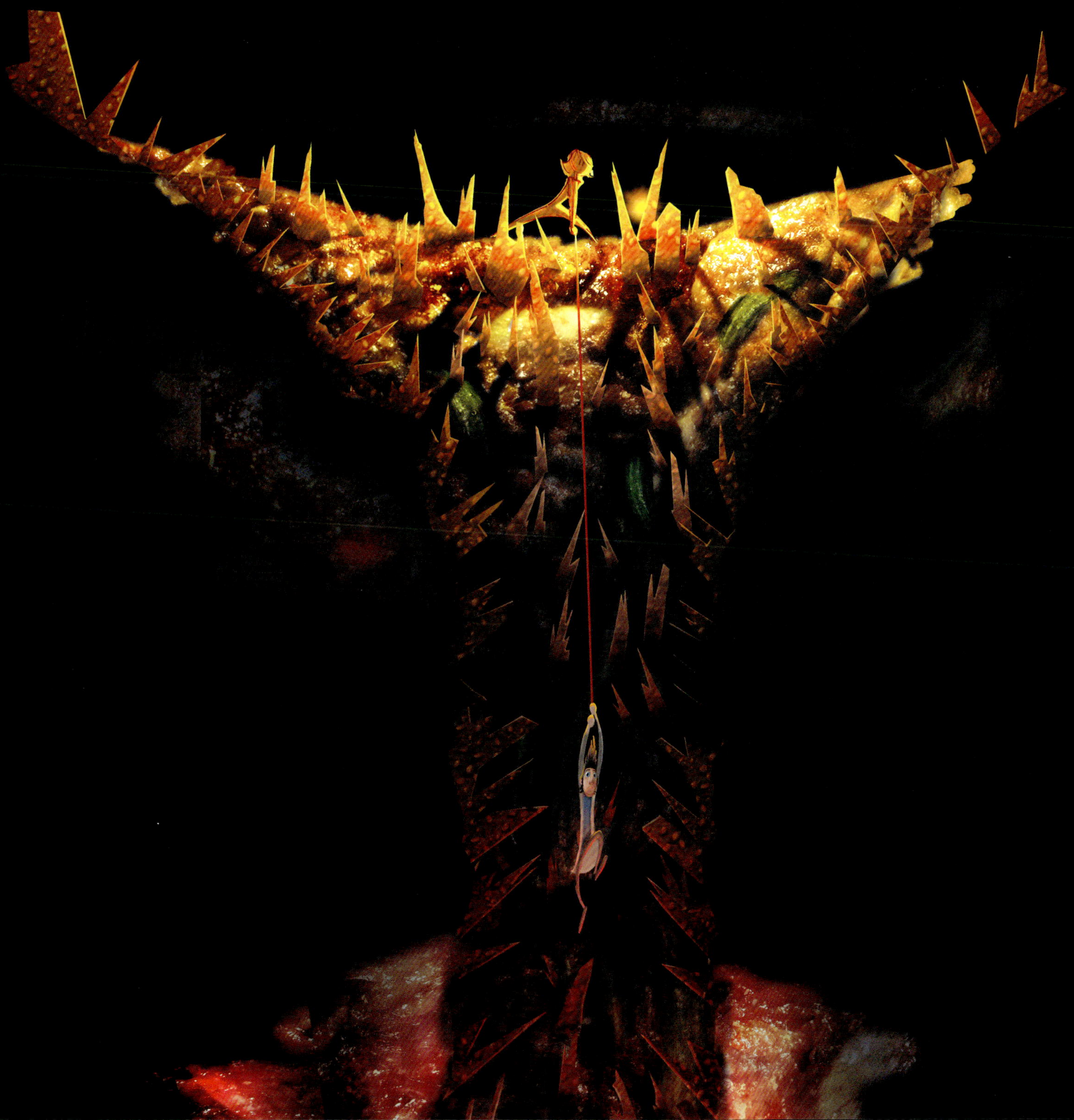

# International House of Pandemonium

Meanwhile, back on the "real" world, reports of food damage have started coming in from other cities around the planet. New York City is barraged by bagels, the Great Wall of China is flattened by a corncob, and other iconic landmarks around the globe are plagued by Flint's out-of-control creation that was fueled by Mayor Shelbourne's greed. The matte painting team, led by Dave Bleich, brought these locations into final color for the film, reveling in the challenge of balancing the style established in 2D by the art director with the look of the 3D effects created by Imageworks.

The crew had so much fun brainstorming what could happen that, in the interest of time, a few sites had to be edited out of the Weather News Network telecast, such as Stonehenge and Tokyo.

↗ Egypt and London ★ *Design: Simon Rodgers, Paint: Dean Gordon*

↑ Manhattan under attack ★ *Design: Armand Serrano, Paint: Jerry Loveland*

↗ Paris ★ *Design: Armand Serrano, Paint: Noelle Triaureau*
→ New York City's Times Square ★ *Marcelo Vignali*

↑ Mount Rushmore ★ Simon Rodgers
↓ The Great Wall of China ★ Design: Armand Serrano, Paint: Michael Kurinsky

# 3D

After creating such an imaginative world for Flint, the *Cloudy* crew was thrilled to take it to the next level by inviting audiences to enter this environment in three dimensions. "It's the perfect film to immerse the viewers in a 3D world. What could be more fun than inspiring everyone in a theater to reach out and grab burgers as they rain down from the clouds?" asks visual effects supervisor Rob Bredow.

The 3D presentation of *Cloudy with a Chance of Meatballs* draws upon years of stereoscopic filmmaking at Imageworks, ensuring that the audience experience will be both comfortable and dynamic. 3D effects supervisor Rob Engle recalls reading the original book to his daughter and imagining the on-screen possibilities. "As a stereographer, I am always drawn to a good story that will provide wonderful opportunities in which we can bring the audience into the action, and *Cloudy* certainly has plenty of them."

> "The 3D experience really allows the audience to explore vast sets and to connect with characters at the height of action. In this scene, you can almost feel the peanut brittle shards grazing Flint's skin."
> —CHRIS JUEN, Co-producer

→ Final Frames ★ *Digital*

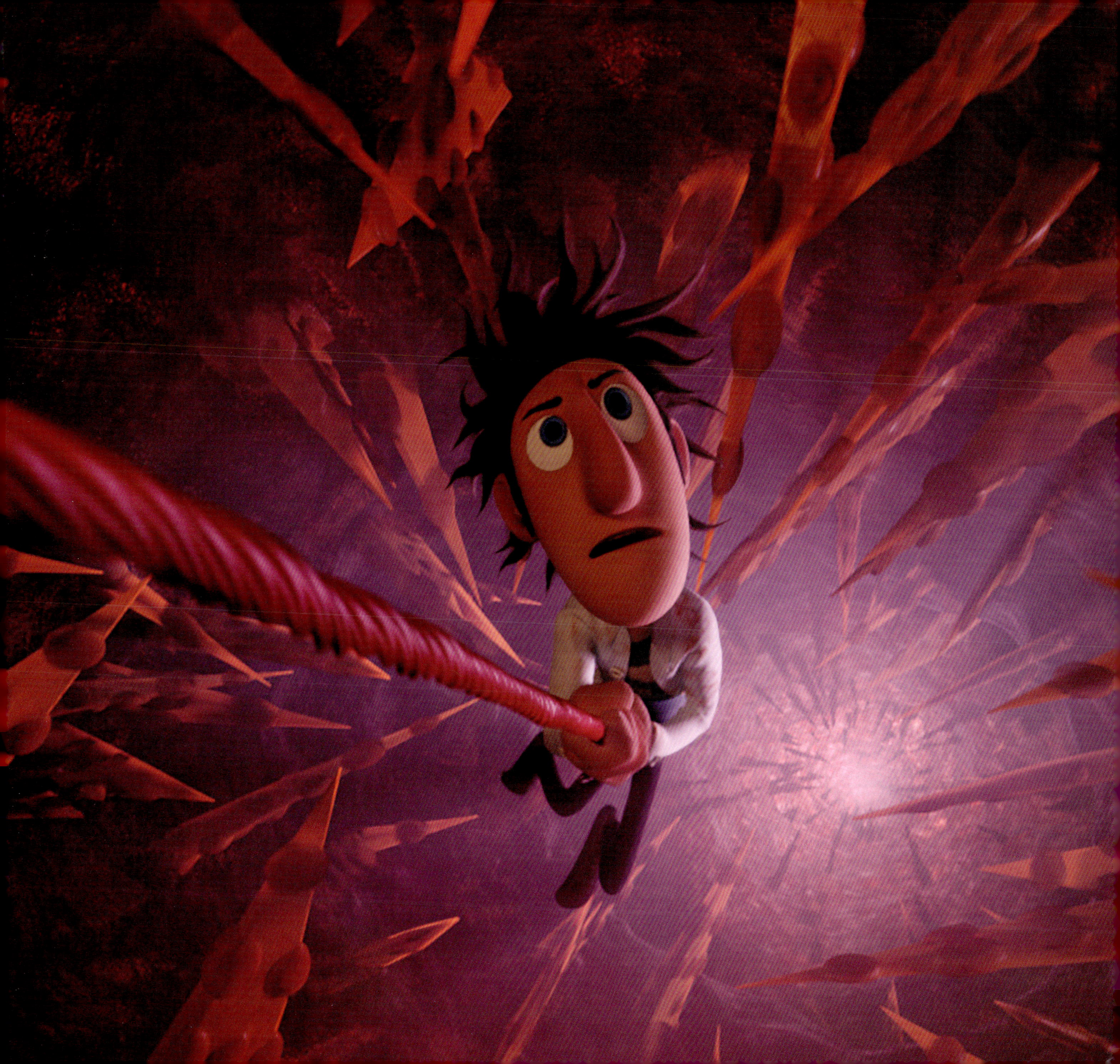

# Afterword

After Flint manages to shut down the FLDSMDFR, the falling food ceases and the fallout assessment begins. The town of Chewandswallow is literally devastated by the ramifications of its gluttonous food fest, which also speaks to the real world about being "addicted to consumption and instant gratification, learning that putting off long-term problems for short-term gains can come back to haunt it," notes director Christopher Miller. Meanwhile, Flint is battered and burned, but even in this state of overcooked exhaustion, he epitomizes a worthy hero. After being delivered to safety via another of his misunderstood inventions, Flint stands before his town as a respectable member of society, having finally taken responsibility for his own creations. "By having the courage to fail and taking action against his own failure, Flint wins the love of a girl and the respect of his father," says head of story Kris Pearn.

Like every successful invention, an animated feature film takes a lot of hard work, a thoughtful balance of elements, and great imagination to bring it all together.

Undoubtedly, it also takes a lot of "throwing spaghetti at the wall and seeing what sticks," and in the case of *Cloudy with a Chance of Meatballs*, what stuck is a perfect combination of artistry, technology, and vision. "*Cloudy* is cartoony on one level and then sophisticated on others. Both adults and kids can appreciate it, which is a balance you don't see very often," notes president of Sony Pictures Digital Productions Bob Osher. Visually, it is a stunning mix of the photorealistic and the whimsical, inspired by the illustrations of the original book and paying direct tribute to such throughout the film, most especially in the energized, unexpected twist of the film's cross-hatched coda.

Although making things look cool and stylish "is reflective of what Flint would do, and generally less of an aesthetic and more of an ethic for us," according to director Phil Lord, the top goal of the inventive directing efforts on this film was to create "a fun, immersive experience that makes the audience laugh while inspiring them to nurture their nerdiness," says Miller. "We hope people can learn to embrace intelligence, curiosity, creativity, and uniqueness—indeed, to insist on it. We celebrate our nerds when they become successful artists and scientists and comedians and senators, but we punish them for their entire lives before that. I wish nerdiness could be socially useful, not a social liability," explains Lord.

Even if the story told in this film is simply another invention from Flint's ever-creative mind, *Cloudy with a Chance of Meatballs* serves up some interesting food for thought that, it is hoped, gives its audience the appetite for multiple helpings.

*"The messages of the film feel organic, suggesting what happens when your eyes are bigger than your stomach, or when you mess with Mother Nature and abuse your natural resources. These topics are timely and provide a smart way to open up discussions between parents and kids."*
—**BOB OSHER** President of Sony Pictures Digital Productions

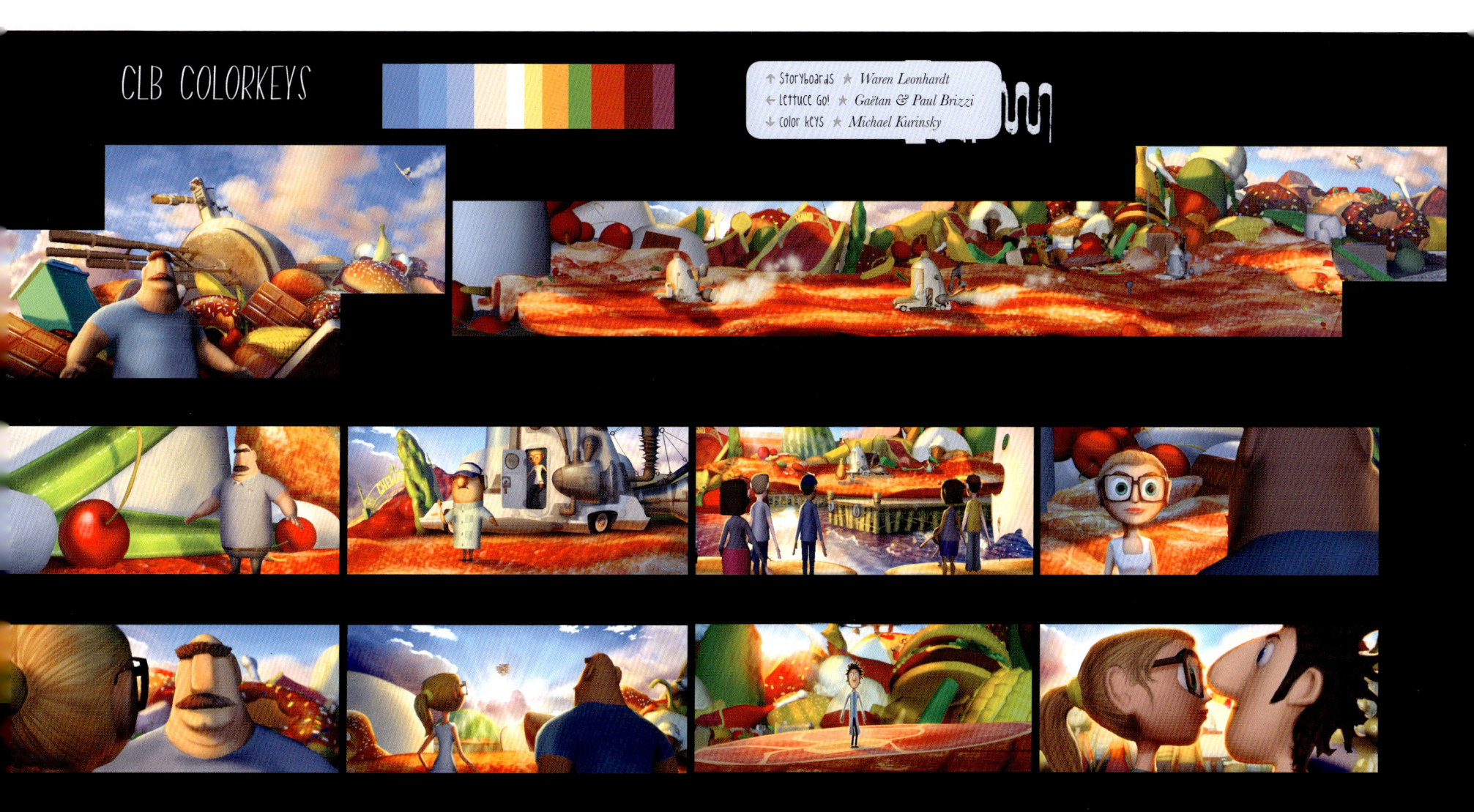

## CLB COLORKEYS

↑ Storyboards ★ Waren Leonhardt
← Lettuce Go! ★ Gaëtan & Paul Brizzi
↓ Color Keys ★ Michael Kurinsky

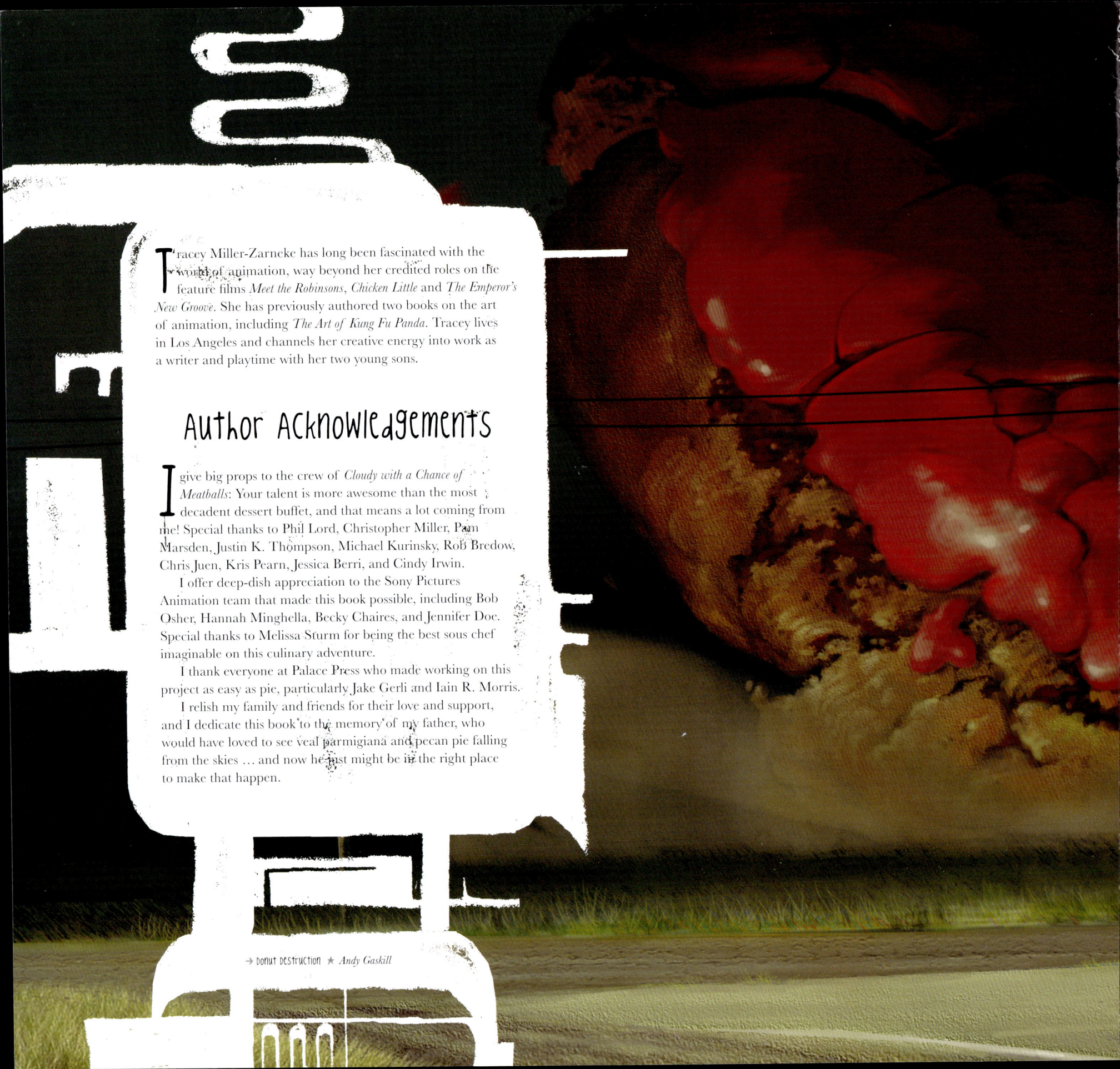

Tracey Miller-Zarneke has long been fascinated with the world of animation, way beyond her credited roles on the feature films *Meet the Robinsons*, *Chicken Little* and *The Emperor's New Groove*. She has previously authored two books on the art of animation, including *The Art of Kung Fu Panda*. Tracey lives in Los Angeles and channels her creative energy into work as a writer and playtime with her two young sons.

## Author Acknowledgements

I give big props to the crew of *Cloudy with a Chance of Meatballs*: Your talent is more awesome than the most decadent dessert buffet, and that means a lot coming from me! Special thanks to Phil Lord, Christopher Miller, Pam Marsden, Justin K. Thompson, Michael Kurinsky, Rob Bredow, Chris Juen, Kris Pearn, Jessica Berri, and Cindy Irwin.

I offer deep-dish appreciation to the Sony Pictures Animation team that made this book possible, including Bob Osher, Hannah Minghella, Becky Chaires, and Jennifer Doe. Special thanks to Melissa Sturm for being the best sous chef imaginable on this culinary adventure.

I thank everyone at Palace Press who made working on this project as easy as pie, particularly Jake Gerli and Iain R. Morris.

I relish my family and friends for their love and support, and I dedicate this book to the memory of my father, who would have loved to see veal parmigiana and pecan pie falling from the skies ... and now he just might be in the right place to make that happen.

→ Donut Destruction ★ *Andy Gaskill*

# colophon

**Cloudy with a Chance of Meatballs**
ISBN: 9781848565036

Published by Titan Books
A division of Titan Publishing Group Ltd
144 Southwark Street, London, SE1 0UP

Copyright © 2009 Sony Pictures Animation Inc.
All rights reserved.

10 9 8 7 6 5 4 3 2 1

A CIP catalogue record for this title is available from the British Library.

Visit our website: www.titanbooks.com

Did you enjoy this book? We love to hear from our readers. Please e-mail: *readerfeedback@titanemail.com* or write to Reader Feedback at the above address.

To receive advance information, news, competitions, and exclusive Titan offers online, please register as a member by clicking the 'sign up' button on our website.

No part of this publication may be reproduced, stored in a retrieval system, or transmitted, in any form or by any means without the prior written permission of the publisher, nor be otherwise circulated in any form of binding or cover other than that in which it is published and without a similar condition being imposed on the subsequent purchaser.

Originally published in the US by Insight Editions
www.insighteditions.com

**Insight Editions**
Publisher: *Raoul Goff*
Creative Director & Designer: *Iain R. Morris*
Design Assistant: *Gabe Ely*
Acquiring Editor: *Jake Gerli*
Managing Editor: *Kevin Toyama*
Editor: *Lucy Kee*
Production Director: *Leslie Cohen*

Palace Press International, in association with Roots of Peace, will plant two trees for each tree used in the manufacturing of this book. Roots of Peace is an internationally renowned humanitarian organization dedicated to eradicating land mines worldwide and converting war-torn lands into productive farms and wildlife habitats. Together, we will plant two million fruit and nut trees in Afghanistan and provide farmers there with the skills and support necessary for sustainable land use.

Printed in China by Palace Press International
www.palacepress.com

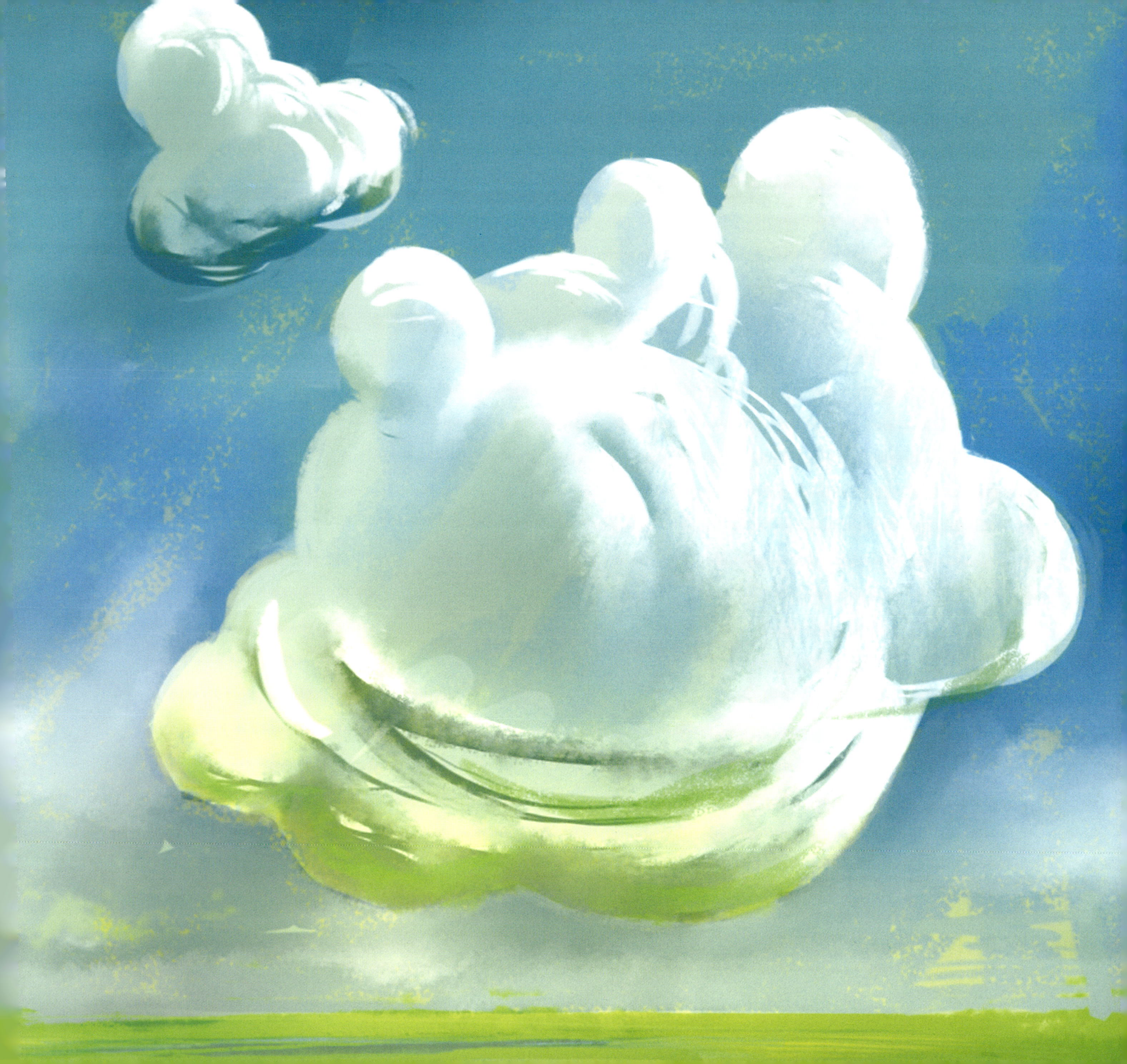

ELEVATOR SECURE

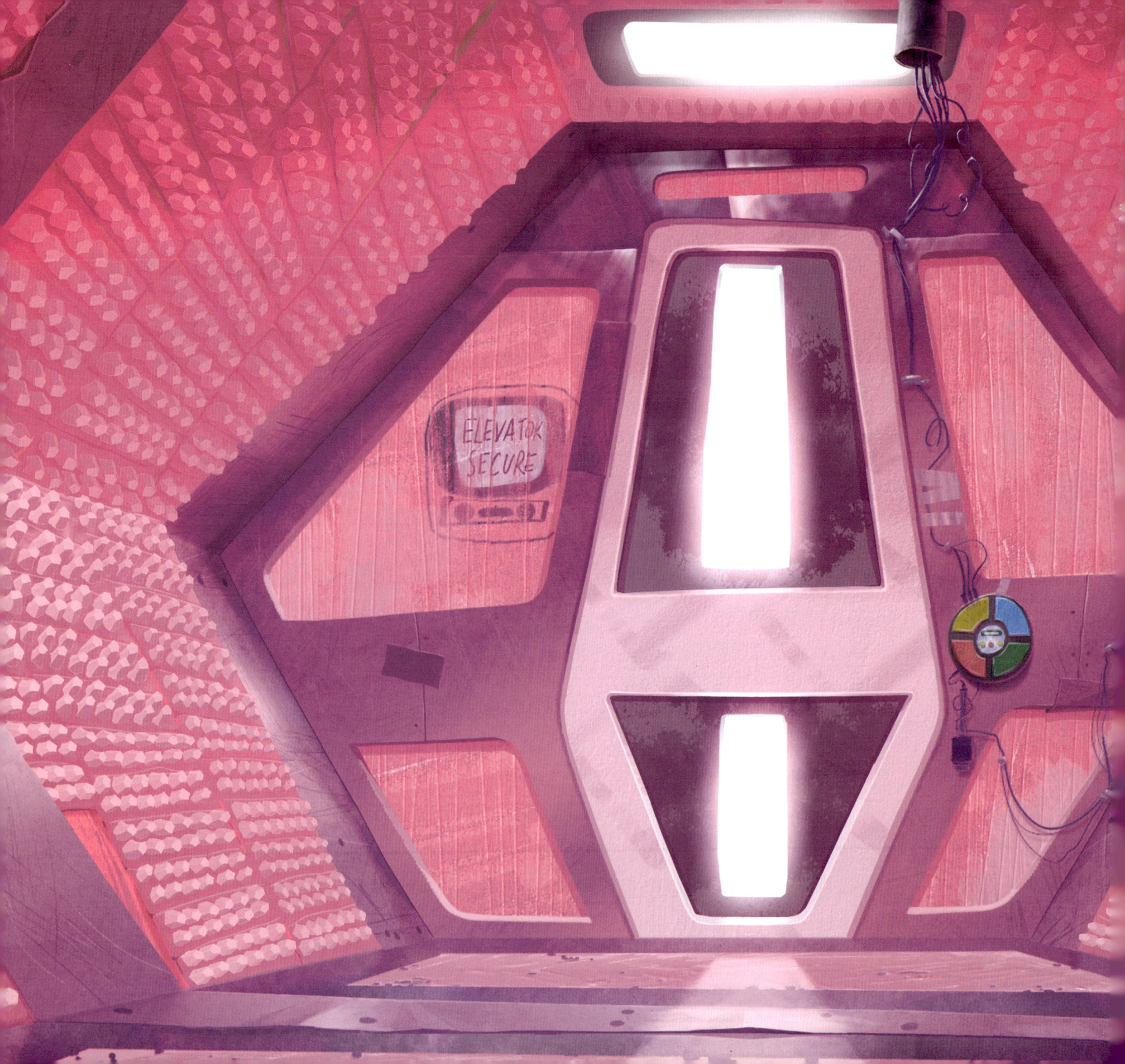